Striding With Economic Giants

Striding With Economic Giants

Business and Public Policy Lessons
From Nobel Laureates

David Simpson

BEP
BUSINESS EXPERT PRESS
Leader in applied, concise business books

Striding With Economic Giants:
Business and Public Policy Lessons From Nobel Laureates

Copyright © Business Expert Press, LLC, 2023.

Cover design by Charlene Kronstedt

Interior design by Exeter Premedia Services Private Ltd., Chennai, India

First published in 2023 by
Business Expert Press, LLC
222 East 46th Street, New York, NY 10017
www.businessexpertpress.com

ISBN-13: 978-1-63742-461-2 (paperback)
ISBN-13: 978-1-63742-462-9 (e-book)

Business Expert Press Economics and Public Policy Collection

First edition: 2023

10 9 8 7 6 5 4 3 2 1

Description

During the last century, policy makers and the public acquired a heightened awareness in economics. As a result, this elevated attention has enhanced the well-being of society.

In 1969, the Nobel Foundation initiated a new prize category of economic sciences and started awarding the prize annually. At the forefront of their field, prize winners have introduced innovative ideas beneficial to society. Moreover, the study of their ideas reveals valuable nuggets of wisdom to enrich the lives of noneconomists.

Drawing on publications written by these laureates, *Striding With Economic Giants* presents the essence of their thoughts in easy-to-understand concepts for nontechnical academic, business, and general readers. This book is perfect for economics students, business executives, and public policy makers.

It begins by describing logic and experimental frameworks in mathematics, econometrics, behavior modeling, and game theory. Next, *Striding* presents microeconomic contributions, including production theory, theory of institutions, fundamental ideas of markets, and consumerism. Then, it reviews financial theory in capital markets, portfolio choice, and asset pricing.

The book moves on to spotlight contributions to the rule of law, public administration, and political science. It highlights a growing understanding of human capital by tracing demographic trends and describing health, education, minority, and labor economics. Enhancements to macroeconomic theory are featured in economic mechanisms and cycles, managing the economy, and policy making.

Striding explores the economic modernization process by outlining the economics of agriculture, growth theories of economic development, and problems with growth. It illustrates contributions to international economics in trade, finance, and global public policy. Finally, the book showcases social justice contributions to social equality, income redistribution, and climate change.

Keywords

nobel laureates of economic sciences; public policy; macroeconomics; microeconomics; human capital; game theory; social justice; technology; the rule of law; the role of government; behavioral economics; modernization; growth theory; institutional theory; financial theory; international trade; econometrics; business cycles

Contents

Testimonials

"Simpson has done a Herculean job of summarizing virtually all of economics in one concise book. He explains how economists make decisions and why they often disagree. He then goes on to summarize leading views on various topics from inflation and the stock markets, to climate change and social justice. This book is a good place to whet your appetite for learning economics."
—**Wilfrid W. Csaplar Jr., PhD, Emeritus Professor of Economics, Bethany College, Bethany, WV**

"David consolidates all the best economic thinkers of the last 100 years and their major contributions into a single book. The historical knowledge summarized in a few hundred pages is a masterpiece. This should be required reading for college economics courses or anyone wanting to gain a broad economics background."—**Milt Best, CFA, Partner, Pathway Capital, Irvine, CA**

"Synergizing the conflicting views of the most brilliant minds of economics into an easy to understand digest is what Simpson has wonderfully achieved. Starting with the building blocks, including terms, tools, and constructive reasoning, Simpson weaves the simple concept of how bread prices are set, into a full educational array of economics from finance to government and human capital to social justice. A talented read of how the world of economics has evolved!"—**Jerry Slusiewicz, President, Pacific Financial Planners, Former Mayor, City of Laguna Niguel, Laguna Niguel, CA**

Preface

Harnessing the concepts and innovations of the contributions of the Nobel Prize for Economic Sciences winners can benefit our well-being. The winners' body of knowledge provides fertile ground to examine the economic behavior of humans as we interact with individuals and institutions.

The laureates concepts might deal with complex social issues, but the challenges are not rocket science. Moreover, the scope and body of their work aren't widely known to the public. Economists intentionally publish literature in a fashion suitable only for other economists. It is a style not always understandable to the general reader. John Maynard Keynes thought the best way to get his ideas disbursed broadly was to first engage with the experts.

Striding With Economic Giants highlights these concepts for the nontechnical reader. This book serves as a gateway to the publications of international Nobel-winning economists and summarizes their thoughts. In addition, the book provides biographical information.

Striding's writing style distills and conveys the concepts using an informal approach. Readers don't need prior experience in economics to enjoy the fruits of the winners' contributions. The author advises the reader to start from the beginning. However, you can jump in anywhere with enough background to understand the topic.

The subject matter of *Striding With Economic Giants* sometimes extends beyond the level of elementary economics. However, in its presentation, the author assumes the general reader has some or a little economics instruction.

CHAPTER 1

Introduction

Remember in childhood when your mother dispatched you to the store to buy a loaf of bread? There were usually five or six offerings with varying sizes, appearances, and smells (supply factors). To preserve wealth, the rational choice would be the one with the lowest price, but are there other considerations (demand characteristics)? What level of satisfaction (utility) are experienced by—your family, your mother, the store owner, the baker, the farmer, or yourself?

Economics is a social science concerned with human consumers and the processes for producing, distributing, and using their goods and services. It examines how individuals, businesses, and governments allocate the available resources. Pilfering Socrates, society's primary objective is to distribute these resources efficiently to yield happiness for its members.

Economics is complicated but not rocket science. It's not rocket science because the variables and patterns are observable to us. It doesn't require the rigor of the physical sciences trying to decipher unseen structures and interactions while using nonsensical terms to describe what's going on. Moreover, you don't have to sport foggy goggles paired with a starched white lab coat.

We can think of economics as an interaction with nature, constantly influencing our daily behavior patterns. The vast quantity of personal interactions and other variables provides the complexity. The challenge for economists is helping society comprehend this abundance. Unfortunately, progress beyond a functional understanding of the basic issues has eluded thinkers for hundreds of years and probably will continue for hundreds more.

But all is not lost. Economists have uncovered fragments of the puzzle, formed plausible concepts, and released their discoveries to the public. As a result, individuals, businesspersons, and public policy makers can benefit from the economists' discoveries.

Our story presents these puzzle pieces in usable forms. It wanders through the established concepts of the economists. The story's main characters are not individuals but *parcels of demonstrated truths* formed into actionable solutions. These headliners of our story are wisdom chestnuts in innovation, institutions, rules of law, accurate measurements, and forms of governance. Think of these gems as individual but related rafts of capital and labor, bound tightly by technology.

The narrative features a solid supporting cast of characters, including the *international Nobel laureates* who develop the gems, often in collaboration. The antagonists of our tale are the *forces of nature* and the *irrationality of individuals*.

The path through our material is not always straightforward and sometimes controversial. For instance, finding solutions to social justice issues requires examining many disparate components. As a result, it is challenging to expect brilliant minds to agree on the proper recipe to fix inequality, income redistribution, or climate change.

Regarding our bread purchase in the opening paragraph, there are several moving parts in this simple transaction. These elements are the result of a plethora of processes in the economy. The meme of the relevance of a fluttering butterfly's wing in China may apply to our quest.

To manage our mission, we limit its scope to the ideas of the leading practitioners in the field. Accordingly, our voyage explores the findings of the winners of the Nobel Prize for Economic Sciences. We begin with austere topics, such as lab experiments and game theory, and finish with complicated ones like inequality and climate change. We explore helpful concepts such as behavioral economics, technology, government role, human capital, and international trade. Learning these concepts will enhance our understanding of economics and assist us in connecting the dots of life.

Nobel Prize in Economic Sciences

Our journey commences by describing the prize selection process of the creative individuals who mined our economic gems. Sveriges Riksbank (the central bank of Sweden) sponsored a new award, the Prize in Economic Sciences, in 1968. The Royal Swedish Academy presents the award annually using the same principles and procedures for the other Nobel Prizes awarded since 1901.

Each September, the academy's Economics Prize Committee, which consists of five elected members, solicits nominations from thousands of scientists, members of academies, and university professors. An academy rule also authorizes members and former laureates to make nominations.

The academy receives 200 to 300 nominations yearly, covering over 100 nominees. However, the committee does not consider unsolicited suggestions. Then, the Prize Committee reviews the proposals.

The committee relies on outside experts who examine the contributions of the most prominent candidates. These experts are sometimes Swedish but usually foreigners. Based on the expert's analysis, the committee selects potential laureates. If there is a tie, the committee's chairperson casts the deciding vote. Finally, the committee presents its proposed award to the Social Science Class of the academy in a report. It includes an extensive survey of the primary candidates considered for a prize.

Based on this report, the class suggests a laureate. They usually follow the committee's recommendation. Occasionally, two or three laureates share the prize. As with the other Nobel Prizes, no more than three people can share the yearly prize. The winners must still be living at the time of the prize announcement in October. The academy doesn't publicly disclose supporting documentation concerning the prize nominations for 50 years.

The Prize Committee and the academy embrace a broad interpretation of economic sciences in presenting their awards. There are established essential criteria for the awards. The academy awards prizes for a single contribution, two specific ones, or lifetime contributions. The selection committee examines the originality of the gift, its scientific and practical importance, and its impact on scientific work. The academy may award scholars from neighboring disciplines who make significant scientific contributions to economics.

Among the various branches of economics, the academy gives prizes in macroeconomics. This branch of economic analysis explains the national economy's behavior in broad aggregates. The academy also offers awards for contributions to microeconomics theory, which involves decision making by individuals, households, and firms. This branch also highlights the allocation of resources among different uses and production sectors in the economy. The academy awards prizes to economists who widen the interdisciplinary domain of economic analysis in new areas. Their work is often on the borderline of economics with political science, sociology, law, history, and philosophy.

The committee recognizes new ways of looking at the economic system. Their awards reflect the economics of information, human capital, game theory, and the role of institutions. However, the committee seeks not to influence the direction of new economics research. They try to maintain a broad approach and take a pluralistic outlook in their decisions. They emphasize the multidimensional nature of economic analysis. Unfortunately, innovations take more time in economics than in physical sciences to determine whether the new contribution is solid and not a fad. So it's essential to wait for scrutiny, criticism, and repeated test of the quality and relevance of a gift.

Economic behavior, like human behavior, is complex and varies over time and place. Moreover, we learn from previous experiences, making it challenging to estimate patterns of behavior. Thus, new results may be relevant only to a temporary intersection of circumstances.

The awarded prize sequence reflects the trail of historical features of economic analysis through the last century. The United States had a dominant role during this period, with 70 percent of the winners being U.S. citizens. Others were born and trained in other countries but spent their professional career at universities in the United States. Because the academy initiated the prize in 1969, the passing of time has sorted out worthy candidates. The committee worked off a heavy backlog of apparent candidates during the first decade.

Table 1.1 lists the recipients, the year of their award, and their year of birth.

Table 1.1 Winners of the Nobel Prize for Economic Sciences

Last Name	First Name	Nobel	Birth
		Year	
Akerlof	George	2001	1940
Allais	Maurice	1988	1911
Arrow	Kenneth	1972	1921
Aumann	Robert J.	2005	1930

Last Name	First Name	Nobel	Birth
		Year	
Banerjee	Abhijit	2019	1961
Becker	Gary	1992	1930
Buchanan	James M.	1986	1919
Coase	Ronald	1991	1910
Deaton	Angus	2015	1945
Debreu	Gérard	1983	1921
Diamond	Peter A.	2010	1940
Duflo	Esther	2019	1972
Engle	Robert F.	2003	1941
Fama	Eugene F.	2013	1939
Fogel	Robert	1993	1926
Friedman	Milton	1976	1912
Frisch	Ragnar	1969	1895
Granger	Clive	2003	1934
Haavelmo	Trygve	1989	1911
Hansen	Lars Peter	2013	1952
Harsanyi	John	1994	1920
Hart	Oliver	2016	1948
Hayek	Friedrich	1974	1899
Heckman	James	2000	1944
Hicks	John	1972	1904
Holmström	Bengt	2016	1949
Hurwicz	Leonid	2007	1917
Kahneman	Daniel	2002	1934
Kantorovich	Leonid	1975	1912
Klein	Lawrence	1980	1920
Koopmans	Tjalling	1975	1910
Kremer	Michael	2019	1964
Krugman	Paul	2008	1953
Kuznets	Simon	1971	1901
Kydland	Finn E.	2004	1943
Leontief	Wassily	1973	1905
Lewis	Arthur	1979	1915
Lucas, Jr.	Robert	1995	1937

(Continues)

Table 1.1 (Continued)

Last Name	First Name	Nobel	Birth
		Year	
Markowitz	Harry	1990	1927
Maskin	Eric S.	2007	1950
McFadden	Daniel	2000	1937
Meade	James	1977	1907
Merton	Robert	1997	1944
Miller	Merton	1990	1923
Mirrlees	James	1996	1936
Modigliani	Franco	1985	1918
Mortensen	Dale T.	2010	1939
Mundell	Robert	1999	1932
Myerson	Roger B.	2007	1951
Myrdal	Gunnar	1974	1898
Nash	John F	1994	1928
Nordhaus	William	2018	1941
North	Douglass	1993	1920
Ohlin	Bertil	1977	1899
Ostrom	Elinor	2009	1933
Phelps	Edmund S.	2006	1933
Pissarides	Christopher	2010	1943
Prescott	Edward C.	2004	1940
Romer	Paul	2018	1955
Roth	Alvin E.	2012	1951
Samuelson	Paul	1970	1915
Sargent	Thomas J.	2011	1943
Schelling	Thomas C.	2005	1921
Scholes	Myron	1997	1941
Schultz	Theodore	1979	1902
Selten	Reinhard	1994	1930
Sen	Amartya	1998	1933
Shapley	Lloyd S.	2012	1923
Sharpe	William F.	1990	1934
Shiller	Robert J.	2013	1946
Simon	Herbert	1978	1916
Sims	Christopher	2011	1942

Last Name	First Name	Nobel	Birth
		Year	
Smith	Vernon L.	2002	1927
Solow	Robert	1987	1924
Spence	Michael	2001	1943
Stigler	George	1982	1911
Stiglitz	Joseph E.	2001	1943
Stone	Richard	1984	1913
Thaler	Richard	2017	1945
Tinbergen	Jan	1969	1903
Tirole	Jean	2014	1953
Tobin	James	1981	1918
Vickrey	William	1996	1914
Williamson	Oliver E.	2009	1932

Text Organization

Striding With Economic Giants arranges the concepts into chapters, subchapters, and topics. The first chapter of our journey introduces the Nobel selection procedure, lists the recipients, and lays out the text organization of the book.

The rest of the book presents the contributions of the Nobel laureates found in their various publications, including books, articles, and speeches. The narrative organizes the material according to the topic in approximate chronological order of publication. Winners' contributions may appear in multiple sections throughout the book.

Laureate contributions to model design, behavioral economics, and game theory are laid out in Chapter 2, "In the Laboratory." Chapter 3, titled "Small-Scale Economics," reviews concepts influencing microeconomics in firm factors, institutional theory, basic market theory, and consumerism.

Chapter 4, "Finance Theory," highlights the winners' impact on financial economics in capital markets, portfolio choice, and asset pricing. Chapter 5, "Role of Government," focuses on areas where the laureates advanced the study of economics in law and the public sector with sections on the rule of law, public administration, and the political economy.

Chapter 6, "Human Capital," highlights the essential production factor of human capital by outlining demographic trends, principles of labor economics, and human development concepts.

Chapter 7, "Domestic Big Picture," showcases contributions in macroeconomics. It includes economic cycles, managing the economy, and macroeconomic theory. Chapter 8, "Modernization," outlines developmental economic growth theory contributions with sections on agriculture, growth theory principles, and problems of growth.

Chapter 9, "International Economics," describes international trade economics, finance, and global public policy advancements. Finally, Nobel contributions to applied economics in equal opportunity and outcomes, income redistribution, and climate change are brought to the forefront in Chapter 10, "Social Justice."

As our first lap draws to a close, in this chapter, we introduced the book, described the prize selection process, listed the winners, and described the text organization of the book. We next look at some of the discoveries found in the economics laboratory.

CHAPTER 2

In the Laboratory

Not all of this tale of economics is riveting. Sometimes, you have to eat your vegetables to gain an understanding of more complex concepts. This chapter investigates the fundamentals of economic model design, behavioral economics, and game theory.

Model Design

The mathematics of economics is an application of mathematical methods to describe economic theories and perform problem analysis. It allows economists to form meaningful, testable propositions. These propositions involve wide-ranging and complex subjects that they can't express informally. Further, the use of mathematics enables economists to make specific, descriptive claims involving controversial or contentious issues that are difficult to convey without mathematics. The math uses differential and integral calculus, matrix algebra, mathematical programming, and other computational methods.

This section explores mathematics, methodology, and models, which represent the blocking and tackling of economics. It segments the basic elements into several areas, including economic mathematics, econometrics, and applied studies.

Building Blocks in Economics

Model designers construct economic models based on standard structures adopted by their community. In addition, logic systems expressed in mathematical terms underpin their designs. This topic excavates these basic foundations of economics by mapping out its mathematics, methodology, and computational experiments. The discussion includes field experiments, forecasting essentials, and self-selection problems in modeler bias.

Mathematics in Economics

Designing a model begins with a review of the mathematics behind the architecture. In the early 20th century, before the heavy use of the computer, economists presented their models using formulas stitched together to form theorems. These formulas relied heavily on algebra and calculus to show relationships and statistics. Trygve Haavelmo (1954), a Norwegian economist, explored the underlying methodology for mathematics in economics, which focuses on *regression* and *stochastic* modeling approaches. The most widely used model in economic analysis is the linear regression model. Economics appropriated this well-established workhorse from physical science. Economic regression models describe associations between a dependent variable and one or more independent variables.

Tjalling Koopmans (1957), a Dutch American mathematician and economist, introduces *linear programming* to economic theory to describe specific maximization problems. The technique presents the elements as a case of the classical competitive equilibrium model. He structured his model primarily in terms of production theory. However, its mathematical structure lends itself to various other interpretations and applications.

The usefulness of the regression model only goes so far. Skeptically, Haavelmo thought regression models in economics belong to the world of fiction. Nobody expects these models to paint an accurate picture. Nonetheless, researchers can strike a reasonable balance between reality and theory if they precisely present the facts. Moreover, Haavelmo suggests independent observers will question the validity of the model's outcome if the researcher crunched the wrong data or made an error of measurement.

Another approach to modeling borrowed from physics is the *stochastic process*. Unfortunately, these models' sources of stochastic predictions are irregular and either external or internal to the data. These source examples include shocks to an economy from discovering technology, a change in the political landscape, or a war. They are Donald Rumsfeld's unknown unknowns that make modeling difficult.

Methodology of Postulates and Theorems

Tjalling Koopmans (1957) from the University of Chicago dives into the dry and unpopular subject (his words) of the *methodology* of economics. Nevertheless, he promotes the potential of new tools available to economists. As in any empirical science, researchers use these tools to derive progress through the continuous observation of economic interactions, proceeding from causal to systematic. The early informality of economics is firmly rooted in methodology.

Initially, economists observe actionable facts involving their inquiry in daily life. Then, they develop these ideas into concepts in understandable proposals. Finally, in democratic environments, a group of enlightened noneconomists must be able to comprehend these policy recommendations to facilitate acceptance in the general community.

Koopmans explores the structure of logic in economics that's discernable beneath the polished prose of professional practitioners. He distinguishes between the *positive* and *normative* analytical approaches. A researcher forms conclusions or predictions, tests possibilities, and verifies or refutes by observation in *positive* analysis. In *normative* analysis, analysts don't limit the purpose of the study to empirical testing of theorems. Instead, they want to right a wrong and develop suggestions for society to normalize their ideas.

Postulates describe any independent premises used as building blocks in economic analysis. Economic postulates are concerned with human outcomes and their choices for achieving them. Once analysts adopt a set of postulates, they tie them together and develop the core reasoning bound by rules of logic. The opportunities to verify predictions and implications derived from the postulates in economics are scarce, and the verification results remain uncertain. This uncertainty is due to the vastness of the economy and the inability to measure it accurately.

Koopmans contends that economists should try to explore all available direct and indirect evidence in these unverifiable conditions. He suggests a researcher should view economic theory as a series of concept models expressed simply. They should consider their theory a prototype to protect this more realistic but simpler theory from unreality and the more complicated next model.

Analytical Tools and Problems

When planning their approach for scientific inquiry, researchers should identify a target phenomenon to study. Then, their specifications should focus only on the problem to investigate. According to Koopmans, the best analytical tools converge on the selected area of concern and the extent it uncovers partial answers.

New research tools introduce severe communication difficulties within the professional economic community due to a lack of common terminology. The oldest mathematical tools in economics were simple numerical examples and diagrams. Later, economists demoted these numerical examples and charts to the humble role of presentation tools.

Then, in the late 1950s, theorists introduced more formal mathematical concepts and theories in economics. Koopmans recalls this paradigm shift encouraged economists to take up mathematical training, which was a departure from the past. This mathematical transformation increased the sensitivity of economists to the significance of the basic postulates of economic theories. Problems in practical operations, such as scheduling, programming, and resource allocation, were where computers proved valuable. Fortunately, progress in these areas was the unintended result of World War II.

Koopmans emphasizes that *modern statistical theory* increases the flexibility, power, and precision of the economists' procedures for drawing interferences from their observations. Researchers use statistical methods extensively in the *econometric* measurement of behavior equations. Koopmans explains that the objectives of econometrics range from demand or supply equations for an individual market to the systems of equations for related, more significant needs.

Field Research Design

Economists need a systemic platform in *field studies* to analyze the rational behavior of subjects from empirical data. For example, Michael Kremer (2003) studied the randomized evaluations of educational programs in developing countries. He used *randomized controlled trials* (RCTs) or randomized impact evaluations to examine target social programs' statistical underpinnings. As a result, RCTs help limit researcher bias and generate valid impact estimates.

By contrast, a *retrospective evaluation* is a research platform where researchers study the area of inquiry by exclusively examining historical data. It allows the study of rare phenomena and is less expensive. Another advantage is that it works with smaller sample sizes and without long-term tracking of subjects to determine outcomes.

Koopmans also suggests purpose-designed *sample field surveys*. They are the primary tool for actively observing qualitative variables. Moreover, they can be quantified or classified. Therefore, sample surveys are the only suitable method for measuring buyers' intentions, attitudes, and expectations. Sample surveys can also contribute to understanding economic behavior's underlying structure. However, researchers face difficulties with their interpretation or identification. These complexities include ones arising from the inferences of aggregate time series.

Regression Methods of Forecasting

Clive Granger (1980), a British econometrician, uses regression models in economic forecasting. The primary challenge in model construction is gathering the appropriate independent variables. In one example, he uses regression models for forecasting corporate dividends. He bases his model on the patterns of previous annual dividends to gaze into the future. It is also helpful in explaining a firm's determination of dividends in terms of earnings.

One practical problem he encountered was measuring the elements of error. To illustrate, he used *error margins* to express the prediction's confidence level. Another source of error is the *degrees of freedom* which deal with the number of variables and how well they explain the data. Granger also touches on the concept of *causality*, which philosophers and research workers dispute. Everyone agrees that the cause occurs before the effect. But is the cause connected to the outcome, or is it a coincidence? The relationships between cause and effect are profound and should not be affected by another variable.

Self-Selection Bias

James Heckman (1990), an American economist, investigates the problem of *self-selection bias* of researchers. This bias occurs when they misinterpret the variables and parameters of their model. He isolates the researcher's self-selected parameters to examine the degree of prejudice. Then, he evaluates the remaining variables not having researcher bias for their effectiveness. Finally, he reviewed the relevant literature and zeroed in on unbiased theories that studied interesting and economically valuable areas. For example, some models used assumptions for smoothing and continuity to manage bias errors.

In other bias examples, researchers didn't adopt solid independent assumptions. Instead, they incorporated the conditional functions of mean indexes. This method was their point of departure for handling sample selection problems. Heckman thinks the more straightforward methods are the most robust of all. The general case models may feature the most variables but appear to be the least empirically fruitful.

Economic Regularities

Maurice Allais (1997), who taught at the University of Paris, maintains that *behavioral regularities* to analyze and forecast should be the prerequisite of economic science. A thorough analysis of economic phenomena should display the presence of frequencies like those found in physical science. Researchers should accept or reject the model and the theory it represents. The idea becomes devoid of scientific interest when the facts from the real world adversely confront the hypothesis.

The expanding interest in practical numerical applications marks Allais' work based on the data provided by observations. All genuine scientific progress advances against a dominant tyranny of ideas generated by the establishment. Nevertheless, along with other economists, he concludes human psychology remains the same worldwide.

Computational Experiments

A Norwegian economist, Finn Kydland (2006) developed *computational* experiments as another tool for economists. His innovative model positions individuals in targeted environments and independently records their behavior (versus traditional aggregate data). These individuals interact in granular settings and are linked together to become computer representations of national economies. The individuals in the model independently make consumption and savings decisions corresponding to their counterparts in real life. Preference for goods and leisure projecting into the indefinite future characterizes his model of people's behavior. First, economists calibrate the model to mimic the world with carefully specified dimensions. Then, they use computers to process the data to answer hypothetical questions.

The model economies in these computational experiments consist of households and governments. Kydland's model also contains thousands of firms combined into an aggregate production function. Computational experiments generate a time series of the aggregate decisions of the people in the model. He uses the model to observe government behavior under various contingencies and policy rules.

In this topic, we discussed how model designers construct standard models based on logic systems expressed in mathematical terms. We mapped out mathematics, methodology, and computational experiments. The discussion included field investigations, the essentials of forecasting, and the problem with modeler self-selection bias.

As a result of the explosion of computer capacity, economists could now construct a general model that describes regional, national, or global economies in purely mathematical terms. Next, we take a peek at econometrics. The field's early pioneers were John Maynard Keynes, John Hicks, and Lawrence Klein.

Econometrics

Our inspection of economic models to study bread choice has a long way to go. So far on our journey, we looked at generic models of isolated sectors in the economy. This topic examines econometrics involving large scale. It's a branch of economics where practitioners base their mathematical models on empirical data to describe more significant phenomena. The scope of their models ranges from regional, national, and global economies.

A Magic Formula

John Maynard Keynes (1936) and John Hicks (1939) were two economists based in the United Kingdom when a significant revolution was brewing in the 1930s. At the time, economists began developing comprehensive models for the general economy. Their early models were based on *collective aggregate levels* for economic variables and assumed firms attempted to maximize profits. However, these theories were misleading for not considering the essential behavior of individuals, as Kydland later incorporated into his *conditional* model.

An *index number approach* is an alternate way of integrating these behavioral inputs and outputs relationships into models. Lawrence Klein (1943), an American economist, describes how *econometricians* build their dynamic models for studying cycles, forecasting, simulating alternative policies, and understanding the structures of complicated systems. Econometric models are magical formulas divulging all complex world secrets in a single equation.

Soon after World War II, policy makers studied the economy's aggregate investment and savings aspects. They wondered what levels of these aggregates the economy required to reach optimum GDP levels. Solving this question involves developing an aggregate schedule of demand and supply. This analysis of the GDP level also considers the time lags between investment and resulting income.

Initially, econometricians measured past relationships among consumer spending, household income, tax rates, interest rates, and employment. Then, Klein incorporated a scheme of a time lag between investment and outcome. This innovation drew much attention from the economics community. However, the essence of these systems of business cycles is that authentic relationships don't perfectly correlate with the internal dependent variables. Instead, they are interrelated stochastically. Using a stochastic approach, economists can study the dynamic characteristics of relational variables and their timing in the research of economic cycles.

In the 1960s, Klein helped develop the Wharton models. Economists still widely use these models in forecasting GDP, exports, investment, and consumption. The original model used 51 stochastic equations. The models' estimation of time lag resembled the time measurement methods of electrical engineering. It was also desirable to provide analytical tools for public economic policy independent of the researcher's judgments. Computer integration into econometrics expanded its focus. Other researchers advanced the science by combining the Wharton model's *input–output analysis* with *mathematical economics* (statistical inference).

By the 1970s, the older Keynesian demand-oriented models could no longer account for the problems of short, mild cycles with persistently high inflation. So Klein expanded his new basic models to reflect the shift away from the Keynesian models by focusing more on the supply side.

Statistical Modeling of Monetary Policy

Christopher Sims (2012) is an American econometrician and macroeconomist. He thinks that the study of economics adheres to higher constraints and deeper tensions among highly regarded practitioners, unlike other sciences. As a result of these characteristics, individual theories come and go rather than building on a unified body of knowledge over time. This ebb and flow theme is evident in his chronicling of the transition from demand orientation to monetary supply focus in the 1950s. The clash involved *theoretical* Keynesian models versus the Haavelmo/Tinbergen *statistical probability* models. Critics felt the weak spot in Haavelmo's approach was his heavy use of the ranges of chance or randomness in variables and policy intervention.

Milton Friedman (1962), an American economist and statistician, embarked in a different direction, developing models using a shorter list of variables. The variables are limited to measuring the money supply, high-powered money, broad price indexes, and actual activity such as industrial production and its behavior. He embraced a simpler view where monetary policy has powerful effects on economic systems and is the primary driving force behind business cycles.

None of these models consider public policy behavior. Contrarily, James Tobin (1997), an American economist, thought observed patterns of money supply arose from high correlations with public policy timing. Therefore, erratic monetary policy can't be the source of cycle fluctuations. Furthermore, Tobin feels the changes to the money supply are exogenous.

At the same time, Sims (2012), a Princeton University professor, sees these fluctuations as testable.

By the 1980s, Keynesians also struggled to incorporate money supply into their models. In contrast, monetarists used simpler models to explain the correlation between income and interest rates. Monetarists isolate monetary policy. To them, the rest of the economy is a black box. Researchers use these simpler monetary models to make conditional policy projections. However, central banks don't widely adopt them. Instead, the banks want to incorporate other scenarios involving the price ranges of commodities due to supply disruptions, ranges of productivity growth, currency value declines, and changes in fiscal policy. Despite early confusion in incorporating data time series, the eventual adjustments to the Keynesian model resolved the controversies between Keynesians and monetarists.

The changes in interest rates engineered by the Federal Reserve substantially affect the economy, primarily real output and inflation. The influence of monetary policy on output is immediate, but the effects on inflation take longer. Unfortunately, the financial crash of 2008 woke everybody up. No one predicted it because the event significantly departed from the existing probabilities in historical data. Recognizing the likelihood of large and rare model errors is a technical challenge and why they receive little attention.

This section examined econometric models of regional, national, and global economies. It highlighted the basics of econometrics, Wharton models, and modeling monetary policy. In the next area, we will discover places where society can harness the advances of econometrics. We can also determine how effectively their model contributes to the decision-making process in setting public policy.

Applied Studies

Economists develop these econometric models to provide more precise insight into an economy for policy makers. This section highlights two applications contributing to this insight: Wassily Leontief's *input–output tables* and Robert Engle's intriguing advance in *measuring the variance* in a data set. The input–output table uses a spreadsheet style to describe how sectors interact. Engle, a New York University professor, introduces a class of stochastic processes to improve forecasting.

Input–Output Tables

Wassily Leontief (1947), a Soviet American economist, revolutionized economic modeling and is the father of *input–output analysis*. His insightful models view a region, country, or even the world's whole economy as a single system. It interprets all its functions in terms of specific, measurable properties of economic structures. Leontief considers a competitive economy as a gigantic, natural computing machine tirelessly grinding out the solutions to an unending stream of quantitative problems the economy automatically feeds in. Input–output tables can also present the streams of goods and services among all the different economic sectors of nations.

The essential structure of the input–output method is a squared matrix like a spreadsheet with the same number of rows as columns. The labels for rows and columns are identical. The horizontal rows show how the economy distributes the output of each sector group among the other sector inputs. Conversely, the vertical columns show how each sector obtained its needed inputs of goods and services from the others. The amount in the field where the rows and columns intersect represents the related economic flow between the labeled sectors.

The tables reveal the fabric of an economy that the model weaves together. It uses the flow of commerce linking each branch and industry to all others. The central concept of input–output analysis is the fundamental relationship between input volume and industrial output.

The U.S. government released the first official input–output table in 1947. The tables of developed countries yield recipes for the structures of modern technology for fully functional economies. For example, efficient economic systems naturally combine the global division of labor with the minimization of the cost of transportation.

Autoregressive Conditional Heteroskedasticity

Robert Engle (1995) is an American economist and statistician. He explains that traditional econometric models assume a *constant one-period forecast variance.* In other words, the average difference from the mean for errors is consistent throughout the model. However, a class of stochastic processes introduced by Engle, a professor at New York University, proves this assumption is implausible. He developed an irreverently named but insightful concept, autoregressive conditional heteroskedastic (ARCH), to demonstrate this implausibility.

Researchers find that their ability to predict the future varies from one period to another. This critical finding is significant as minor errors tend to cluster irregularly in continuous periods. For example, economists can use ARCH to explain the variances of predicted long-term interest rates by using traditional expectations hypotheses.

Economists find evidence of these variations in monetary and finance theory. The precision of the expected future varies significantly over time. For example, ARCH made regularly accurate forecasts in quiet periods of capital markets, such as the mid-1960s. However, in volatile periods like the early 1970s and 1980s, the estimates were less specific when speculation was more pronounced. Therefore, markets adjust the *risk premia* (the required spread of investors over the return of the riskless asset) to induce investors to absorb the more significant uncertainty associated with holding the asset.

This section reviewed input–output tables and new mathematical applications for practical use. The value-added comes from sharpening the precision of decision-making resources generated from the output of the models. These models determine the precise relationships between sectors of an economy and enable policy makers to make accurate decisions.

Behavioral Economics

We don't always make the best decisions. In contrast, economists rely on models of perfect *rational decisions* where they assume the decision makers have complete information about variables. These model decision makers also have the time, cognitive ability, and resources to evaluate each choice against the other options. Our journey in search of how the economy provides bread compels us to find the nature of the *discrepancy between real-life decisions and perfect rationality.*

Behavioral economics is primarily involved with the bounds of rationality for decision makers. Models of behavior typically integrate psychology, neuroscience, and microeconomic theory insights. Behavioral economics includes how the collective market makes decisions and the mechanisms driving public choice. Rational thinking is the capability to consider the relevant variables of situations and access, organize, and analyze the appropriate information to arrive at sound conclusions. This information includes facts, opinions, judgments, and data.

In this section, we acquaint ourselves with the nature of rational thinking. Then, the journey moves to behavioral models involving cognitive processing systems and bias. Finally, we look at how decisions are affected by uncertainty.

Rational Decision Making

This topic explores rational thinking theories, advances in the laboratory, and psychological models describing two-channel systems of thought processes.

Rational Behavior Theories

John Harsanyi (1977), a Hungarian American economist, focuses on how we ideally promote our interests. Yet, at the same time, his theories predict and paint a picture of the behavior of real-life humans. Despite this goal of directness in behavior, humans fall short of rationality due to unconscious emotional factors. American political scientist Herb Simon's (1945) theory of *bounded rationality* offers an alternate reason for limiting our thinking capacity: available information and time. Despite these limitations, Harsanyi develops theories of perfectly rational behavior that generate approximate predictions about actual social patterns over various situations. Behavior conforms to at least some form of persuasive rationality when rationality can't directly explain what's going on.

From experience, we tend to give lesser weight to other individuals' interests than our own. We also tend to give even less importance to the interests of a stranger than acquaintances. As a result, we are confident we assess social situations from impartial and impersonal points of view.

Harsanyi feels that when we judge moral values on the merits of alternative social cases, we hold clear ideas of our station in life.

A controversial point in utility theory is whether comparing the utility of two individuals who often have different frames of reference is acceptable. Harsanyi thinks comparing the utility between two or more individuals, in principle, shouldn't be more problematic than comparing the sets of the utility of the same person.

Studying Behavior in the Laboratory

Elinor Ostrom (2005), an American political scientist, maintains that studying human behavior in an experimental laboratory is an excellent way to understand the components of human action. Evaluating these active components is an effective way to learn behavior and outcomes. Within her *institutional analysis and development* (IAD) framework, the concept of a situation with human action generalizes a device to allow for internal changes in its rules. She explores the potential of her core concept to serve as a foundation for systematic approaches. This base foundation leads to more elaborate models of complex policy networks.

She explores how changes in the structure of action situations in experiments affect outcomes. The researchers' instructions given to subjects initiate these desired changes and the adopted procedures of the investigation. Interestingly, Ostrom finds participants engage in more cooperative behavior than predicted when using behavior models based on purely monetary returns. Vernon Smith (2008), another American economist, and other researchers also observed this mutual behavior. Trust and reciprocity depend on the relative social positions of the subjects when they possess critical information and can administer sanctions.

Ostrom notes subjects with opportunities for face-to-face discussions share their understanding of how their actions affect the joint outcomes. The subjects are willing to promise things to others they deem trustworthy. They adopt standard plans of mutual action. Most individuals keep their promises. However, if they break agreements, the other individuals become indignant and use verbal chastisement when available. Ostrom also observes that when subjects cannot communicate face-to-face, they overuse the shared pool of resources.

Elinor Ostrom's and Vernon Smith's conclusions aren't consistent with the predictions derived from the classic game theory models. In game situations, the participants focus on monetary returns. However, the findings of Ostrom and Smith are consistent with evidence gathered from empirical research in the field.

Systems of Rationality in Economics

In experimental economics, Chapman University professor, Vernon Smith (2008) found that impersonal exchanges in repeated market interactions converge to equilibrium states. However, the economic theory implies this under weaker information conditions than the idea specifies. In personal, social, and economic exchange, cooperation exceeds the traditional predictions of game theory. Smith thought in cultural exchanges, the role of *constructivism* (his term), or reason, provides variation. Another parallel process, the role of *ecological* processes (his other term), selects among the norms and institutions serving the well-being of society.

Smith introduces these two processes as a guide to illustrate the two types of patterns of human reasoning. They are like the two-channel systems of rational human thought developed by Daniel Kahneman (2011), an Israeli American psychologist and economist, and Richard Thaler and Cass Sunstein (2008), American economists. These three models developed independently have similar characteristics.

Smith's *constructivism*, Kahneman's *system 2*, and Thaler and Sunstein's *reflective system* share similar traits. These slower channels process thoughts more deliberatively along a logical path. This path is based on established truths to reach reasoned conclusions, much like the character of Dr. Spock in "Star Trek."

In the other channel, the decision making resembles Captain Kirk and his "shoot from the hip" style. Smith's *ecological* approach, Kahneman's *system 1*, and Thaler's *automatic system* loosely characterize this process. Instead of a logical progression, this channel of impulsive reasoning does a quick recall of similar prior individual experiences and impressions. It then arrives at a "gut feel."

Smith seems to think many other economists and individuals don't distinguish between these two channels of rationality. Experimental economics enables economists to study and understand rationality and how the two channels work together. He suggests that his two kinds of rationality interact daily in the exchanges of ordinary humans. However, this exchange process is invisible to our conscious experience.

Smith explains *cooperation* in anonymous two-person game theory situations is where researchers observe unexpected behaviors. Like Ostrom's (2005) findings, this benevolence suggests we solve decision problems by drawing on context-laden experience. However, rational theoretical thoughts with abstract properties independent of context do not solve it. Face-to-face interactions swamp the impact of subtle processes entirely to yield outcomes with efficient cooperation. Nonetheless, Smith thought this interaction was the preferred way of real-world bargaining. Curiously, these tendencies fade away in double-blind settings of experiments where participants aren't interacting face-to-face.

The key conclusion from these context-related experiments is that neither the experiment subjects nor their real-life counterparts think about the problems of the decision rationally. In this topic, we looked at rational thinking theories, advances in the laboratory, and psychological models describing two-channel systems of thought processes. The next subject describes models built on these theories, advances, and psychology.

Behavioral Models

In this section, we further investigate the thought process models of Vernon Smith, Daniel Kahneman, and Richard Thaler. We discuss their similarities and how to apply their insight in our daily lives. Finally, our journey wanders through factors influencing our thinking and ponders some of our mistakes.

In nuanced distinctions from Smith's views, Daniel Kahneman (2011), a professor at Princeton University, also develops theories for thinking processes and the biases of intuition. However, he doesn't focus on the reasons for the errors because most of our judgments and actions are often appropriate. Instead, Kahneman explores our ability to identify and understand these errors in ourselves and others. Furthermore, he provides a rich, precise language to discuss the process.

Kahneman suggests that individuals usually respond if we ask them what they think. This condition occurs because they believe they know what's happening in their minds, but Kahneman doesn't think that's how the mind works. Instead, the impressions and thoughts of most of us arise in our conscious experience. But, often, we don't know how the ideas got there.

Mental Processing Systems

When faced with a decision, we search our memory collection of prior similar situations and produce an intuitive answer. Kahneman labels this process *system 1* (Captain Kirk). When intuition fails, we switch to a slower, more deliberate, and effortful process of thinking called *system 2* (Dr. Spock).

The mind activates both systems when we are awake. System 1 runs automatically, generating suggestions for system 2. Most of the time, system 2 adopts system 1's recommendations until system 1 runs into difficulty. When a surprise event occurs at odds with our perception of the world, we experience a conscious surge of attention.

The primary function of system 1 is to maintain and update a model of our world representing what we expect. This structure usually works well, but system 1 has biases or makes systematic errors in specified circumstances. For example, system 1 answers the more straightforward questions but does not understand the underlying logic and statistics. Another problem is that the mind can't turn it off.

System 2 has limited capacity. When it's overloaded, it protects the most critical activities. System 2 assigns more attention to secondary activities as disk space frees up. The performance of secondary assignments improves as the primary activity becomes less demanding.

Causality and Biases

Our mind doesn't like to contemplate the unknown beyond what is required to form our opinions. Kahneman calls this limiting mechanism *what you see is all there is* (WYSIATI). Another effect, *anchoring*, occurs when we settle on a value for an unknown quantity in preparation for estimating an amount. Thaler and Sunstein (2008) also address this anchoring and adjustment effect. Finally, Kahneman suggests that when judging the frequency of events, our mind draws on past experiences. For example, this bias occurs when evaluating the truth in media reporting. Thaler and Sunstein also found this aid of availability for learning and discovery.

The *narrative fallacy* is how flawed past stories shape our perception of the world and expectations for our future. Kahneman contends that the core illusion of ourselves is what we believe we understood from the past. A general limitation of our mind is its imperfect ability to reconstruct our past states of knowledge or beliefs when they change. The *bias of hindsight* has harmful effects on the deliberative process of decision makers.

The *halo effect* refers to stories of success and failure. This effect is the process of accepting the opinions of influencers and celebrities over our own. This acceptance is appropriate if our subjective confidence in judgments is not a reasoned evaluation of probability. Experts try to think freely, but the complexity of the problem usually reduces their validity. Kahneman claims our worldview has a pervasive bias of optimism. We see the world as more benign than it is. As a result, society makes numerous attempts to train us to express our confidence level, reflecting our imprecisions of judgment.

Economists root *utility theory* on measuring our resulting happiness when making decisions. It's a model of individual choice based on the arguments. A rational individual makes their decision to maximize utility. In a related concept, Kahneman (2011) and Harry Markowitz (1959), an American economist, hold that we focus on maximizing the change in wealth rather than the absolute level of wealth.

Well-Being

Memories shape tastes and decisions but are often wrong. The well-being we experience as we live is only one aspect of well-being. Kahneman claims more education is associated with a deeper evaluation of one's life, but not greater well-being. He finds a low correlation between our circumstances and our satisfaction with life. Instead, our temperament determines the way we experience them.

The possibility of using a measure of well-being as an indicator to guide public policies is attracting the attention of policy makers. Although we aren't irrational, we often need help to make more accurate judgments and better decisions. In some cases, policies and institutions help. Institutions are better than individuals when preventing errors because they naturally think slower and have the power to enact orderly procedures. As a result, they process judgments and decisions with a broader range of rationality. However, Milton Friedman (1962) and the Chicago school draw a distinction. They firmly believe in human rationality. Using institutions to protect us against our choices is unnecessary and immoral.

Biases and Blunders

In a departure from Friedman's and Kahneman's views, Richard Thaler and Cass Sunstein (2008) advocate *libertarian paternalism*. Their term appears to be an oxymoron. Libertarianism implies freedom of thought. Their form of paternalism suggests government and other institutions should guide us to make decisions serving our long-term interests. Thaler and Sunstein present solutions to help us make good decisions without curtailing our freedom. They suggest that *architects of behavioral choice* are responsible for organizing the selection context so we can make good decisions. There are parallels between choice architecture and traditional physical architecture. Critically, there is no neutral design.

The libertarian aspect is a straightforward insistence that we can do what we like. But, on the other hand, the paternalistic component presents the claim: It's legitimate for choice architects to influence our behavior to make our lives longer, healthier, and better. Policies are paternalistic if they affect the choice to make the chooser better off as judged by themselves.

Thaler and Sunstein's *nudge* is any aspect of choice architecture altering our behavior in predictable ways without forbidding any options. Their primary field of study is the science of choice. Critics rejecting paternalism insist we do a terrific job of making decisions. They feel we favor freedom of choice and reject any form of paternalism.

One of Thaler and Sunstein's thinking channels is reflective and rational, called the *reflective system*. This Dr. Spock thinking process is like

Vernon Smith's constructivism and Kahneman's system 2. The reflective system is more deliberate and self-conscious. Thaler and Sunstein's other channel, the *automatic system* (Captain Kirk), is rapid and doesn't involve thinking. It's associated with the oldest parts of the brain we share with animals.

The reflective system develops conscious thought while the automatic system expresses gut reactions. Gut feelings are pretty accurate but are often mistaken when relying too heavily on the automatic system. We are busy, and our lives are complicated. A "rule of thumb" is an aid to representativeness or similarity in learning.

Unrealistic optimism explains our risk-taking, especially for taking risks in life and health. However, Thaler and Sunstein maintain that we could benefit from an outside nudge because we take unnecessary risks when we possess unrealistic optimism. Architects of choice try to influence our choices made by their automatic system. We choose whatever options require the least effort or path of least resistance. They believe the required choice, favored by many who like freedom, is sometimes the best way to go.

In this last section, we investigated thought process models. We discussed their similarities and how to apply their insight to our daily lives. Finally, we contemplated factors influencing our thinking and pondered why we make mistakes. Uncertainty places a strain on our thought processes when we make decisions. This next topic examines choices made under uncertainty and distinguishes the differences between likes, wants, and needs.

Decisions Under Uncertainty

Choice Under Uncertainty

Peter Diamond was an American economist. Diamond and Rothschild (1978) examine our choices when making a decision under uncertainty. They present the relevance of the maximization of expected utility for positive and normative theories of personal preference. They examine why we expose ourselves to the risk of injury, damage, or loss while having some notion of benefit or gain.

Risk-taking can be constructive, creative, and healthy. Moreover, it frequently generates positive results for society and us. However, there are other forms of risk where the benefits are less apparent and the risk is more prominent. Here, we take risk-taking actions with less deliberation, with incomplete planning, for negative reasons, and without taking responsibility. Extreme risk is neurotic risk-taking, where the dangers of reality outweigh the benefits of fact. These neurotics motivate themselves primarily by negative aims rather than achieving a positive goal. They choose this path to relieve a psychological feeling of pain.

Likes, Wants, and Needs

Abhijit Banerjee, an Indian American, and Esther Duflo (2019), a French American, are economists and the only husband–wife Nobel winners. They are alarmed by the expressions of absolute hatred of individuals toward individuals of different races, religions, ethnicity, and gender. They suggest we must sharply distinguish between a preference and a belief to understand this hatred. For example, choices reflect whether we prefer cake or cookies. We may have wrong ideas, but we can't have unfair preferences.

Gary Becker (1962) and George Stigler (1986) are American economists. They believe asking why irrational choice makes sense when closing our minds to its possible logic is more beneficial. They attribute this paradox to collective hysteria. This standard view of preferences is influential because it treats the choices as coherent and stable.

Banerjee and Duflo contend that fads are social conformity. They result from a small group of individuals' rational decisions with no intention of conforming with social norms. We believe this smaller group possesses better information than we do, so we follow the influencers. Banerjee and Duflo suggest these superficial fads are examples of herd mentality. Standard preferences also rationalize social norms. The rest of the community punishes those violating these norms. Folk theorems in game theory are the formal demonstrations of this argument. It's logically coherent and explains why standards are so powerful.

A more precise picture forms once society correctly acknowledges its beliefs and perceives these preferences. However, Jean Tirole's (1988) work on motivated ideas of individuals suggests economists should not take these beliefs too seriously. Instead, he thinks emotional needs shape the views of society. The role of preferences is crucial. Discussing growth, inequality, and the environment without considering needs, wants, and preferences are impossible. Wants aren't needs. We often use irrational thinking in choices.

This last topic examined decisions made under uncertainty and distinguished the differences between likes, wants, and needs from a psychological perspective. In contrast, the following section uses a mathematical approach to portray human behavior.

Game Theory

Game theory is one of the most significant branches of social sciences developed in the last 50 years. An American economist, Roger Myerson (1991), defines game theory as the study of mathematical models of conflict and cooperation between intelligent and rational decision makers. It provides general mathematic techniques for analyzing situations where two or more individuals influence one another's welfare. Even though the name suggests it, game theory isn't a recreational activity. Myerson felt conflict analysis, or the theory of interactive decisions, is a more accurate term. Still, social science is stuck with game theory.

Myerson recalls that researchers worked on game theory during World War II in the same intellectual community where many theoretical physics researchers toiled. The theory's position in the mathematical foundation of social sciences provides appeal and promise. Game theorists try to understand human conflict and cooperation by studying quantitative models and examples of hypotheses. Their models are unrealistically simple. However, this simplicity makes fundamental conflict and collaboration easier to evaluate in controlled settings.

This section explores the world of game theory. First, we walk through the basics, study simple games, and expand our investigation into complex games. Then we show how we can use these ideas.

Simple Games

A game in game theory refers to any social situation involving two or more individuals. A decision maker is rational if they make decisions consistently in pursuit of their objectives. For example, maximizing the expected payoff of personal utilities isn't necessarily in line with maximizing the expected monetary gain. Bayesian decision theory, an approach to estimation and inference, forms the root of game theory. The model expresses the uncertainty of known parameters in probability distributions.

Analysis of games or conflict situations begins with the specifications of the model describing the game. Like the development of parameters in statistics, the distributions found in empirical data form the basis of the distribution of structural parameters of the game theory model. Games with incomplete information start at the point where players begin to plan their moves in the game.

The following topic covers rational behavior theory basics and the Nash equilibrium, and applies them to social settings. We also go over the Shapley value and a model of impulse behavior.

General Theory of Rational Behavior

John Harsanyi's (1977) general theory of rational behavior produces game *solutions*, such as the solutions corresponding to vectors of unique payoffs for each game. In addition, his theory specifies *strategies* where rational players most effectively advance their interests against other rational players. These solutions furnish predictions about bargaining outcomes among rational players. Results depend on each player's rewards and penalties for each additional player. Players face several problems when developing these strategies. First, the payoff distribution of bargaining should center on an efficient payoff vector. In simple bargaining games, the rules specify the vectors of conflict-payout or the points of conflict where it confines the players.

John von Neuman was a Hungarian American mathematician and physicist who worked on the Manhattan Project. Oskar Morgenstern was a German American economist. They met on the faculty of Princeton University and collaborated to found the field of game theory. Harsanyi's theory is a departure from the concept of stronger and sharper behavior presented by the seminal work of von Neuman and Morgenstern (1944). Instead, Harsanyi evaluates how the expectations of a rational player considers the other player's behavior. Each function of a player's utility determines the utility derived from any physical outcome, called the payoff. Each player plans by deciding in advance what moves they make in any situation before the game begins.

Economists and others extend these same concepts to real-life settings. For example, in social situations with more than two players, the bargaining literature in the 1970s developed cases where rational players form overlapping *coalitions* of two or more. Harsanyi's theory finds a middle ground by predicting the emergence of different structures of coalitions and social situations of indifference.

Nash Equilibrium

Von Neuman and Morgenstern (1944) didn't furnish defined solutions for bargaining problems. John Nash Jr. (1950), an American mathematician, was the first to use Von Neuman and Morgenstern's cardinal (ranking) utility function. This function led to a fixed theory when it integrated biological rationale. Russell Crowe portrayed Nash in the 2001 film *A Beautiful Mind*. Nash made several landmark contributions to game theory, but the most significant is the *Nash equilibrium*. He used an analysis of best choices to generalize a game situation. For example, there is a minimum requirement for strategic pairs of options to be candidates for the optimal solution of a two-person game. Each strategy is the best response to the other, known as the *Nash solution*. In other words, given perfect information, no alternative outcome would yield more utility for each player.

Nash also recognizes the process of interactive adjustments, where players possessing Simon's (1945) bounded rationality observe the strategies played by their opponents over time. As a result, they gradually adjust their plan to earn higher payoffs, leading to a Nash equilibrium.

The theory of *cooperative* games is more freewheeling than the *noncooperative* game theory. The cooperative game theory concerns situations where players negotiate before the contest begins. First, they decide on what choices to make in the game. Then, these negotiations wrap up with the signing of a binding agreement. Before Nash, theorists thought this *pregame bargaining* was vague. These theorists didn't identify principles about how two rational players settle their differences. Nash demonstrates a solution set encompassing the whole problem, producing a unique solution. This solution includes pregame bargaining and the game itself. The bargaining outcomes depend on the players' results and preferences over the complete agreement.

Nash from Princeton University distinguishes between haggling and bargaining. *Haggling* is the case where information on the preferences of each player is incomplete. Real-world *bargaining* is where information on players' circumstances is common knowledge. A *solution* means determining the satisfaction everyone expects from the situation or what it's worth to bargain. Examples of real-world examples are monopoly versus monopsony, international trading between two nations, and employer and labor negotiations.

Harsanyi (1977), a professor at the University of California, Berkley, contends that analyzing two players' *mutual* expectations about the other's behavior justifies Nash's postulate. This justification holds because neither player expects a rational opponent to grant them better terms than they are willing to concede in an asymmetrical game. In cooperative games, Harsanyi suggests game rules don't uniquely determine players' conflict payoffs if they can't agree on outcomes. They must rely on their strategies of *conflict* instead.

Each player implements a *threat* only at a specific cost to oneself. In conflict situations, each player prefers to save the cost of danger. In cooperative games without an urgent threat, if negotiations break down and conflict arises, any threats made in the earlier stages don't restrict the freedom of action of a player.

Actual Social Settings

Theories of bargaining games directly apply to social situations where two economic or political units are anxious to expand and preserve their relative positions of power. In these cases, Harsanyi assumes these players make only one choice simultaneously. However, there are situations where one player irrevocably commits themselves to some demand. This demand is their *ultimatum*. These ultimatum games arise when one player commits to the agreement before others respond. Asymmetries occur when there's a substantial difference in size between bargaining units.

Theorists regard ultimatum games as degenerate games of bargaining where circumstances reduce practical bargaining. If both parties expect to agree, theorists don't judge the conflict strategy's net payoff.

The American economist, Thomas Schelling (1960), suggests that participants don't always take *enforceable promises* for granted. Enforcement depends on establishing a legal authority to punish or coerce. This authority also possesses the ability to determine whether the behavior warrants punishment.

Schelling also demonstrates that an available tactic is *delegation to an agent*. At issue is the portion of the player's total interest. It can also be a component of all the initiatives for decision. However, the agent becomes another player in the game. Theorists view the role of *mediator*, whether imposed on the game by original rules or adopted by players, as an arrangement of communications. Irrevocable authority surrendered by players converts this mediator into an arbitrator. As a result, Schelling suggests game tactics and situations depend on the communication structure.

The Shapley Value

American mathematician and economist Lloyd Shapley (1988) proposes determining the total worth of all payouts from playing a game. This amount became known as the *Shapley value*. Other economists derived the same function of value but from entirely different assumptions. Earlier, von Neumann and Morgenstern (1944) found a way to summarize each choice facing a player with a single number. Shapley's 1953 work further outlines the complex possibilities facing each player in a function of characteristics. But, again, it uses a single number to represent the game's total value.

A simple game is no more than a list of winning coalitions. Nevertheless, they are often the model of a natural situation where circumstances don't justify the total weight of usual assumptions about a game of function of characteristics.

Impulse Balance

Reinhard Selten (2015), a German economist and a University of Bonn professor, developed a theory of *impulse balance* based on the path of player learning. It predicts a *mixed strategy* (personal and random chance moves) for every player in an arbitrary *n-person* game (n means any number). A mixed method employs a *randomizing device*, such as a coin toss or dice, to select between two or more actions in addition to player choice. Rational deliberation can't evaluate this mixed strategy because of the randomness element. Instead, it's a pure distribution of strategic behavior in a long section of a super game. As the game's length approaches infinity, the process of pure strategy choice settles into a stationary state with a corresponding plan featuring a stable group of *mixed-method activities*.

The theories of Nash equilibrium and impulse balance are both free of parameters. They don't depend on estimating parameters from the data of experiments. Approaches that are not parameter-free in this sense aren't genuinely predictive.

The previous topic covered simple game basics and the Nash equilibrium and applied it to social settings. We also went over the Shapley value and a model of impulse behavior. While the games discussed thus far involved a few subjects, designing the game theory to describe society requires handling additional factors. The following two sections describe the complex game theory, take a reality check, and analyze auctions. They also look at voting and games with incomplete information.

Complex Games

In more complex games, Nash (1950) explains that *n-person* games are games where each player has finite sets of pure strategies. Groups of payout to n players correspond to each *n-tuple* of pure methods. So there's one strategy for each player. Harsanyi (1977) adds that in n-person games, players often form *coalitions*. Suppose two or more players form a team and function as one bargaining unit. In that case, this coalition weakens the bargaining position of the remaining players. As a result, the alliance is less willing to risk a conflict or receive less incentive to press for better terms. Instead, they share any concession they obtain with partners of the coalition.

The payoff functions are the expectations of players for a *mixed strategy* with random chance and personal moves as a probability distribution. A *dominant* situation exists when one player is always best in choosing actions, whatever others do. In *transfer-utility games*, the rules permit a player to transfer unlimited utility between one another without changing their joint payoff. These games of transfer utility aren't strictly games of bargaining.

Reality Check

Individuals and institutions can utilize these game theory principles in many real-world situations, from buyer and seller to politics to international diplomacy. Let's explore some of the applications.

Shapley suggests measuring the value of role-playing in an n-person game helps determine the equitable distribution of wealth available to players through game participation. In addition, it allows us to assess their prospects by playing the game. For example, players want a framework that is advantageous to them when forming a coalition in an unsymmetrical situation. This phenomenon is well known in the real world at many levels, from decision making in organizations, such as corporations and universities, to international negotiations.

The simplest model for a negotiation framework is a structure of a *coalition. Competitive equilibrium* is a notion of a noncooperation equilibrium based on the optimization of individuals. When analyzing large games, *technology* describes the payoffs achievable by any group of players in ways continuously dependent on a player's attributes.

In the real world, different solutions become equivalent in an economic environment where there's perfect competition and no single individual affects the overall outcome. So, for example, labor wages equal their value to the *employer* in perfectly competitive markets. In contrast, rewards proportional to the *employee's* contribution have considerable ethical appeal. This appeal reflects widely held views on what constitutes just compensation without referencing the theory of perfect competition.

Roger Myerson (1991), a professor at the University of Chicago, suggests the most straightforward solution to a strategic game is a *threat*. Without assessing various design probabilities, each player used this solution. He also feels Nash's equilibrium concept is the most critical solution concept in game theory. He suggests that if a player acts as a *theorist*, they try to predict the behavior of other players in each game.

On the other hand, if they function as a *social planner*, they try to prescribe players' behavior.

Auctions and Bidding Games

William Vickrey (1939), a Canadian American economist, theorizes that the strategy of a bidder depends on the possession of information concerning the object's value to other bidders. He assumes all players know this distribution in advance.

Thomas Schelling (1960), a professor at the University of Maryland, distinguishes *rational* and *irrational* behavior among conflict theories. Irrational behavior treats conflict as a crude contest where players try to win. On the other hand, in the sensible conflict of consciousness, players with intelligent and sophisticated behavior seek rational rules of conduct. This pragmatic strategy is significant when participants are actively in conflict. For example, in the case of bargaining in international diplomacy, each side wants to win in the proper sense. These participants also want to understand how other participants behave in these situations. They might want to control or influence the behavior of others. They want to know what variables are subject to their control.

The pure conflict between the opposing interests of two antagonists is a particular case and leads to war. In this situation, strategy isn't about applying efficient force but projecting potential energy. Schelling stresses that *deterrence* is a cornerstone of the U.S. national security strategy. However, the characteristics of institutional and structural negotiations make commitment tactics easy or difficult to employ. He suggests that limited war requires limits. The study of *tacit bargaining* applies to minor conflict or little competition, where communication is insufficient or impossible. We coordinate our intentions or expectations with others if we know the other is trying to do the same.

Coordination of tacit bargaining doesn't apply to *explicit negotiation*. Schelling suggests zero-sum games yield essential insight and advice in pure conflict strategies. However, real-life situations where secrecy plays a role still need the element of intention-signaling and meeting of the minds. Games of coordination underpin the stability of institutions and traditions besides leadership itself. An individual's character appears as a matter of convergent expectations in these institutions and practices. A key advantage is hiding one's strategy from opponents. Genuine ignorance is an advantage to a player when recognized by opponents. However, a danger exists where too much ambiguity changes the nature of the game.

The presence of *randomness* precludes adversaries from gaining intelligence about one's play mode. Typical with threats, punitive action is painful or costly to both sides if it fails, and the player takes corrective action. If *surprise* carries an advantage, it's worth averting by striking first. Fear that other players are about to hit first in the mistaken belief that the player is about to strike first gives the player a motive for attacking.

Simple Majority Voting

Shapley (1988), a University of California, Los Angeles professor, suggests analyzing voting rules in the real world with game theory. One approach is to model them into a simple game. This simplicity removes existing personalities and political interests present in a voting environment. But this removal requires the analysis to focus on rules rather than other aspects of the political climate.

James Buchanan (1962), an American economist, maintains that modern game theory focusing on two-person games also contributes to understanding the voting of a simple majority. However, such games don't go far in predicting enough outcomes of the rules of the vote in the political process. For example, suppose a group must agree on voting rules that dictate only a plurality of the total. In that case, the case for the symmetry of effective coalitions is stronger. Members of a winning alliance are satisfied with shares of symmetrical total gain. It isn't because they expect a larger fair share. Instead, they know an alternate player stands ready to join new coalitions if they demand more.

Modern welfare economists evaluate given situations for changes in efficiency or optimality. This criterion has a premise of individualism. Economic welfare is successful if it improves every individual in the economy, or at least one member is better off without making anyone worse off. Situations or social states are efficient when it's impossible to change without some individual becoming worse off. So instead, Buchanan suggests those individuals and groups of direct beneficiaries of the most productive projects form a coalition. The application of game theory to the majority's voting is straightforward. Still, it is helpful only to a limited extent of the political problem. A more relevant theory to the problem is the n-person game theory.

Repeated Games With Incomplete Information

Applying game theory to real-life situations is not like a once-played game. Robert Aumann was an Israeli American mathematician. Aumann and Maschler (1995) observed that conflict situations usually lead to other conflict situations in the real world. When a player acts, they consider immediate payoffs *and* the future effect actions have on different conditions of conflict. In theoretical game situations, participants assume all players knew all available strategies and profits. However, in the real world, each participant usually has only partial knowledge of the available designs for both players. Therefore, the actual gain is impossible to determine because of the lack of relevant facts.

According to Aumann and Maschler, concealing or revealing information is crucial. This information includes military secrets, trade secrets, hiding weaknesses, and covering embarrassing circumstances. A secret means something one knows or possesses and others don't. Or it's something known or owned, which others don't know the holder knows or keeps secrets. It's essential to manage information during diplomatic negotiations carefully. It's not enough to divulge information one wants to hide or supply incorrect information. Opponents can guess the correct information by detecting a lie or observing attempts to conceal it. How one expresses oneself is sometimes as important as the substance.

Aumann, a professor at the Hebrew University of Jerusalem, contends that diplomacy's primary objective is to reveal or partially reveal information. It should present this disclosure to make it possible to gain immediate profits and a better position in the latter stages. The holder often must show they possess this item or piece of knowledge. This tactic employs the fact that it's known the individual has possession of a specific item or amount of expertise.

What we have been discussing may seem complex when you are initially exposed to it. So the early takeaway should be to look at personal situations for simple underlying patterns. Then, as you gradually contemplate the contours of the problem, you can begin to apply the lessons learned from this chapter. Recognizing there is a structure to each encounter is a valuable start.

The last two topics described complex game theory, took a reality check, and analyzed auctions. They also looked at voting and games with incomplete information. We examined mathematics, methodology, and models in this chapter. While we didn't find the answer to the bread choice, we came across some valuable market demand/supply framework tools. The models helped us strip away superfluous elements and focus on demand structure. Even though individuals are not perfectly rational, they use a good approximation. Game theory allows us to portray this process mathematically with implications for real-world settings. In the next chapter, economists arrange these models in combinations that help discern functional patterns in isolated sectors of the economy.

CHAPTER 3

Small-Scale Economics

Our civilization features groups of individuals grouped around organizing objectives. To live happily, we must navigate this thicket of markets, corporations, and governments. Fortunately, economists have developed theories on how these institutions tick and interconnect. Strolling through this garden of ideas will help us better understand the economic process for choosing bread loaves. In this chapter, we explore the world of microeconomics. We examine entrepreneurial firms factors, introduce institutional theory, discuss how markets operate, and investigate consumer markets.

Firm Factors

The last chapter's behavioral economics and game theory sections focused on how isolated individuals make decisions. We now turn to economic principles where these individuals work together as a unit. The emphasis is coordinating decision making to produce a greater good, like harnessing a team of horses to pull a stagecoach. This section analyzes administrative structures, discusses firm strategy, and investigates industry structure.

Organizational Administration

Herb Simon's (1945) theory of organizational administration addresses the processes of group decision making and actions. Decision making doesn't end when the decision makers initially install the structure of a general organization. Instead, perpetual decision making permeates the entire organization's operation throughout its existence. This topic discusses organizational principles, bounded rationality, and how an organization assimilates employees.

Simon points out that the actual physical tasks of the organization's operations center on the people at the lowest hierarchical level of the organization. However, the personnel above this base level, the managers and support staff, also play an essential role. These nonoperational staff participate to the extent they influence the decisions in operations. In small organizations, the influence of a supervisor is usually on direct reports. On the other hand, in larger units, there are several layers of intermediate supervisors.

Simon maintains the construction of an efficient organization is a problem of social psychology. The financial performance of the bottom line is the measure of the structure's success. All behavior involves conscious or unconscious actions. In forms of actions other than physical ones, the decisions are a product of complex activities such as *planning and design*. In planning and design, *propositions of facts* are statements that are established about the observable world and how it operates. *Decisions* can be something more than factual propositions. The correctness of administrative decisions is, therefore, a relative matter.

Simon, a professor at Carnegie Mellon University, believes a single individual can't attain higher degrees of rationality in isolation. He calls this *bounded rationality*. There are limits to our knowledge base. What managers think they should do is often different from what they do. The group activities of people become more efficient only when they are permitted participation in the organization, to influence the group's decisions and behavior.

Simon suggests there are two aspects of social psychology that influence how organizations fit our behavior into an overall pattern of operation:

1. The *stimulus* the organization uses to trigger activity
2. The *response* of individuals to this stimulus

Simon asserts that communication is essential to the success of the organization. Available technology determines the way it distributes decision making throughout the organization. The most common communication forms are the *spoken word* and *written memos* sent to participants. Also, existing *policy* transforms flows of messages and letters to more formal control than casual communications. *Operation manuals* communicate the organization's practices with a relative application of permanence. They specify actions and designates who prepares the documents, including occasions and content. Otherwise, these practices are only temporarily embedded in the participant's minds and cease to have a profound influence. *Records* and *reports* are also crucial components of the standard system in every organization.

Simon suggests that in for-profit organizations, the efficiency criterion stimulates actions yielding the most significant net return to the organization. On the other hand, the government administration focuses on budget documents in its decision-making process.

Initially, the administrative process imposes the values and objectives of the organization on employees. Gradually these employees internalize these values and incorporate them into their personal psychology. This identification process of the employee forges ties of emotion to employers. This connection engages a personal interest in the institution's success. Simon summarizes organizational behavior as a complex network of decision processes that influence operatives' behavior.

This topic discussed organizational principles, bounded rationality, and how an organization assimilates employees. The next topic builds on the administrative organization and maps out strategic planning.

Firm Strategy

To be successful, firms need to plan their activities. This section considers firm finances, organizational decentralization, and supply chains.

Firm Leverage and Liquidity

Bengt Holmström is a Finnish economist and Jean Tirole (2011) is a French professor of economics. They assume a firm either finances its capital needs by applying for a loan or issuing new securities secured by its cash flows. A firm usually monitors its current and forecasted cash requirements to meet its liquidity needs. They don't wait until the cash register is empty. Instead, they arrange this financing in advance, backed by assets and liabilities on their balance sheet. The net present value of the reinvestment must be favorable to their investors before they agree to supply the needed funds.

A firm usually has known outcomes, but only part of its return is pledgeable to the investors. When this pledgeable income is insufficient to cover the investment costs, the firm has to cover the gap with funds retained from the past. A firm generally has a bias toward less risky projects. Its net worth limits which project to invest. The diversification of projects helps reduce the need for funds. For example, two identical, half-sized projects can replace a single project.

Decentralization Within Firms

A firm aims to maximize profits. Organizational economists debate whether it's better to make business decisions in a *central executive entity* or farmed out to decentralized *independent line units*. The centralized executive administrative teams primarily gather available information relating to the aggregate firm. On the other hand, the autonomous decentralized units are numerous and resemble markets of capitalism without the complete picture.

Leonid Hurwicz was a Polish American economist and a professor at the University of Minnesota. Arrow and Hurwicz (1977) explore how the top levels of management can improve the firm's efficiency on mission-critical decisions where a wide degree of information is available. In addition, they explore how much latitude a firm should leave to individual departments closer to the action. In cases where the firm directs each process manager independently to maximize profits using market prices, complete decentralization is possible. Moreover, this decentralization is advantageous in economizing the transmission of information. The department retains the information without transmitting it to the central office.

Jean Tirole (1988), a Toulouse 1 Capitole University professor in France, suggests it's customary in economics to evaluate aspects of horizontal and vertical structures depending on the firm's size. *Horizontal* dimensions refer to the production scale in a single-product firm or its scope in a multiproduct one. The *vertical* dimension reflects whether the firm purchases goods and services from outsiders or produces them in-house.

Unfortunately, in the early days antitrust regulation approached various trade practices as evil manifestations of the power of a monopoly. However, firms can bypass these industry frameworks by internalizing these practices. They can quietly exercise monopoly power because internal transactions are unobserved.

One primary determinant of the optimal firm size is the extent to which it exploits *economies of scale*. Elevated levels of production permit the use of more efficient techniques. In addition, these high volume levels allow workers to be more specialized, while unit costs decrease by spreading fixed costs over a longer production run.

Tirole thinks of consumer goods as sets of product characteristics. Consumers usually evaluate the quality of most goods before purchasing. However, Tirole observes that some purchased products still have low quality or fail. *Discrimination* in price occurs when a producer sells two units of the same physical good at different prices, either to the same consumer or to other consumers. *First-degree* price discrimination occurs when a single or several identical consumers demand a single unit. Producers can extract a surplus from the consumer in environments of incomplete information using self-selecting devices such as advertising. Discrimination in quality has the same effect as discrimination in quantity. Also, the producer can offer different quantities of the same good at different prices with varying tastes of consumers for goods, such as seats on an airliner or policies of cancellation.

Intermediate Markets

Tirole refers to the *vertical control of the supply chain* as the relationship between the upstream supply firm possessing monopoly power in a middle market and the downstream firm using the goods. In these situations, the monopolist isn't supplying end users. These vertical relationships are more complex than those between retailers and consumers.

In the short run, price is often the primary resource allocation device. Firms can change it easily. In noncooperative game situations, each firm behaves in its self-interest. The Nash equilibrium is the essential solution to the game and strategy of the industry. Ironically, competition on price among even a few firms yields optimal competitive and social outcomes. Dynamic models of repeated price interactions are complex but provide the best approach for examining tacit collusion.

George Stigler's (1986) central thesis is the theorem of Adam Smith (1776). The core theory focuses on the unitary function of the firm and industry. Stigler uses historical context to describe firm elements. He applies this theory to vertical integration and suggests broader theorem applications. Adam Smith, a Scottish professor at the University of Edinburgh, observed the extent of the final market limits the degree of labor division. The entrepreneur gains by combining or expanding operations while driving out rivals when a more aggressive division of labor offers lower costs for more significant outputs.

Economists usually characterize the firm as purchasing a series of inputs to obtain one or more saleable products. The firm's output quantities are associated with the amounts of inputs by a *production function*. This process links the cost of the production function to technology. Smith's theorem suggests that economists expect vertical disintegration to develop in growing industries and horizontal integration to expand in declining industries. Therefore, researchers can evaluate the significance of his theorem by analyzing the integration factors.

An American economist, Oliver Williamson (1985) feels markets in advanced societies need a complex organizational approach to support the growth of technology. This comprehensive structure should organize integration back into the materials supply chain, laterally into the components, and forward to distribution. His orientation of *firm-as-production-function* accomplishes efficiency by combining fungible inputs that yield an output according to engineering specifications. A typical example is the integration of iron and steel making. Keeping the product heated in the transition between these steps is more efficient.

Apart from the results of the natural order of technology, the transactions of products in intermediate markets are more numerous than commonly known. Williamson maintains integration should consider the decision to integrate as a source of efficiencies in the *cost of transactions*. He believes that when markets evolve separately, bureaucratic failures appear and limit the process' efficiency. Vertical integration mitigates the problems of contracts between an independent buyer and supplier because the parties can toss out the existing arrangements and reallocate production resources at a reduced cost.

However, the advantage of external organizations is that markets illuminate high-powered incentives to act. They also restrain bureaucratic distortions more effectively than internal ones. However, Williamson points out there are boundaries of efficiency where firms shouldn't consider integration. The uniqueness of assets determines the degree of integration.

Another challenge with forward integration is competing with distributors and their relationships with independent retailers. In large cities, manufacturers can eliminate the go-between layers by setting up their network of sales offices to coordinate marketing and distribution. Vertical integration in industries with low or moderate degrees of firm concentration poses fewer problems.

Williamson concludes that minimizing transaction cost involve examining alternative ways to govern the exchange interfaces. Firms, markets, and mixed modes are alternative structures of governance. The most suitable model depends on the characteristics of the underlying transactions.

Successful firms plan their activities. This last section considered firm finances, organizational decentralization, and supply chains. The next topic looks at industry structure.

Industry Type

Oliver Williamson felt the monopoly of supply is commonly efficient where *economies of scale* are large relative to the market size. However, it also triggers organizational difficulties, such as miscommunication and geographical dispersion. He maintains that an enterprise's efficiency depends on finding the optimum size of the firm's organization. This optimal size should address all entrepreneurial problems, such as relations with labor, innovation, regulation, and unstable markets. In this topic, we discuss economies of scale, barriers to entry, and the role of research and development.

Stigler's (1986) theory of economies of scale embraces the relationship between the use of scale and the enterprise's output rates in carefully chosen combinations of inputs to production. This relationship is a crucial element of the economic theory of social organizations. For example, analysts can determine the optimal size in an industry by comparing the costs of actual firms with varied sizes. Another method involves evaluating techniques of survival among the more efficient firms.

Once analysts settle on the firm's optimal size, they can explore the relationship between size and other external variables. For example, spending on advertising is often an explanation, though not conclusive, for the optimal growth of large firms, especially in markets for consumer goods. Technology and research also explain a wide range of variables. Complicated processes of production require large companies to operate large plants.

Industry Barriers to Entry

Tirole (1988) contends that high fixed costs generate an imperfectly competitive market structure, thus limiting entry. But even when fixed costs restrict market access, the market doesn't guarantee above-normal profits. Other nonprice entry barriers can prevent firms from exploiting profitable situations. For example, the government can restrict access by introducing permits, licenses, patents, and taxi medallions. Suppose the minimum efficient scale is a considerable proportion of the industry's demand. In that case, the market supports only a small number of firms making super-profits without inviting entry. In the *blockaded* entry, incumbents compete as if there aren't any access threats. An incumbent has more incentive to deter entry than an entrant can muster to enter because the new competition destroys the industry's profits. *Preemption* entry fails when the incumbent doesn't possess the competitive technology of the new entrant.

Market variables affect oligopolists when they can't observe or estimate them precisely. These include their function of costs, the role of rivals' expenses, the state of demand or market potential, and decisions of the strategy of their competition. Interactions in a market with asymmetric information are a noncooperative game. Circumstances incentivize established firms to manipulate data that prospective entrants and established firms possess. Strategies with big budgets rely on financial imperfections.

Research and Development

Evaluating research and development (R and D) is crucial in analyzing industries and economies. In the early stages of R and D, Tirole suggests that firms derive knowledge of fundamentals through *primary research*. Later, *applied research* is associated with engineering and development, which brings products and processes into commercial use. Finally, *post-research* stages distribute innovation throughout the industry through licensing, the imitation of patented inventions, or the adoption of unpatented innovations. Product innovations create new goods and services, while production innovations reduce the cost of producing existing products.

The main theme of Joseph Schumpeter (1942), an Austrian-born political scientist, is that monopoly situations and R and D are interrelated. Monopolies are natural breeding grounds for R and D. Public policy makers must accept the creation of a monopoly as unavoidable to benefit society. It is the only way to encourage firms to undertake R and D efficiently. Innovations are public goods. Therefore, our system of patents should encourage them. In practice, such compensation comes through the grant of patents that provide the innovating firm with a temporary monopoly, allowing it to recoup its R and D costs.

The progress of technology in society depends on the new adoption of technology and its inventions. However, it adopts few innovations instantaneously. Positive externalities of industries arise when a good is more valuable to a user, as more users adopt the same interest or compatible ones. An example is social media.

This last topic discussed industry fundamentals, including economies of scale, barriers to entry, and the role of R and D. The section analyzed administrative structures, discussed firm strategy, and investigated industry structure. Our laureates build on these elements and create comprehensive theories describing institutions in the following section.

Institutional Theory

One alternate approach to classic economic theory is *institutional theory*. It examines how an organization's structures, schemas, rules, and routines develop authoritative guidelines for social behavior. It explores how such systems come into existence, how they diffuse, and discusses their role in supplying stability and meaning to social behavior. Though one of the dominant theoretical perspectives at the end of the 19th century, other approaches eclipsed institutional theory during the first half of the 20th century. In recent decades, however, institutional theory has experienced a remarkable recovery. As a result, it enters the new century as one of the most vigorous and broad-based theoretical perspectives in the social sciences. This section investigates the origins of institutional theory, the efficiency of transaction economics, and institutional frameworks.

Evolution of Organizations

Individuals have banded together to use resources more efficiently for hundreds of years. This topic discusses the division of labor, the nature of the firm, human interaction diversity, and organizational authority and incentives.

The Division of Labor, Coordination Costs, and Knowledge

Adam Smith (1776) thought the *division of labor* led to significant improvement in the productive power of work. These human capital improvements include personal skill, talent, and judgment. Gary Becker (1962) confirms this by implying that later economists refined labor division to the extent that the market and other factors limit specialization.

Becker explains that the cost of combining specialized workers grows as the number of workers in a firm increases. On the other hand, cumulative knowledge derived from this combination improves a worker's productivity. These two variables tie the division of labor to economic progress. This progress is dependent on human capital and growth in technology.

Individual artisans don't specialize or allocate working time and investments to specific tasks to maximize standard output. Workers can become more efficient by specializing in subsets of tasks and combining their efforts with other workers specializing in different subsets. However, the disadvantages of specialization include personal conflicts among members of a team. In addition, the chances of a production breakdown due to poor coordination of efforts or misleading communication multiply with the number of workers.

Economic systems that encourage entrepreneurship have lower costs of coordination and a more widespread division of labor. Becker observes that the division of labor and specialization, both within and between countries, increased enormously over several centuries, making the world vastly richer.

Oliver Williamson (1985), a professor at the University of California, Berkeley, believes that when rational individuals know the relevant costs, they maintain a heightened self-interest orientation. Herb Simon's (1945) bounded rationality assumes that desired rationality exists. Enhanced rationality is a process related to evolutionary institutions. However, circumstances limit it to the solitary person's competence. Limitations include the problem's difficulty, the cognitive capacity of the mind, and the time available to make the decision. In this view, multiple decision makers in institutions function as compromisers, seeking a satisfactory rather than an optimal solution.

Contract enforcement implements the law to achieve a favorable outcome by treating the identity of parties as irrelevant. Contracts narrowly define remedies in case initial agreements fail to materialize because of nonperformance. When a breakdown of classical contracting develops, participants avoid the transactions altogether. Highly standardized transactions don't require a specialized structure of governance. Only recurrent transactions of a complex nature need a highly specialized form of governance. Williamson observes that market governance is the primary structure for nonspecific transactions in infrequent and recurrent contracting. Commerce needs the authority of government for more complex but occasional and specific transactions.

The measurement of contract effectiveness binds solutions to assure a closer correspondence between actions and outcomes. For instance, the firm sacrifices economies of scale and scope if it attempts to make in-house what it could buy more cheaply. Williamson explains that the theory of cost of transactions employs a comparative approach to analyzing institutions. The organizing elements are transaction costs while assuming ownership of technology and assets. But it goes beyond examining incentives and governance under a unified ownership roof compared to the market alternatives.

The Nature of the Firm

Ronald Coase (1988), a British economist and author, assumes price mechanisms determine the allocation of production factors. While there is some planning in a capitalistic economy, it differs from the planning of an individual artisan. The capitalist type is the planning of the entrepreneur.

Outside the firm, movements in price govern production. Within the firm, the structure eliminates these market transactions, and in their place, the entrepreneur becomes the coordinator of output. The amount of vertical integration varies from industry to industry. Coase, a University of Chicago professor, thinks it's sometimes profitable to establish a firm using the cost of price mechanisms as its basis. Using an outside specialist who gathers this price information independently, reduces the internal effort of discovering these prices. In addition, this arrangement eliminates the cost of negotiating and concluding a separate contract for each exchange factor.

Firms aren't the only type of organizations undertaking economic activities. Many agencies of government undertake economic activities, some of immense importance. It's instructive to study why they are conducting these activities. How the industry organizes depends on the relationship between the cost of executing the transactions in the marketplace and the cost of managing the same operations in-house.

The Coase theorem states that the market corrects externalities. This process implies there's no need for government intervention regarding externalities except to ensure it clearly defines and protects property rights. However, Paul Samuelson (1948), an American academic economist, argues unconstrained self-interest leads to problems of bilateral monopoly, with their vagueness and inefficiencies. Samuelson has been familiar to many first-level economic students for decades as the author of the universal primer, *Economics: An Introductory Analysis*, first published in 1948.

Diversity of Structured Human Interactions

Elinor Ostrom (2005), an Indiana University and Arizona State University professor, viewed institutions as behavioral prescriptions. We use them to organize all forms of repetitive and structured interactions of groups at all scales. We interact within a structure of rules and face choices regarding actions and strategies we take. This interaction leads to consequences for ourselves and others.

Contemporary life offers a diversity of situations for interaction. We depend on others to do their work well, so we all can work efficiently. We must learn the basic rules of conducting economic games and find others to engage in this activity repeatedly. There are many subtle changes from one situation to another, even though variables stay the same. These factors of institutions and culture help form our expectations of the behavior of others.

In institutions, policy makers can construct a diverse system of regularized social behavior which can be observed at multiple scales, from universal components organized in various layers. Ostrom develops and applies her theoretical framework to understand these underlying components. First, her framework formalizes mathematical action games (game theory). Then, her method digs deeper into the structures that constitute a situation of action. Finally, she evaluates narrow models used in game theory. She anchors them to one end of a continuum of models of human behavior.

Rigorous analysis of essential elements eventually requires examining many variables. Ostrom presents her framework at scales ranging from fine-grained to broad-grained. Her *arena of action* consists of a situation of action with participants. She views arenas of action as dependent variables. She suggests that working rules are the rules participants reference to explain and justify their actions.

Biophysical and material conditions define:

- What activities are physically possible
- What outcomes they produce
- How they link actions to results
- What's contained in sets of participant information, affected by the outside world

Ostrom presents three types of institutional statements: rules, norms, and shared strategies. The grammar of institutional theory ensures these statements are guidelines that predict influence. Statements often apply to a subset of participants. Conditions indicate when and where the institution uses these statements, such as weather conditions or jurisdictions. No single classification of rules is helpful for all purposes.

Incentives and Authority Within an Organization

James Mirrlees (2006), a British economist, found that firm employees exhibit established interaction patterns. Also, there isn't a sharp line between perfect markets and intraorganization relationships. Instead, circumstances base the structure of hierarchical compensation within organizations on their incentives.

When the firm finds an employee's work satisfactory, they promote them. The organization's managers and owners can thus determine who performs effectively. Workers are intimately aware of their abilities and choose to work accordingly on this personal basis. However, employers can't distinguish talent among job applicants. Instead, they offer compensation schedules that the employer equally applies to all hires.

In this topic, we examined the division of labor, the nature of the firm, human interaction diversity, and organizational authority and incentives. The following section focuses on the recent theory of economic transactions in organizations.

Transaction Efficiency

Economists have advanced a theory centering around the nature of transactions instead of focusing on the firm as the central basis for analysis. This topic describes transaction theory and explains how it operates. We look at the constraints of antitrust regulation and how the direction of enforcement has changed to match evolving markets.

Cost of Transaction Economics

Peter Diamond from MIT and Rothschild (1978) suggest markets attract consumers to obtain commodities through an exchange. They can also make these commodities from scratch through a transformation from technology or production. It is only advantageous to make this internal conversion if sets of commodities acquired fetch higher market value than sets given up. Recent interest in institutional economics started to pick up in the early 1970s. A firm's concept as a *governance structure* supplanted the firm's idea as a *function of production*. As a result, the cost of transaction economics became the basic research component.

Williamson (1985) grounds his orientation on the cost of the contract. He maintains that a firm can formulate any issue as a contracting problem. This way, it's possible to investigate the advantages of economizing a transaction's cost. Every relationship of exchange qualifies. Ones that don't still have an implicit quality of contracting. He also uses transactions as the basic unit of analysis and insists that evaluating the organization of transactions is relevant. The firm categorizes the transaction cost by assigning transactions to the governance structure.

Kenneth Arrow (1951), an American economist and political theorist, sees contract transactions as the cost of running the economic system. He distinguishes these from production costs, forming the classical theory's basis. Instead, the price of a transaction is the economic equivalence of friction in physical systems.

Williamson also analyzes the preliminary cost of the contract transactions, including drafting, negotiating, and safeguarding the agreement. Firms prepare complex documents where parties recognize contingencies and appropriate adaptations. They stipulate and agree to them in advance.

Post-transaction costs include:

- The cost of compensation when transactions drift out of alignment
- Haggling costs incurred if participants make bilateral efforts to correct transaction misalignments
- Setup and running costs are associated with governing structures
- Bonding costs affecting secure commitments

He divides property rights matter into three parts: the right to use the asset, the right to receive asset returns, and the right to change the form and substance of an investment. Once the arrangement is established, the utilization of the investment aligns with the owner's purposes.

Antitrust Enforcement

Oliver Williamson (1985) observes that the thrust of antitrust enforcement has transformed since 1935. Some recent reforms were attributable to a growing appreciation for the cost of transactions. Policy transitioned from a firm-centric focus to a structure of governance for transactions.

This shift transformed public policy toward emphasizing the organization of firms and markets.

The early emphasis on the power of markets was inadequate for specifying the circumstances. First, there was a general undervaluation of the efficient benefits of society. There was a widespread tendency to regard efficiency narrowly, primarily in technology. The focus of antitrust lasered in on the purpose and effect of monopoly. This narrow formulation facilitated easy enforcement, but sometimes at the expense of social welfare issues. Moreover, policy makers thought the cooperation of an oligopoly occurred commonly. Therefore, they held barriers to entry to be anticompetitive and antisocial.

At the time, economists described business firms as production functions with the objective of profit maximization. Technology determined their efficient boundaries. Efforts by policy makers to reconfigure the structures of firms and markets violate these natural boundaries. They have their origins in market power.

Change in Focus

Williamson recalls that the focus of antitrust enforcement started to shift in the 1970s when the emphasis on analysis transitioned to a framework of price theory. Other developments included reformulating modern corporation theory. The new direction emphasizes economizing the cost of transactions. Intellectual bias experienced a substantial change in assessing alternative merits of transactions or nonstandard contracting costs. Its criteria narrowed in focus. History is essential for evaluating competitive rivalry. It involves the advantage of leadership by incumbent monopolists and the consideration of comparative cost.

Strategic behavior occurs when established firms take advanced positions relative to actual or potential rivals by responding punitively to the new rivalry. Williamson thinks this creates a dilemma for policy makers to resolve.

This topic described transaction theory and explained how it operated. Next, we looked at the constraints of antitrust regulation and how the direction of enforcement has shifted to reflect evolving markets. The following section provides a discussion of the structural frameworks for institutions.

Institutional Framework

Douglass North (1990) is an American economist like Ostrom. They hold that institutions are the game rules of society. These organizations are human-devised constraints that guide the interaction of humans. They construct incentives in human exchanges, whether political, social, or economic. How they shape societies evolving through time is critical to understanding historical changes. These institutions are analogous to game rules in competitive team sports. They consist of formal written rules and unwritten codes of conduct. Sometimes, we violate laws and informal regulations, and the referees throw a penalty flag. This topic discusses institutional change, expected utility theory, and political decision making.

North views institutions as groups of individuals bound by a purpose in common to achieve objectives. The institution's framework fundamentally influences how they come into existence and evolve. Institutions affect economic performance by shaping the cost of exchange and production. Together with the technology employed, they determine the cost of transaction and transformation as components of the total cost.

Institutional change is complicated because changes at the margin result from changes in rules, informal constraints, or certain enforcement types. An entrepreneur brings about this incremental change in institutions to become more efficient. However, through Herb Simon's bounded rationality constraints, they frequently act with incomplete information. These unintended constraints result in paths of inefficiency.

North contends that a framework of game theory best evaluates problems of cooperation. For example, teamwork is difficult to sustain when the players don't repeat games, when information on other players is missing, or when there are many players. In addition, some approaches to behavior rely on an assumption of expected satisfaction.

The theory of *expected utility* doesn't imply that the behavior of everybody is consistent with rational choice. North suggests determining an institution's weakness involves evaluating incentive motivation and deciphering the environment. Empirical evidence indicates a trade-off exists between wealth and other nonmonetary values. Of our actions, 90 percent appear to be regular, repetitive choices requiring little reflection. Institutions exist to reduce uncertainties involved in our interaction.

North, a professor at the University of Washington in St. Louis, constructs theories of institutional behavior combined with the relevance of the cost of a transaction. Emphasis on the cost of exchange separates this theory from the traditional classic approach of Adam Smith. He feels formal laws and property rights seem to order life and the economy. Informal constraints come from socially transmitted information and are part of our culture. The difference between casual and formal constraints is one of degree.

Political decision making specifies and enforces property rights and hence individual contracts. North suggests contracts are self-enforcing when it incentivizes contracting parties to live up to them. Enforcement by a third party is a newer development. It positions the government into a more coercive force to monitor property rights and enforce contracts effectively.

The framework of institutions also shapes the direction of acquiring knowledge and skills. Yet, North suggests institutions' incentive to invest in knowledge of production has been absent throughout history. The features of these incentives are crucial. Change agents are individual entrepreneurs responding to stimuli embodied in the framework of institutions. Complex structures of constraint accomplish stability by including formal rules nested in a hierarchy.

Wars, revolutions, and natural disasters are discontinuous sources of institutional change. North contends that under these circumstances, formal rules change, but informal constraints don't. Consequently, the shifting dynamics develop ongoing tensions between calm conditions and new legal restrictions.

This topic discussed institutional change, expected utility theory, and political decision making. The section investigated the origins of institutional theory, the efficiency of transaction economics, and institutional frameworks. The following section sketches out the basic concepts of markets.

Basic Market Theory

Private market exchange is the most efficient way of allocating resources for most goods and services. This section examines markets by discussing information and knowledge, presenting a theory of asset value, and introducing the production function.

Information and Knowledge

Information binds an economy. Adding technology makes the economy more efficient. This topic discusses price dispersion, search costs, and market competition.

The Economics of Information

George Stigler (1986), a professor at Columbia University, evaluates price changes in markets experiencing varying dynamics. Unless policy makers centralize a market, no individual knows the prices sellers quote at a given time. A buyer hoping to find the best bread price must search among multiple sellers. Stigler thinks the dispersion of prices is a manifestation and measure of *ignorance* in free markets. But unfortunately, it's a biased measure of ignorance because there's never absolute homogeneity in commodities.

Whatever the exact pattern of the price distribution, it's a foregone conclusion that additional searches will deliver diminishing returns. Economists measure this characteristic of markets by the expected reduction in the minimum price of bids from buyers. If the distribution pattern doesn't have this characteristic, it is unstable. Stigler maintains that the efficiency of a personal search for buyers and sellers is extremely low in markets of unique goods. The more significant the portion of repeat sellers, the higher the correlation between successive prices.

The needs of supply and demand change over time. Stigler believes the element of ignorance of price is due to changing identities of buyers and sellers. Advertising is a method of providing buyers with the identity of the seller. The advertisement of prices has a decisive influence on the dispersion of prices.

Perfect Competition

Milton Friedman (1962) laments that the concept of *market competition* didn't receive economists' explicit and systemic attention until around 1870. Then, economists using mathematics took the first steps in advancing competition analysis. Industrial competition requires market competition within each supply chain industry. Therefore, the market continuously obtains equilibrium of industrial competition if resources are instantaneously mobile or if they eventually transfer at a finite time rate.

He also emphasizes that competition has two different meanings. In non-technical conversation, competition refers to a *personal rivalry* where we seek to outdo our known competitors. In economics, competition means the opposite. Personal rivalry doesn't exist in competitive markets. The essence of competitive markets is their *impersonal character*. No participant can determine the exchange terms when other participants can access alternate goods or jobs.

In contrast, a monopoly exists where a specific group of individuals or enterprises have enough control over the product or services to determine the practical terms of exchange when consumers access the market. In some ways, a monopoly comes closer to the economic concept of competition because it involves a lack of personal rivalries. But on the other hand, monopolies mean there are limitations on voluntary exchanges by reducing alternatives available to consumers.

Friedman surveys the extent of monopolies, sources of a monopoly, appropriate policies of the government, and social responsibility of business and labor. He thinks monopolies of private firms are unimportant from an economic point of view due to the vast competition. There are also similar tendencies to overestimate the importance of labor monopoly. Monopolies arise because technological considerations make it more efficient or economical to allow a single firm to produce the good rather than many.

Friedman observes that opportunities for private collusion or private cartels are constantly present. The critical role of antitrust laws should be to inhibit this secret conspiracy. Rather than breaking up a firm, the primary mission of the government's policy should be to eliminate those conditions that directly create monopolies.

The wokeness gaining acceptance by corporate management and labor leaders is adopting social responsibilities beyond serving the interests of stockholders. However, Friedman strongly suggests only one corporate social responsibility in free-market countries: the shareholder. He asserts that similar trends could thoroughly undermine the foundation of our free society.

We examined this topic's price dispersion, search costs, and market competition. Now, we turn to a simple but helpful system for determining asset value and characteristics developed by Gerard Debreu.

Theory of Value

In our quest to understand price determination, particularly bread, it is helpful to develop a working definition of value. In this topic, Gérard Debreu (1959), a French-born economist and mathematician, creates a self-evident foundation for determining asset value in competitive markets. He also establishes the existence of equilibrium using a novel approach. Finally, he presents a price system where the excess of aggregate demand vanishes. Debreu, a professor at the University of California, Berkley, divides economic activity into finite numbers of elementary time intervals of equal lengths, such as a minute, week, or year. Similarly, he divides the economic activity of physical space into finite numbers of smaller elementary units.

Among the problems of primary value addressed by Debreu is an explanation of the price of a commodity. This price results from agent interactions through markets in an economy with private ownership, much like the price of bread. He highlights the role of price in the optimal states of the economy. The simplest type of commodity is an economic good. Many varieties of goods are specified by their grade or time and location of their availability. Debreu's theory expresses the quantities of goods in units.

A second type of good is more complicated, such as a tractor. Its specific description includes its model, mileage, date, and location. Unlike more straightforward goods, his theory can't divide this type, so it measures them in units of tractors. Finally, the land is a particular case. The nature of its soil and subsoil, trees, planted crops, and construction specifies its condition. Again, his theory expresses a quantity of land with a specified condition, such as location and date in acres.

An economic service is the labor of humans. Its description specifies a performed task. When the situation adds date and location, it becomes a well-defined commodity. Debreu's theory expresses the quantity of a specified type of labor in hours worked. A different kind of service involves an inanimate object, such as using a truck. Its life is a succession of time intervals during which it stays in the same condition. The length of its intervals depends on the intensity of its use. His theory expresses its quantity by the rendering of the service.

A more complex type of service includes a location such as a hotel room. The situation dates and locates its description, including a list of everything performed for occupants. Its quantity is expressed in several days or weeks. Time doesn't specify quantities for other services, such as storage. Instead, economists describe them as the beginning and ending dates when the provider renders it and its location. The theory describes its quantity in cubic feet and the time specified between several dates.

Conditions under which providers render services, locations, and dates describe transportation services. His theory expresses its quantities in terms of transported weight or volume of goods. These specifications of time require several dates and locations.

Debreu suggests a commodity is a physically, temporally, and spatially specified good or service. By focusing on changes in dates, he can describe a case of the general theory of commodities. Debreu also expresses a view of savings, investment capital, and interest. Similarly, by focusing on location changes, he lays out another case of the same general approach with a theory of location, transportation, international trade, and exchange.

Prices

Each commodity is associated with a price. His theory interprets this price as the amount an agent pays for every commodity unit made available to them. Contracts of sale define the providers of the goods delivered at a specified date or area.

The cost of a commodity is positive, null, or negative. In the negative case, a buyer's need is where providers dispose of the buyer's output (i.e., garbage). This buyer pays another entity to haul it away; the removal entity characterizes the garbage as an input. A commodity with a positive or negative value isn't intrinsic to the product. Instead, it depends on the economy's technology, tastes, and resources.

If the commodity is money, his theory calls the price of holding and borrowing a quantity of it from one date to a subsequent date: interest.

This interest is associated with payment, location, and date, like delivering a physical good. The economy organizes systems of prices and dates into exchanges. The price is roughly the same for all regions or nation trades. Markets can then establish exchange rates for all deals in one country when paired with another nation.

Role of Agents

Debreu suggests that an economy consists of a fixed number of participants. Their collective role is to choose an action plan to decide each commodity's quantity of input or output. Limitations of choice and their criteria for selection characterize these participants' decisions. For example, given options representing limited knowledge of technology known by producers constrain the production plans of producers. As a result, producers select *production plans* at prices to maximize their profits.

A producer specifies quantities for all inputs and outputs in a production plan. Inputs include raw materials, semifinished products, land, equipment, labor, supervisor, and managers at various dates and locations. In contrast, the outputs can include more than one commodity if the production process involves several dates. For example, land and equipment are inputs on one date. However, they might reappear as outputs later in another condition.

Debreu thinks of consumers as typically individuals or households. They hatch a collective plan in the present for activities in the future. It involves the specification of quantities of all inputs and outputs. A state of the economy governs each specification of actions of participants. For example, a price mechanism becomes attainable if each participant's actions is possible and their actions is compatible with total resources.

In his simple, uncomplicated model, a particular class of economies with private ownership has a set of attainable states. These simple two-party economies feature consumers owning resources and controlling producers. Given a system of prices, each producer maximizes their profits, which they distribute to consumer shareholders. This distribution of profit determines the wealth of consumer shareholders. They satisfy their preferences under the constraints of wealth. As a result of these prices, each participant chooses an action. Unfortunately, these actions aren't always compatible with the availability of resources. The quantity of all commodities accessible to participants provides the total economic resources. They include existing financial capital.

Debreu's theory defines an optimum state as attainable within limitations imposed by consumption, production plans, and total economic resources. One couldn't satisfy more efficiently any consumer preference without satisfying less efficiently those of another, as in a Nash equilibrium.

This topic examined Drebeu's self-evident foundation for determining asset value in competitive markets. It also established the existence of equilibrium using a novel approach. Finally, the section presented a price system where the excess aggregate demand vanishes. It made great strides in explaining the price of our bread. The next topic introduces the production function.

Production Function

The production function is one of economics' most widely used model concepts. This topic discusses the origin of the production function, single commodity production, the conditions of the technology process, and empirical investigations.

Allocation of Economic Knowledge

Tjalling Koopmans (1957) points out formal similarities in various problems arising from diverse parts of the economic theory first introduced by Paul Samuelson (1948). During Koopmans' time, scientific progress introduced mathematical tools to economics. Moreover, this advancement permitted economic perceptions to be articulated with greater clarity. It also provided an avenue to express the logical structure of the theory.

These new tools shed light on older problems of fundamentals. They operate through a system of prices compatible with the efficient utilization of resources. As a result, economists formulated propositions in economics more succinctly. Elementary concepts and theorems borrowed from the mathematical theory of linear spaces also aided them.

A *linear space* (also called a vector space) is a collection of vectors. In the earlier period, economics was a *descriptive* competitive equilibrium theory. The most valuable properties of these new constructions for economists were highly elementary to the mathematician. Therefore, presenting some of the properties in prose text was challenging.

Koopmans bifurcated the economic decisions of supply and demand into distinct processes. Decentralizing these decisions spreads production decisions among groups of entrepreneurs or managers, all on the producing side of consumer goods markets. He develops the notion of decentralizing decisions, their incentives, and the information economy. Finally, Koopmans uses the two sets of theorems to construct models where they first separate supply and consumption decisions. Other economists had already developed several similar models with diverse uses. For example, the concept of perfect competition runs through all classical and neoclassical literature. It achieves efficiency for our maximization of satisfaction.

After examining *interpersonal utility comparison*, Koopmans believes this view isn't sustainable. Economists perceive competitive equilibrium can't remain stable in any technology environment, whether efficient or not. In a study of relationships between competitive stability and *Pareto optimality*, Koopmans follows the investigations of Arrow and Debreu. Pareto optimality is the state where a given system optimizes resources so that one dimension cannot improve without a second worsening with a steady state. Koopmans' prototype is a device for separating reasoning within the model from applying its relationship to reality. Even if they are Pareto optimums, competitive equilibriums involve more unequal income distributions than society considers desirable. A term such as the *efficiency of allocation* of incomes accurately describes the concept.

The Production Function

Koopmans recounts that traditional economists portrayed choices of production decisions not as a fixed set of decisions but by the unique concept of only the production function. Regarding a firm or industry producing a single commodity, the production function is a function of available quantities of input commodities or flows of productive labor, also called factors of production or inputs. However, Koopmans maintains that the best choice of operational modes and combinations of processes manifests the general problem. Regarding problems of allocation of an entire economy, there are good reasons for starting with a model construction of production possibilities before researchers evaluate the assumptions of institutions.

Postulates of linear activity concern two original entities: commodities and activities. Specifications about the addition and subtraction of identical items imply that each is homogenous. The total net output for each commodity characterizes an activity. Koopmans proposes that there are systems of prices compatible with technology where all desired things are favorable. Economists call a point of net output resulting from efficient bundles of activity a *point of efficiency*. One application of the activity model analysis yields the input–output model adopted by Wassily Leontief (1947) of Harvard University long before the development of linear programming in activity analysis.

Koopmans focuses on the time element complexities of his production function model. To overcome this limitation, the model adjusts the length of the horizon. The horizon of the model now becomes the union of all period components it recognizes.

Ragnar Frisch (1965) was a Norwegian economist and one of the initial winners of the Nobel Prize for Economic Sciences. He suggests *technical production* means any transformation directed by humans or in which humans are interested. Transformation indicates certain things (goods or services) and factors of production enter the process and lose their identity. They don't exist in their original form. Instead, other things come into being, products, and emerge from the process. This transformation doesn't need to alter the actual qualities of the material but only needs to be a movement, selection, or conservation. The production of commerce consists of choices or activities in time and place.

Single commodity production results in a single, technically homogeneous link of goods or services. This particular model measures its production in units produced. Most theories of production are concerned with this single production process. On the other hand, the joint production model contains an element that makes it impossible to produce one product simultaneously. According to various values of products, there are primary products, by-products, and waste products.

Frisch suggests relative quantities of joint products produced aren't always determined strictly on technological grounds. Instead, production organization refers to how labor, machines, and natural resources operate together to obtain production results. He surmises that the circumstances influencing the results of production are endless. Analysts select certain factors to consider more closely and label them as *specified factors*. When circumstances can't alter capacity without great expense, analysis of product quantity assumes a fixed constant capacity, while other factors vary.

Discerning which circumstances fix the factors or variables depends on the length of time of the process. Conditions in the technology process change constantly, and new inventions open new production fields. Also, changes in the production function often occur when the designation of factors remains unchanged, but laws evolve that connect factors and products. Production takes time as specific periods of production elapse.

Empirical investigations into several production processes show the production function path passes through rising volumes stages. Then, it transitions to diminishing return stages if a single factor is varied while allowing others to remain constant. Frisch observes that social and economic institutions evolved to make perfect competition and pure monopolies less compatible with reality in modern times. These elements reduce competition while, at other times, they sharpen competition. These alternate forms of markets and different economic strategies need more refinement by economists for classic theory.

Frisch suggests describing any economic situation by a particular set of attributes is possible. If it's possible to define a parameter, an individual or organization fixes the size of the parameter and executes production. These variables are labeled *parameters of fixation*. We act autonomously if, in our deliberations, we assume other parameters won't change when we change our own. For example, analysts regard the plant's maximum capacity as permanent. This capacity is the highest quantity of products the plant can produce when running at its best level of performance.

This topic discussed the origin of the production function, single commodity production, the conditions of the technology process, and empirical investigations. The section examined markets by discussing information and knowledge, presenting a theory of asset value, and introducing the production function. It provided plenty of insight for our investigation of bread prices. The following section analyzes consumer markets.

Consumerism

Consumer markets represent 70 percent of GDP. Therefore, a study of their operations is fruitful. This section delves into consumer preferences, analyzes matching markets, and examines retail credit markets.

Consumer Preference

This topic focuses on defining *consumer preference*, elements of consumer decision making, and taking a personal risk. In theory, Tirole (1988) thinks the price is the only rational variable to focus on in a homogeneous product market. But, in practice, some consumers prefer buying a firm's brand, even at a slight premium. They purchase it if it's available at a closer store, delivered sooner, or has superior postsale services. Other consumers remain faithful to firms with soaring prices because they are unaware of alternatives. Still, other consumers are concerned that other options don't have the same quality or won't satisfy their preferences.

Daniel McFadden (2006), an American econometrician, suggests economists assume consumers' preferences are well defined in most economic theories and ideologies. These consumers consistently behave to advance their self-interests. They know their tastes and welcome market opportunities to expand their consumption options. These views of market orientation of well-defined preferences changed economic policy making in the last quarter of the 20th century in the United States and elsewhere. This movement led to the successful deregulation of air and truck transportation, telecommunications, and energy markets. Unfortunately, there were also striking failures, such as the deregulated energy markets in California.

Economists held reasoned discussions on the privatization of public utilities. These discussions centered on information asymmetries, incentives, economies of scale and scope, and risk management. They also looked at the relative efficiency and sustainability of alternative forms of market organization. From the public conversation, they began to detect widespread unease with some market solutions.

With that discussion in the background, McFadden focuses on consumer decision making, the market outcomes achieved as a result, and the influence of effects on their attitudes toward the market. Many of these factors draw opposition from the consumer. These controversial factors include free trade and globalization, privatization of social insurance, and deregulation of energy markets. Free choice has moral appeal, but the moral fiber is strongest when self-interest doesn't sever it. McFadden's focus is finding positive ways to manage information and technology issues in privatization.

He observed studies of consumer perceptions, motivations, and behavior paint a complex picture of self-interest and determinants of well-being. In addition, these images perceive consumers in markets finding product choice troubling due to the risk in the market. Finally, there's also a social risk found in the personal interactions between individuals, which commerce requires. McFadden highlights how consumers deal with their needs, emotional stress, and social risks by studying their thoughts in social contexts and trade exchange.

Personal Risk

The biological evidence indicates that the brain of a human is complex and layered. However, McFadden maintains that economists can generate valuable empirical evidence on a consumer's decision making from experiments in the laboratory. While behavioral complexities sometimes appear in experiments, they aren't crucial for understanding economic behavior. For instance, some consumers may be slower learners than others. Many markets are also inconsistent teachers, sometimes providing more consumer irritation than illumination.

This topic focused on defining consumer preference, elements of consumer decision making, and taking a personal risk. The following section discusses the sister market mechanism to traditional commodity exchanges, *matching markets.*

Matching Markets and their Design

Matching markets have unique characteristics. This section discusses these characteristics, explains how matching markets operate, and points out how they sometimes break down. Finally, it outlines how pervasive they are in daily activity, laws and regulations, and asymmetric information.

Matching Versus Free-Market Exchanges

Alvin Roth (2015), an American economist, thinks economics should seek the best public policy for efficiently allocating scarce resources. At the same time, the process should also develop ways to make essential resources less scarce. *Economic matching* (versus free-market exchanges) is one avenue where we obtain many things we choose in life, which also chooses us. Often, there are situations of structured matchmaking where courtship and choosing occur. It's a process of application and selection. This process and how well we navigate it is crucial in determining some critical turning points in our lives and many smaller ones.

Until recently, researchers often passed quickly over this matching economic phenomenon and focused primarily on commodity markets. In commodity markets, prices alone determine who gets what. With commodities, we decide what we want. If we can afford it, we buy it. But in matching markets, prices don't work the same way. Roth contributed to the creation of this new field of market design.

The first task of successful matching market design is gather participants wanting to find the best transactions. Markets help organize potential transactions. Therefore, participants must evaluate them quickly. Next, economists identify the strategic decisions where choices depend on what other individuals are doing. Roth notes that every market has a story to tell. He offers insight into potential markets of matches that society faces. *Congestion* becomes a problem a market faces once they've achieved *thickness*.

Markets Throughout the Day

Roth suggests the existence of market design is so pervasive that it touches every facet of human lives, starting when waking up in the morning. For example, advertisements and social media embody various markets' hidden workings. While most market configurations make it easy to participate, they often disguise apparent simplicity in sophisticated market designs.

Type distinctions aren't thin bright lines between commodity markets that are perfectly anonymous and matching markets with specific relationships between participants. Instead, markets are positioned at different points along the spectrum, from pure commodity to pure matching.

To understand the ways matching fails, Roth starts even before the beginning. An *exploding offer*, sometimes found in job offers, is a temporary take-it-or-leave-it offer. Firms make these offers to recruits before gathering enough information on how candidates might have performed in school. Roth also suggests that the breakdown of participant self-control unravels markets. Markets collapse despite the collective benefits of having thick markets. That's why self-control is not a solution. People can only control themselves.

Roth thinks markets can also move too fast. Although the Internet operates at computer speeds, we still need time to consider and act. Moreover, matching markets often deal with congestion since each offer isn't a uniform set of terms. He believes making markets safe is a long-standing market design problem, going back to well before the invention of agriculture. But there are other more straightforward risks of markets. For instance, buying something from easily identifiable merchants in legal markets is safer than illegal transactions.

While markets need lots of information to work well, there is sometimes too much information. Policy makers dramatically improve markets when their design encourages people to communicate only essential details they otherwise keep to themselves. Roth suggests there is a paradox in market design. As communication gets more straightforward and cheaper, it sometimes conveys less information. Markets work best when they allow participants only to transmit essential information reliably.

Roth implies laws and regulations apply to a wide range of markets. A few laws provide the standard framework for the design of many markets. While good designs of markets emerge slowly over time, designers also modify old rules and regulations. The principle of market design open for political debate is understanding how markets should operate and how society governs them. The market designers in both government and private sector have roles. Good design is a moving target. Because markets and languages are complex social tools used collectively, they are sometimes hard to redesign even when they work poorly. Sometimes, society redesigns markets to perform badly. Roth points out markets are human artifacts, not natural phenomena.

Asymmetric Information

James Mirrlees (2006) considers what happens in a market with asymmetric information. The participants know less about relationships between input and output than the producers choosing input. Producers also exhibit some ignorance. Each consumer may know something about the effects of labor income. However, it's different for different individuals. There are two natural periods during this process. First, the consumer chooses what to do, and then the outcomes become known to the consumer in the next period.

The abovementioned transaction is one-sided because producers always set the contract terms, and participants respond accordingly. Many economic relationships are one-sided, but many aren't. These multiple-sided relationships involve cooperative arrangements or bargains between individuals in similar situations.

The last section featured matching markets. It discussed matching market characteristics, explained how they operate, and pointed out how they sometimes break down. The topic looked into how pervasive matching markets are in daily activity, related laws and regulations, and the handling of asymmetric information. The next segment assesses credit markets.

Credit Markets

Money is the glue of an economy. Without it, markets would be less efficient. Several financial markets accessible to the consumer satisfy their basic needs. Studying these markets helps build a better understanding of essential consumer behavior. This topic examines mortgages, financing college, government intervention, and choice architecture.

Retail Credit Markets

Richard Thaler and Cass Sunstein (2008) remember when shopping for a mortgage was easy. Most mortgages had fixed rates for 30 years with a 20 percent downpayment. However, in the last decades, mortgage shopping has become more complicated. Variable-rate loans, interest-only loans, and prepayment fees became popular. These additional options have the potential to make consumers better off. But they can realize this potential only if they choose the right loan for their circumstances. When mortgage markets became more complicated, complexity significantly disadvantaged unsophisticated and uneducated individuals. Thaler and Sunstein propose a very mild form of government regulation called *RECAP* to regulate the practices of lenders. Their goal is to inform customers of the types of existing fees and terms. RECAP compels lenders to disclose their fee schedules in a spreadsheet format publicly.

In another example of consumer market design, college costs are rising faster than inflation. Scholarships and part-time jobs typically don't cover all college expenses, thus creating the need for a loan. Shopping for a student loan is as complicated as searching for a mortgage. Thaler and Sunstein propose a RECAP solution to reduce the number of questions on applications for a student loan. Also, credit cards are a ubiquitous feature of modern life. But unfortunately, life is far more complicated than it needs to be for mortgages, student loans, and credit cards.

Thaler and Sunstein offer one objection to their behavioral nudge: the slippery slope where government propaganda machines progress from general education to outright manipulation. But, in many cases, nudges are inevitable. Also, sometimes architects of choice have a personal bias in proposing a helpful nudge. Alternatively, skeptics argue that we can be wrong in a free society. Forced choosing may not always be best.

Thaler and Sunstein endorse the principle of using publicity in the architecture of public choice. This publicity principle is a good guideline for constraining and implementing nudges. However, in many situations, the government can't be purely neutral. They maintain that there are no fixed boundaries. Instead, policy makers must decide where to stop and when to call a nudge a shove. Circumstances justify flat bans in some contexts, but they raise unique concerns.

Studying these consumer markets helps us better understand consumer behavior. This past topic examined mortgages, financing college, government intervention, and choice architecture. In addition, the section delved into consumer preferences, analyzed matching markets, and reviewed retail credit markets.

In this chapter, we explored the world of microeconomics. We examined entrepreneurial firms' factors, introduced the institutional theory, discussed how markets operate, and investigated consumer markets. Unfortunately, the answer to our bread choice problem may still be elusive, but we can see it has rational and subjective components. Still, we were able to build on an understanding of the supply side of economics and see how demand combines with supply to form an equilibrium. In the next chapter, we move on to capital markets.

CHAPTER 4

Finance Theory

We began our voyage looking at the basic building blocks of economics: mathematics, models, and methodology. Then, in the last chapter, we looked at the basics of small submarkets. The path now leads us to a specialized market, the capital market. Unlike physical goods markets, it is mainly invisible with relatively few moving parts. However, it is global, it has many complexities, and few theories capture its vast underlying foundation. This chapter looks at financial economic theory. It discusses capital markets, introduces investment management concepts, and presents capital asset pricing theories.

Capital Markets

In market economies, the allocation of economic resources is the outcome of personal decisions. Prices are signals operating in a market economy that direct resources to their best use. Financial assets are intangible. The primary benefit or value of a financial instrument is the claim to future cash payments. The entity that agrees to make future payments is the *issuer*. The owner of the financial asset is an *investor*. This section discusses capital markets. It explores the basics of these markets, explains rational exuberance, and describes the current environment.

Basics of Capital Markets

Franco Modigliani was an Italian American economist. Fabozzi, Modigliani, and Jones (2013) co-wrote a textbook on financial markets. These markets are where participants exchange financial assets. Most economies create and subsequently trade in some form of financial market. This topic covers the basics of financial markets. It includes a discussion of financial globalization, treasury markets, and stock markets.

Globalization doesn't limit entities in any country seeking to raise funds for their domestic market. This global integration resulted from the deregulation of markets. Also, technological advances help monitor world markets, analyze opportunities, and execute trades. However, governments find it necessary to regulate certain aspects of these markets due to their prominent roles in their economies. In their regulatory capacity, governments have a hand in influencing the development and evolution of financial markets.

The U.S. Treasury issues debt securities and backs them with the full faith and credit of the U.S. government. As a result, investors consider these issues risk-free. Their interest rate structure, based on maturities, forms the basis for all interest rates throughout the U.S. economy and, to a lesser extent, worldwide. The treasury is the largest issuer of debt. Moreover, the volume and size make the market for treasuries the most active and liquid in the world. As a result, the bid/ask quote spread is narrower than in other sectors, and most issues trade quickly.

The treasury directly issues new securities through the *primary market*. It determines the procedure for the auction, the time of the auction, and the maturities offered. The *secondary market* for treasury securities is a larger over-the-counter market where government securities dealers provide continuous bid and ask prices. There is virtual 24-hour trading of U.S. Treasury securities with the primary trading locations in New York, Tokyo, and London.

The treasury market is three times the size of the stock market. In the stock market, investors express their opinions about a firm's prospects through trades they make in the common shares of these corporations. An aggregate of these trades reveals the consensus opinion of participants about capital market prices. These equity securities represent an ownership interest in a corporation. They entitle equity holders to corporate earnings when firms distribute them in dividends. They also entitle holders to a prorata share of a remaining entity in case of liquidation. This topic covered the basics of financial markets. It included a discussion of globalization, treasury markets, and stock markets. In the following section, we tackle the psychology of markets.

Irrational Exuberance

Former Federal Reserve Chairman Alan Greenspan first used the term *irrational exuberance* to describe the behavior of stock investors in 1996. An American economist, Robert Shiller (2000) highlighted the meme and made it famous. The term applies when traders bid market prices up to unusually high and unsustainable levels under market psychology influences. Shiller studied speculative bubble episodes where prices surge, spurring investor enthusiasm. The contagion spreads from individual to individual. This process amplifies stories justifying the price hikes which attracts larger volumes of investors.

Shiller feels the same forces of human psychology driving markets of stocks and bonds can influence other markets. Real-estate markets, mainly residential homes, display booms of speculation occasionally. Experienced observers should identify these bouts of irrational exuberance for the public. They should specify the precipitating factors. However, historical events don't have simple causes. When these events move markets in extreme directions, it's usually because of a confluence of several factors. This topic introduces irrational exuberance, discusses precipitating factors and amplification mechanisms, and draws parallels in the real-estate markets.

Historical Perspective

The 1990s' capital market surge occurred in many countries around the world at the same time. Before their surge in 1992, corporate earnings were depressed but rebounded vigorously. Similarly, stock markets peaked simultaneously in many countries in the early 2000s. Shiller explains this behavior is due to robust profits enjoyed by public corporations throughout the period. Profits doubled, which hadn't occurred in a half-century. At the waves' peak, the stock market's elevated levels puzzled the public. They were unsure if these levels made sense. They wondered if the froth reflected unjustified optimism permeating their thinking. This optimistic impulse also affects many other personal decisions.

According to Shiller, the path of interest rates through time is often an intense public concern. Central banks set short-term interest rates. However, long-term rates are more speculative and depend on public expectations of rates and inflation. As a result, central banks can only jaw-bone the long maturity market. In 1997, Greenspan discovered significant negative correlations between yields of 10-year bonds and price-earnings ratios of stocks. Analysts often use this relationship, known as the *Fed Model*, to justify levels of the stock and bond markets.

Precipitating Factors and Amplification Mechanisms

Shiller hunted for the causes of factors influencing stock markets that economic fundamentals don't warrant. He looked at public reactions to market movements, not just those of professionals. Some professionals are more sensitive than others and work to offset public exuberance. The Internet was born at about the same time. It made the public more conscious of the pace of technology. More vividly than television, it conveys changed expectations of future conditions. In addition, people acquire a sense of world proficiency when using search engines.

According to Shiller, a professor at Yale University, there's no single cause for bubbles but many factors at work. These factors have aspects of self-fulfillment and are impossible to evaluate in scientific, predictable ways. For example, the proliferation of online trading, favorable policies of legislation, and cuts in capital gains taxes are undisputable market enablers. Other factors, such as the rise of *defined contribution* (DC) plans, the popularity of mutual funds, a decline in inflation, and expansion of trade volume, are associated with booms. Shiller suggests enabling mechanisms that reflect investors' confidence, investor expectations of future gains, and related influences on investor demand, expand the effects of these factors. Moreover, these social mechanisms work through *feedback loops*.

New common wisdom has taken over investor thinking in recent years: Stocks are now the best investment, and investors can't go wrong investing in them. This notion sharply contrasted with prevailing ideas when the public considered real estate the best investment. In the theory of feedback loops, the initial surge in stock prices leads to more gains in prices, as the effect of the initial drive increases investors' demand. The loops amplify the initial impact of these precipitating factors, resulting in more significant increases in price than the fundamentals suggest.

The dynamics of feedback loops generate complex and even random behavior. Many types of feedback loops operate in the economy with precipitating factors. The tendency to create sudden market movements for no apparent reason may be explainable. However, the idea that this psychological feedback drives market prices isn't well known to the public. The enthusiasm we sense during bubbles is often inconsistent with widespread awareness of the bubble. We wouldn't get so excited if we knew herd mentality was approaching an abrupt end.

Real-Estate Bubbles

A bubble in *real estate* occurred in the early 2000s in many places worldwide, but not everywhere. In the aftermath, home prices cratered, and the financial malaise lingered for a few years. These crashes followed the booms in most countries. One widely held explanation was that circumstances built population growth pressures to a point where the land became scarce. Another belief was that the resources used to build houses, including labor, lumber, concrete, and steel, were in such heavy demand that they became expensive.

The public's attitude toward real estate shifted during this period. Shiller suggests that the speculation of home prices has become more entrenched in the national or international psyche than ever before. He constructed an index of historical home prices from 1890 called the *Case–Shiller* index with Karl Case. His analysis determined that the elevation in home prices after 1998 was unprecedented. Moreover, they rose faster than the growth in personal incomes.

Shiller searched the literature and found little public discussion of home prices until the 1990s. As a result, there weren't high-quality home price indexes until the Case–Shiller index. Therefore, accurate general information on home prices, which would have generated irrational exuberance, wasn't available in the earlier period. There were infrequent newspaper articles mentioning subjective price changes, but the articles referenced anecdotal evidence or biased opinions of real-estate brokers. Life was simple before the 1990s. Families saved and then bought a home when the time was right. They expected buying a home to be part of everyday living. They didn't worry about what happened to the house price after they moved in. Price activity was local and associated with the conditions of regional infrastructure.

Shiller thinks real-estate prices are more predictable than stock markets in a one-year time horizon. However, few market participants can take advantage of these predictions because of the high costs of getting in and out of real-estate markets. He doesn't mean to exaggerate its usefulness but feels that knowing at least half of the variability is valuable.

This topic introduced irrational exuberance, discussed precipitating factors and amplification mechanisms, and drew parallels in the real-estate markets. The following section describes the new environment for markets.

New Era Thinking

The news media often portray themselves as detached observers of market events. However, Shiller suggests they are integral to these feedback events. They are constantly competing to capture the public's attention to survive commercially. As a result, competition forces them to find and present exciting news. They focus on material with word-of-mouth potential. They maintain ongoing storylines to encourage audiences to remain steady customers. This topic will discuss the media, speculative bubbles, and a new way of thinking.

Stock markets possess star quality. The financial news has the potential for human interest. It deals with actual humans making or breaking fortunes. Shiller observes there is no shortage of media outlets reporting the day's events, but very few offering relevant facts or considered explanations. Instead, the media create most stories under deadlines and produce anything that fits the bare facts.

The media thrive on superlatives and mislead their audiences into perceiving that recent movements in stock prices are unusual. They are big on announcing historical records. Fortunately, in recent years, they shifted their focus to the *percentage change* in stock prices, which is more appropriate than changes in *absolute index levels*. Reactions in the markets often delay the impact of a news event due to incomplete information. This lag has the effect of setting in motion sequences of public attention. Facts previously ignored find new prominence in the wake of breaking news. These cascades of sequences occur as one focus of public attention leads to another.

Speculative market expansion is associated with popular perceptions of a brighter future or less uncertainty than in the past. Moreover, this notion of a dawning era has momentum. Over prior centuries, the general trend has been that standards of living increase, and the economic impact of risk declines. However, Shiller laments economists sometimes miss cultural trends by focusing on the data and not on what's unique about technological changes or institutions. The public also often misses the bigger picture while overreacting to obscure stories suddenly made popular. As a result, they don't take an interest in forecasts of the aggregate economy in the long run. The economic theory presumes they should, but acquiring a comprehensive interpretation of forecasts is too abstract, technical, or boring. Likewise, the public is dazzled by the new capabilities of technological innovations but ignores their impact on the economy.

Speculative bubbles and their associated new era thinking don't often end abruptly with a sudden final crash. The minds of millions of investors who buy or sell in the markets shape speculative prices. Therefore, it's unlikely that people will simultaneously arrive at sudden and enduring changes in their long-run expectations. The focus of the public debate becomes no longer upbeat at the end of new eras. Someone may have a bright future vision but lacks the credibility to express it. Eventually, optimistic ideas no longer achieve levels of public awareness. There are times when audiences are receptive to optimism and other times when they're not.

Individuals who communicate regularly with one another think similarly. At any place and time, there's a spirit of the times. Ideally, markets tend to discount any inconsistent thinking if investors are genuinely independent. On the other hand, if irrational thinking is pervasive among many people, it becomes the source of booms and busts. Shiller thinks we become ready to embrace the majority view even if it contradicts common sense. Most people recall prior experience making mistakes when they rejected the judgments of larger groups. They tend to learn from these experiences.

This topic discussed the media, speculative bubbles, and the new way of thinking. The section discussed capital markets. It explored the basics of these markets, explained rational exuberance, and described the current environment. The following section introduces a more detailed discussion of investments.

Portfolio Selection

Since the 1950s, economists have developed significant theories involving capital markets and how investors can make better decisions. The central theme of these discoveries is identifying the investor's needs and selecting the appropriate securities to meet these needs. This section explores investment management. It introduces investment theory, analyzes efficient portfolios, and describes retirement and endowment fund programs.

Securities and Portfolios

Economists divide investment management into two disciplines: security analysis and portfolio management. The analyst researches capital markets and securities. The portfolio manager matches client needs with these capital market expectations. This topic discusses portfolio selection and presents analysis criteria. In addition, it introduces portfolio theory and describes risk/return and asset pricing models.

Portfolio Selection

Harry Markowitz (1959), a University of California, San Diego professor, examines how to select portfolios that best meet the investor's objectives. He starts by assessing the personal information of the investor's needs and goals. From this, Markowitz determines the investor's desired *risk and return profile*. He then forms an opinion about capital expectations and selects the assets that match the investor profile.

Uncertainty is a primary feature of investments. Unfortunately, analysts don't understand economic forces well enough for predictions to result beyond doubt or error. Moreover, even if they know the consequences of economic conditions perfectly, other external factors are involved. For example, noneconomic influences can change the course of general prosperity, market levels, or the success of a particular security. The existence of uncertainty doesn't mean careful security analysis is useless. On the contrary, thorough and expert judgments concerning security's potential and weaknesses constitute the best way to analyze portfolios.

Markowitz suggests that a second important aspect of investments is the *correlation* among security returns in the portfolio. Like most economic quantities, security returns also move up and down together. However, this correlation isn't perfect. Some securities even move against the general flow of the portfolio and the market.

When security returns aren't correlated, *diversifying* the holdings reduces risk. Unfortunately, when security returns are highly correlated, it implies diversification can reduce risk but can't eliminate it. The degree of correlation among security returns isn't the same for all securities. Analysts expect returns on securities to be more correlated with those in the same industry than unrelated industries. Business connections among firms, servicing the same market, and dependence on military spending also increase correlation.

Analysis Criteria

Markowitz bases portfolio analysis on *investment guidelines*. Managers use them as a clarifier for what's essential or not. One common objective with all investors is to keep the return high. Therefore, a method for measuring risk is needed. Using the technique of *most significant loss acceptable* to an investor as a measure of variability is plausible but not sound. A better measure is analyzing the *standard deviation* of the expected return. The standard deviation of overall portfolio returns isn't determined solely by the standard deviations of individual securities due to the lack of correlation. Instead, the total portfolio's standard deviation is its components' net performance.

Instead of using past performances for input, portfolio managers use the future probability analysis of security analysts in selecting the portfolio. For example, the public expects meteorologists to predict whether rain is likely. Therefore, they ask for their advice on their beliefs about the probability attached to rain tomorrow. Markowitz anoints the security analysts as the meteorologists of stocks and bonds. They form opinions about the future of security regarding general conditions, economic and market prospects, financial structure, and other matters relating to investment opportunities.

Markowitz integrates expected outcomes with the concept of a *weighted average of returns* using probability. He defines an anticipated outcome of an uncertain event precisely like a random variable, except he uses belief probabilities instead of objective probabilities.

Analysts use computers to find the average of *weighted covariances*, consistent with other objectives and restrictions on portfolio choice. The computer supplements rather than supplants the human analyst. The analyst selects the analysis objectives and judgments 'on expected returns, a variance of the returns, and the covariance of security returns. They use a computer for routine and deductive processes, freeing them to focus on induction and judgment. Overall, expected combinations of return and variance that promise the highest returns are necessarily the best combinations that meet the investor's needs. For example, investors sometimes prefer sacrificing long-run returns for short-term stability.

Portfolio Theory

William Sharpe (1970), an American economist, suggests we have an option of consuming all our wealth immediately and sacrificing all future consumption, but in practice, we don't. Our wealth represents the maximum present value of the money we obtain in our lifetime. The difference between wealth and consumption is savings. Our basic savings options are to invest in risky assets, lend the funds out, or hold them in cash. In addition, from the perspective of portfolio theory, we should consider all personal alternatives as investments. Portfolio decisions involve the broadest sense of life decisions, such as job choice, an insurance policy, or a spouse.

Sharpe characterizes the probabilities of portfolio returns with two measures based on computational convenience and familiarity. First, the *expected value of the portfolio return* measures central tendency. This measure is the possible average outcome of weighted returns, with each result weighted by its likelihood. Also, *variance* determines the distribution of the return spread of the portfolio, using a standard deviation of returns, like Markowitz (1959). Analysts suggest the spread distribution is normal (the familiar bell curve). However, these relationships don't always hold. Portfolio theory assumes investors choose securities solely based on these two portfolio measures, and each pair summarizes a probability distribution. However, in reality, such managers don't explicitly use these distributions. This practice is because portfolio theory involves decision making under risky conditions. Uncertainty exists because analysts can't predict the future with enough confidence.

Risk/Return and Asset Pricing Models

Fabozzi, Modigliani, and Jones's (2013) approach to *portfolio theory* involves optimal portfolio selection by risk-averse rational investors. Likewise, their *view of capital markets* considers the implications of security prices for investors' decisions. Together, these theories specify and measure risk and return investment relationships. Analysts measure portfolio performance during a given interval by changes in portfolio value adjusted for additions and distributions. The return is change in market value as a percentage of the portfolio's initial value.

They observe that not every investor agrees on how to assess risk. For example, an investor holding a portfolio of treasury bills to maturity doesn't face an outcome of uncertainty. On the other hand, it's difficult to predict portfolio values in common stock portfolios at any future date. Like Sharpe, they suggest that one way to quantify uncertainty is by specifying probabilities associated with portfolio returns in the future. These probabilities should total one. The portfolio's expected return is a weighted average of returns where weights are relative to the occurrence.

Fabozzi, Modigliani, and Jones found standard deviations of individual stock returns are more significant than those of the overall portfolio returns. Also, the average returns of individual stocks are less than the average returns of the portfolio. Not all risks of individual stocks are relevant, and much of it is diversifiable. Portfolio diversification comes from combining securities whose returns are less than perfectly correlated to reduce the portfolio's risk. This diversification doesn't systemically affect the portfolio's returns. However, it reduces its variability. The systematic risk of individual securities in a portfolio is the portion of total risk not eliminated by diversification. This source of risk is proportional to market risk and expressed as *beta*. It's an index of market sensitivity, indicating how volatile returns are relative to changes in the level of markets.

This topic discussed portfolio selection and presented analysis criteria while introducing portfolio theory and presenting risk/return and asset pricing models. The following section discusses efficient portfolios.

Efficient Portfolio

The Portfolio Management Process

Markowitz (1959) developed the theory of rational behavior, which establishes principles involving the choices made in portfolio management. These theoretical principles describe how rational investors decide. However, unlike *real people*, *rational investors* in models don't make errors in arithmetic or logic while achieving clearly defined objectives. Circumstances limit real investors' information, so actual portfolio results fall short of the best-conceived ones. Nevertheless, the models ideally work out every action and perfectly calculate every risk. This topic discusses efficient portfolios. It introduces a shift in portfolio management thinking, connects objective and subjective probabilities, and explains why dynamic programming isn't appropriate.

Early economists used maximized objectives of *expected returns* of money when formulating principles of behavior. Now, rules of *expected utility* replace these objectives by including an element of uncertainty in the mix. The new rules maximize the combined investor utility of *return and risk*. This arrangement introduces a subjective dimension. However, the probabilities used don't necessarily imply the beliefs are reasonable.

On the contrary, investors readily admit they are currently either always overoptimistic, consistently pessimistic, or in some way biased. Nonetheless, Markowitz emphasizes that the connection between objective and subjective probabilities is close. This connection incorporates the updated calculation of expected utility. In addition, overall relative frequency affects objective and subjective probabilities.

Dynamic programming studies the techniques for obtaining the best investment strategies over time. Economists developed it to model how rational individuals determine their course of action. Its general approach is to look back through time, starting with the latest period and then work backward to the first. This approach determines the best action for each circumstance in the prior periods. Then, with this information, it's possible to derive the best solution for each case in the next period.

However, analysts can't use dynamic programming to make actual portfolio choices. It requires too much input from humans and computers. It's difficult to derive a representative personal utility function for consumption over time. Even simple computations of the process of utility are complex. Nonetheless, the value of dynamic programming is the insight it provides concerning optimum strategies and how the theory computes them. It emphasizes the use of single functions for utility within a period. It demonstrates how the idea generates sequences of utility in a single period.

In addition to its considerable computation cost, Markowitz suggests the other disadvantages of dynamic programming involve the lack of convenience and appeal to the investor. In practice, most investors have little knowledge of portfolio selection and respond in divergent ways. This topic discussed efficient portfolios. It introduced a shift in portfolio management thinking, connected objective and subjective probabilities, and explained why dynamic programming isn't appropriate. The following section discusses retirement and endowment fund strategies.

Retirement and Endowment Fund Plans

This section examines institutional aspects of portfolio management. It provides models of rational thought used in retirement plans, proposes a public pension, and examines strategies for endowment funds.

Save More Tomorrow

Richard Thaler and Cass Sunstein (2008) developed a two-channel model of rational behavior. They use the terms *automatic system* and *reflective system* to characterize it. The automatic system process differs dramatically from reflective system in financial decisions. For example, sensible spending and saving are represented in the reflective system process. They use these two processes to explore how we save, invest, and borrow. In addition, they suggest how public and private institutions might influence our behavior in favorable directions.

They feel we would fare better in handling retirement provisions if we saved more independently. But unfortunately, most of us cannot solve the complicated mathematic problems needed to figure this out. In addition, determining how much to save for retirement without good computer software and a financial background is daunting. Also, individuals don't possess the willpower to implement a relevant plan.

Thaler and Sunstein suggest that the two primary types of pension plans, *defined benefit* (DB) plans and *defined contribution* (DC) plans, have pros and cons. The DB plan automatically entitles the participant to benefits determined by formulas. It has many merits from the perspective of the architecture of choice. The only decision an employee must make is when to start receiving benefits. These plans are adequate for someone who stays in one job for their entire career.

On the other hand, some employees change jobs frequently and end up with no benefits if they quit before they are vested. In addition, DB plans are expensive for employers to administer. In DC plans, employees and sometimes employers make specific cash contributions to these tax-sheltered accounts in the name of individual employees. As a result, employee benefits consumed during retirement depend on pre-retirement contributions and investment decisions.

The penalty for saving too little for retirement is more significant than saving too much. Unfortunately, some people in our society are saving too little. Many employees don't fully participate in available retirement plans. These folks can use a behavioral nudge. Over the last 50 years, the generational switch from DB to DC plans has provided employees with more control, options, and responsibility. However, while determining how much to save is complex, making portfolio selections is even more difficult.

Historically, most DC plans don't have a default investment choice option. Instead, the plan offers enrolled participants a list of fund options. Then, it instructs them to allocate their funds among the funds offered. Through Thaler and Sunstein's architecture of better choices, plan sponsors can guide their participants in many ways. They can demonstrate there are many good plan policies for providing options. For example, participants can choose a set of fund bundles based on risk tolerance. Another strategy is to target a given retirement year. Attention to the architecture of choice is becoming increasingly important because plan sponsors have increased the number of offered options.

A Modest Public Pension System Proposal

The principal objective of a public pension system is to provide a reasonable standard of living in retirement. A British economist,

Robert Merton (1990) presents a comprehensive national pension system proposal that integrates private and public pension plans. The difference in characteristics between public and private pension systems is the mandatory participation feature in public systems. Unfortunately, policy makers can't tailor public plans to meet the specific needs of each participant.

Public pension plans improve the efficiency of risk-bearing. Government can make use of opportunities for diversification, unavailable in private markets. They can also issue financial instruments and employ strategies segmenting risk-sharing between generations. They can use taxes and transfers for more efficient cash flow.

Merton's proposed plan invests contributions and earnings in each participant's account using life annuities indexed to their consumption. The plan defines these annuities as instruments that pay a constant portion of participants' aggregate per capita spending every period. The commencement date for the distribution of benefits is a specified age, whether the participant is retired or not. The plan uses this provision to avoid possible undesirable distortions of retirement decisions. However, the program can stipulate delaying the distribution of benefits to a later age.

In his plan, the government commissions private firms to administer the program. The government holds them accountable for issuing life annuities to participants, where annuities constitute senior liabilities of the firm. The U.S. government retains a residual liability or is an equity holder of the firm with unlimited liability.

Merton suggests limited opportunities exist in existing private markets to accumulate savings in life annuities. So instead, the administration firms invest these savings in spending-linked investments. His proposed plan permits participants to enjoy adequate retirement income by contributing smaller amounts to life annuities. Participants can use the additional funds from this reduced contribution rate for more current consumption or purchasing life insurance. However, the immediate feasibility problem of Merton's plan is the amount of administration required for contributions and account maintenance of individual accumulations. He bases his proposal on the existing Social Security structure, but the funds needed aren't significantly larger.

University Endowment Investment Strategies

Merton also examines *investment portfolio strategies* for university endowment funds. He develops optimal investment and spending policies for these endowments by considering the university's overall objectives and other revenue sources. For endowment portfolio selection, the first step is estimating the market value of each cash flow source of the endowment as if it is a traded asset. Then, Merton computes the university's total wealth or net worth by adding the capitalized values of the sources to the endowment fund value. Finally, the optimal portfolio allocation among traded assets is determined based on the total market value of the university.

Universities receive donations from the type of alumni usually sensitive to the stock market performance. Therefore, the donated levels depend on the wealth effect. Through this process of giving, universities have a shadow investment in the stock market. Consequently, they should lower their allocations of stock more than other universities with smaller amounts of gift-giving. The same effect applies to different classes of specific assets of the university. For example, suppose some gifts to schools specializing in science and engineering come from entrepreneurial alumni. In that case, the school has significant investments in venture capital and tech companies.

Merton's analysis also considers the uncertainty of university *costs* for education, research, and knowledge storage. Estimating unit costs of full-tuition-paying undergraduates and costs of undergraduate education with financial aid further sharpens the focus. Another concern is investing in specific-purpose tangible assets such as dormitories and labs versus financial assets. The endowment returns should strongly correlate with university costs and form a strong hedge against irreversible unexpected expenses that reduce flexibility.

This topic discussed institutional aspects of portfolio management. It described a model of rational thought used in retirement plans, proposed a public pension, and examined strategies for endowment funds. The section explored investment management. It introduced investment theory, analyzed efficient portfolios, and described retirement and endowment fund programs.

Asset Pricing

In the last section, we were concerned with how an investor selects assets for their portfolio. This section on asset pricing will explore how these investor decisions combine to form the aggregate market. Unfortunately, economists have not made much progress in developing a workable theoretical framework for asset pricing due to the complexity of the general capital market.

In financial economics, asset pricing has two primary systems: pricing assets in *general equilibrium* and *rational pricing* of assets. Economists develop models for different situations to illustrate these principles. Under the general equilibrium theory, supply and demand determine prices through market pricing. As a result, the prices of assets jointly satisfy the requirement that supplied quantities and demanded quantities are equal at a market-clearing price. Economists spun off these models from *modern portfolio theory*. The *capital asset pricing model* (CAPM) is the prototype.

On the other hand, rational pricing models calculate derivative prices independent of this supply/demand arbitrage. This approach corresponds to risk-neutral pricing. It focuses on the intrinsic prices of individual securities with simple models. As a result, it creates a unique price for each asset. The classic rational pricing model is *Black–Scholes* (1973). It illustrates the dynamics of the market through equity derivatives. However, economists can also apply rational pricing to fixed-income instruments like bonds.

Theoretical Models

Capital Market Theory

The road through the next section may get bumpy, so tighten your seat belts accordingly. The contributions of our laureates become very technical and challenging to understand and explain. Nevertheless, public policy makers should incorporate these ideas in designing and regulating the markets. Society will benefit from the smooth markets created.

William Sharpe (1970), a professor at Stanford University, notes that a *capital asset* is a contract between an investor and the outside world. In contrast, a *financial security* is a contract between investors. The capital market theory does not distinguish between financial securities and capital assets. Investors' view of the market depends on their predictions and available opportunities to borrow and lend. Ideally, all investors make the exact predictions and agree on optimal combinations of risky securities in the simplest form if they are purely rational.

In an equilibrium of the market, there are optimal combinations of risk securities that include all securities. The proportion of each security represented equals its proportional value to the market total. Economists call this collection set the *market portfolio*. Sharpe suggests that the equilibrium of this market portfolio doesn't remain fixed over time. If conditions of demand and supply change, prices are also likely to change. However, conditions in a market are balanced if the quantity demanded equals the amount supplied.

From a more complex but realistic departure from the basic model of capital theory, Sharpe eliminates the assumption that all investors agree on the expected performance of securities. As a result, two investors from different backgrounds probably won't necessarily face identical prospects.

Analysts use *beta* to measure the systemic risk of securities. It uses a single index as its base. Beta is a measure of *volatility* in the price of a stock relative to the overall market. Volatility is a numerical measure of the return distribution for a given security or market index. In contrast, *variability* measures how much a stock return deviates from its average return and expressed in standard deviations. These models aren't helpful if investors place more faith in personal predictions than those implied in the current prices of securities. Both portfolio theory and capital market theory must deal with future predictions. A third helpful measure is a security's ratio of reward-to-volatility, known as the *Sharpe ratio*.

Random walk refers to the irregular way information becomes known to the market and reflected in current prices. The timing of the announcements resembles the aimless stroll of a drunk wandering down the street. The portfolio theory assumes investors consider expected returns and standard deviation when comparing alternative portfolios. Sharpe emphasizes utility functions (versus monetary gain) represent an individual's preferences.

Certainty and Uncertainty Models

Eugene Fama was an American economist and University of Chicago professor. Fama and Miller (1972) were concerned with how individuals and firms allocate their resources through time. They explain how the existence of capital markets and firms facilitates economic solutions to problems in allocating resources. Under perfect capital markets, a firm policy of maximizing the decision maker's current share of a market leads to operating decisions. Moreover, these decisions are identical to what managers and investment owners with different tastes and resources would adopt independently. Investment decisions are technological in the strictest sense to maximize market value. Capital budgeting becomes financial when it considers the present value of a capital asset. Due to uncertainty, a critical decision is selecting the most efficient financing instrument: bonds versus stocks versus retained earnings.

Econometric Asset Pricing Models

An American economist, Lars Peter Hansen was from the University of Chicago. Hansen, Heaton, and Luttmer (1995) applied statistical methods for assessing asset pricing models using specification-error and volatility bounds. These methods account for market frictions due to the cost of transactions or short-sale constraints. In addition, they are easier to interpret than standard models. Their asset pricing models imply that asset prices represent some stochastic discount factors.

Using the linear methodology, Bengt Holmström of MIT and Jean Tirole (2011) extend their asset pricing model to a pricing model of heterogeneous firms' liquid assets (LAPM). Uncertainty affects all parameters of technology. Their model explains how liquidity premiums determine bond yields and firm values. They suggest that risk management policies typically recommend being fully insured or hedged against external risks like fire hazards in practice. Although Holmström and Tirole's model resembles an Arrow–Debreu equilibrium, demand for firm liquidity drives LAPM premiums entirely. This demand segments investors into healthy entrepreneurs willing to pay a premium and investors-consumers who aren't.

Fabozzi, Modigliani, and Jones (2013) suggest that the most common asset pricing model, CAPM, explains risk and return relationships in capital markets. Economists base it on the principle that the same systematic risk assets should have the same expected returns. CAPM implies that the only relevant risk where an investor requires compensation is systematic because diversification doesn't eliminate this risk. CAPM holds that the expected return of security equals the riskless rate plus a risk premium. The model assumes the riskless rate is the return of a U.S. Treasury bill.

Market Price Behavior

A Dynamic Model of the Asset Market

Merton (1990), a professor at MIT, uses *continuous-time models* to derive relationships of general equilibrium among securities in asset markets. This model is like his model for individual investors' life decisions of spending and saving. He assumes that a firm's value is an independent capital structure. He derives equations for pricing individual security classes within this capital structure. In addition, Merton presents a model where the riskless asset doesn't exist. The rationale for this exclusion is the uncertainty of inflation. Because consumers are interested in investing only for increased spending in the future, a riskless security in nominal terms of money isn't riskless in real terms.

Merton develops equilibrium models for capital markets featuring simplicity. As a result, the consumer-investors know at each point in time the probability of transition returns for each investment over the following trading sessions and the probability of transition returns on assets in future periods. He reformulates his asset pricing model based on pricing models of capital assets that fit the model framework of Arrow–Debreu aggregate markets. The models of Arrow–Debreu require a complete set of pure securities for every state of the world.

Efficient Markets, Random Walks, and Bubbles

Robert Shiller (2000) suggests efficient market theory assumes that financial prices always accurately portray all information known to the public.

In other words, financial assets are always correctly priced, given what is known. Of course, prices may appear too high or low, but appearances are an illusion. His argument for this theory comes from observing that it seems challenging to make a lot of money by buying low and selling high. As a result, we compete against smart money trading in markets, looking for the same opportunities to make money.

Investors who doubt a stock's market value try to *sell them short*. A short seller borrows an asset from somebody else, immediately sells the asset, and holds the proceeds in cash. When the asset price falls, the short seller repurchases the investment at a lower price and returns the shares to the lender. Unfortunately, obstacles limit this strategy. It breaks down when zealots gobble up so much overpriced stock that there are usually not enough shares to borrow.

Shiller notes certain anomalies appear in equity prices. The *January effect* appears when stock prices go up between December and January. The *small-firm effect* occurs when stocks of small firms tend to yield higher returns. Finally, the *day-of-the-week effect* occurs when stock markets do poorly on Mondays. It's argued that these are minor effects that diminish once discovered. They aren't the stuff of bull or bear markets. Miller and Upton (1974) also recognize many minor anomalies. However, they argue they are inconsequential and not worth the cost of taking advantage of them.

It's Shiller's (2000) central position that *news* of future dividends or earnings account for a substantial portion of the volatility of financial markets. There also appears to be less evidence of excess volatility in long-term interest rates. The U.S. stock markets reached overvaluations in 2000, 2007, and 2014 without reasonable justification. As a result, Shiller thinks few market participants feel the need to perform careful research on the long-term value of investments.

The Term Structure of Interest Rates

Fabozzi, Modigliani, and Jones suggest there's not a single interest rate in any economy. Instead, interest rates form a pattern called a *term structure* expressed in *yield curves*. Interest rates depend on many factors, such as the features of bonds, their yield, the base riskless interest rate, risk premiums, and inflation expectations. Fabozzi et al. demonstrate that yield curves illustrate relationships between comparable quality and bond yields with different maturities.

Market participants can construct these yield curves by observing prices and yields in treasury markets. When yield curves, presented in maturities, are sloping positively, investors expect interest rates to steadily rise as maturity increases. This pattern occurs in healthy economies. Market participants measure positively sloped curves based on their steepness. On the other hand, when inverted yield curves are downward-sloping, investors expect interest rates to decline as maturity generally increases.

The theory of *investor expectations* explains why the market shapes these yield curves. Forward rates represent future expectations of rates. Another theory, the *liquidity* theory, suggests investors hold longer-term maturities if the market offers them higher risk premium rates than expected. As a result, these forward rates reflect both rate expectations and risk premiums.

A third theory, *preferred habitat*, rejects assertions that risk premiums rise uniformly with maturity. Instead, many investors wish to carry financial resources forward further in the future. They're concerned the desired funds will be available when they need them and don't care which path interest rates take to get there. A similar theory, *market segmentation*, proposes that the primary reason for the yield curve shape is asset/liability management constraints. Creditors desire to restrict their lending to specific sectors of maturity. This restriction assumes neither investors nor borrowers will shift their maturity preference.

Contingent Claims Analysis

Theory of Rational Option Pricing

Myron Scholes (2000) is a Canadian American financial economist. He developed an alternative to supply/demand models for asset pricing. He explains how analysts should visualize the firm liabilities as a basket of *derivative options*. For example, formulas can determine the intrinsic values of common stock, corporate bonds, and warrants. Analysts also use procedures to derive discounts on corporate bonds with default possibilities. *Warrants* are options for a firm's liability instead of a counterparty on an exchange. Warrant holders have the opportunity to buy the stock on specified terms. The exercise prices of warrants aren't dividend adjusted.

Merton (1990) presents simple models which improve Samuelson's (1948) theory of the rational pricing of warrants. Merton introduces his idea of option pricing by deducing the sets of restrictions of the pricing formulas of options from the assumption that investors prefer more than less. These restrictions are necessary for procedures to be consistent with the theory of rational pricing.

He pays attention to security-specific problems such as firms paying dividends on underlying common stocks while holding the options. Reduced restrictions aren't enough to determine the pricing formulas of options. He introduces additional assumptions to examine and extend the seminal Black–Scholes (1973) option pricing theory.

Merton derives general formulas of security prices whose values under specified conditions are known functions of another security. He demonstrates that derived pricing formulas are continuous first derivatives, and there isn't preselection bias in independent choices of variables. Black and Scholes use continuous-time analysis. Scholes (1998) is a Stanford University professor. The resulting formulas from their model don't require expected returns, expected cash flows, and the prices of risk or return covariance to markets. The market prices all these variables in the valuation of stocks.

Franco Modigliani was a professor at the University of Illinois, Carnegie Mellon University, and MIT. Fabozzi, Modigliani, and Jones (2013) determine the theoretical prices of futures and options contracts using arbitrage arguments. Futures are derivative contracts that obligate parties to transact an asset at a predetermined future date and price. Closely examining underlying assumptions necessary to derive theoretical prices explains how the market changes to price-specific contracts.

This section on asset pricing explored how these investor decisions combine in the aggregate market. The chapter examined financial economics theory by discussing capital markets, introducing investment management concepts, and presenting asset pricing theories. However, we didn't make much progress in determining how the market sets up bread choices. Nonetheless, capital markets play a part. The next chapter investigates the role of government.

CHAPTER 5

Role of Government

While mathematical concepts helped describe financial economics in the last chapter, our journey brings us to a place where things get interesting: the role of government. It is the elephant in the room. Here, mathematics takes a backseat to subjective logic. This subjectiveness is often tinged with personal sentiment, rendering it controversial. This chapter will examine the rule of law, survey the public sector, study political economics, and discuss political wisdom.

Rule of Law

Fredrich Hayek (1960), an Austrian American economist, legal theorist, and philosopher, examined only free countries, not arbitrary governments. Nothing distinguishes conditions in a free country more clearly than the observance of the *rule of law*. The rule of law means governments, in all their actions, are bound by rules fixed and announced ahead of time. These rules make it possible for us to foresee how the government might use its coercive powers in given circumstances. Moreover, it allows us to plan our affairs based on this knowledge. But, of course, it's never perfectly achieved because fallible individuals enforce the law. This section visits the rule of law. It covers property rights, describes contract theory, and aligns the rule of law with freedom and justice.

Property Rights

Property rights are theoretical constructs society enforces to determine how its members use and own a resource or economic good. For example, individuals, associations, collectives, or governments own resources. This topic examines the attributes of these rights, describes the approach, and analyzes firm integration. The characteristics of these rights have four broad components:

1. The right to use the asset
2. The right to earn income from the asset
3. The right to transfer the asset to others
4. The right to alter, abandon, or destroy the asset

According to the property rights approach, owners have discretion over any missing gaps in the contracts they enter. In addition, owners have residual rights of control. Finally, they have the right to determine all asset usage consistent with prior agreements.

A benefit of corporate integration is the incentive for an acquiring firm to expand investments. These investments are relationship-specific because it receives a more significant portion of the revenue created by the assets. As a result, the cost of the developed relationship with the acquired firm decreases, increasing surpluses for the acquiring firm.

Contract Theory

Hayek (1960) maintains that contract freedom is essential for our personal freedom. It's not what we can do, but what types of contracts government will enforce. For instance, the government doesn't enforce agreements for criminal or immoral purposes or contracts in restraint of trade. This topic discusses contract theory. It examines legal boundaries, describes the current bankruptcy procedure, and proposes two policy alternatives to improve these procedures.

Oliver Hart (1995), a British-born American economist, emphasizes that it is essential to identify who owns a piece of private property. Contracting, renting, and owning are different ways of using an asset. Incomplete agreements don't specify all outcomes of property use. According to Hart, owners have residual rights of control over the property. So, for example, if the property breaks down or needs modifications, owners ensure quick repair to keep it productive. As a result, owners are more incentivized to take care of the machines and learn how to efficiently operate them.

One concern of ownership involves the *legal boundary* determinants. Hart thinks firms should set legal boundaries that allocate rights optimally among various parties. These rights are scarce resources. Therefore, the firm should never waste them. Hart also suggests that when a firm acquires another, it owns their inventory, machines, buildings, land, and client lists. Excluded from the transaction are human assets. This ownership of capital assets becomes a power source when contracts are incomplete.

Hart, a professor at Harvard University, observes that firm owners are often wealth constrained and can't buy enough assets outright to run the business. Instead, they must raise funds from outside investors to purchase the required investments. However, this funding method creates a new agency problem for the investor. They should protect themselves from adverse manager behavior by taking a controlling interest in the assets. However, the investors may then abuse their power. Therefore, it's more advantageous for all parties to enter into a financial contract. Empirical evidence suggests firms commonly use long-term loans for property, leaseholds, and machinery improvements. In addition, firms use short-term loans for working capital, such as payroll needs and inventory financing.

Bankruptcy Procedures and Proposals

When a company takes on debt, circumstances sometimes arise from unexpected financial shocks where the firm defaults on this debt. *Default* is an event where the control of assets transitions from a debtor to a creditor. The creditor becomes the new owner of the assets. In the simple case, there's little need for a bankruptcy proceeding. The procedure is little more than ensuring the transfer of ownership and control.

However, Hart observes that matters become more complicated when there are many creditors. With secured loans, creditors can seize collateral assets. With an unsecured loan, the creditor must sue the debtor. Difficulties arise when debtors have insufficient assets to cover their liabilities. Given this, it's in their collective best interests for all parties to conduct the disposition of assets in an orderly manner.

In practice, transactions make it too expensive for debtors and creditors to design their bankruptcy procedure contractually. So instead, parties rely on the standard form of a government-provided approach for bankruptcy. In cash auctions of U.S. Bankruptcy Code Chapter 7, a trustee initially supervises the sale of the firm's assets. Then, the trustee distributes receipts from the sales among the former claimants. However, Hart senses widespread skepticism among the public regarding the efficacy of cash auctions in practice. There's a lack of competition for the assets and few available paths to keep the firm intact.

Because of concerns about the effectiveness of cash auctions, policy makers developed the alternate procedure of Chapter 11 using structured bargaining. First, the court retains creditors' claims and appoints committees representing each claimant class. Then, a judge supervises a bargaining process among the committees to determine an action plan. Problems arise when restructured firms don't have an objective value. There's also a danger that the process will result in the wrong decision for the firm's future.

Hart proposes two alternative procedures for bankruptcy. They differ from existing designs in the treatment of secured debt and the role of judges. The court initially canceled the firm's debt obligations in Hart's first version. Then, the firm starts a new life as an all-equity corporation. The court appoints a judge to supervise the process. The judge allocate the shares in this firm to the existing claim holders and solicits cash and noncash bids for the new all-equity corporation. Once the judge completes these tasks, the court reveals the bid offers. Finally, the court gives shareholders a period to exercise their options before it sells the firm to the winning outside bidder.

The court retains the secured debt in Hart's second bankruptcy proposal. The judge takes on managing the company while the court completes the procedure. The judge should act in the interest of shareholders and optionholders when planning for the firm's future. Hart's basic approach for this proposal is that a bankrupt firm isn't fundamentally different from a solvent firm performing poorly. The solvent firm elects a board of directors to keep it running, sells it, or closes it down if it isn't solvent. This same menu of options is available to claimants in his first bankruptcy proposal.

Freedom and Justice

Friedrich Hayek (1960), a professor at the London School of Economics and the University of Chicago, thought society should reduce situations where individuals coerce others as much as possible. This tranquil arrangement is the state of liberty or freedom. Sometimes, cultures distinguish this state as an individual or personal space. Hayek observes that freedom might differ widely among cultures but only by the degree of independence. This freedom allows us to act according to our own decisions and plans. We are not irrevocably subject to the will of another individual who can coerce us by an arbitrary decision.

An alternate meaning of freedom is psychological or subjective freedom. It's closely related to personal freedom but different. Whether or not we have the ability to choose intelligently between alternatives is a problem distinct from allowing other people to impose their will on us.

Hayek thinks recognition of our ignorance is the beginning of wisdom. This recognition has profound significance for understanding society. We soon become aware of others' ignorance enough to help them achieve their aims.

We can harvest the advantages of social life by acquiring more knowledge than we initially possess. Hayek suggests civilization begins when we collectively have more understanding than we can process to pursue personal goals. Growth of learning and society are the same, only if we interpret knowledge to include all human adaptations to the environment. Our habits, skills, emotional attitudes, tools, and institutions have evolved by selective elimination of less proper conduct.

Transmission and communication of knowledge refers to the transfer of our accumulated knowledge over time. It also refers to communicating information among contemporaries based on their actions. Hayek asserts that the case for our freedom rests primarily on the recognition of the inevitable ignorance of everybody. Therefore, liberty is vital to provide a reserve for the unanticipated and unpredictable while we soldier through the disappointment of expectations. Hayek thinks our aim should be to improve human institutions and to increase the chances of correct foresight.

Freedom, Reason, and Tradition

Hayek stresses that freedom isn't a state of nature but an artifact of civilization. Society didn't initially establish institutions of freedom because people couldn't foresee its benefits. But, once they recognized the advantages, they began to perfect and extend the realm of freedom. This process began in England and France. Historians base the English version on interpreting traditions and institutions *spontaneously developed* but imperfectly understood. On the other hand, the French tradition aimed for *utopia*. However, society has never put utopia successfully in place. The French tradition is rising while the English version is declining.

Contrasts remain, though the two are lumped together as precursors of modern liberalism. The difference is traceable to their view of cultural development. The organic, slow, half-conscious growth of the *empiricist* view in England holds that culture is the accumulated hard-earned result of trial and error. Its counterpart, the *rationalist* approach in France, features doctrinaire deliberateness. They assume society originally endows people with intellectual and moral attributes, enabling them to fashion civilization deliberately.

Hayek believes the most significant difference between the two liberty visions is the role of tradition and the value of all the other products of unconscious growth. The French believe all functional institutions are deliberate contrivances and freedom means chaos. To the English, the value of freedom consists of the opportunity it provides for the growth of the raw spirits. The healthy functioning of a free society rests on such freely grown institutions.

This topic examined legal boundaries, described the current bankruptcy procedure, and proposed two policy suggestions to improve these procedures. The section investigated the rule of law by covering property rights and contract theory. It also aligned the rule of law with freedom and justice. The following section discusses the proper role of a government in the economy.

Public Sector

A primary point of controversy in today's politics is the proper role of government. This section examines the debate on the appropriate duty of a government in an economy. It addresses the factors of government intervention, determines their proper functions, and provides a historical perspective.

The U.S. founding fathers envisioned a limited role in economic affairs to ensure and support economic and political freedoms. As a result, individual buyers and sellers make most economic decisions in market economies, not the government. Economists starting with Adam Smith identify six primary economic functions of governments in market economies:

- Provide a legal and social framework.
- Maintain competition.
- Provide public goods and services.
- Redistribute income.
- Correct externalities.
- Stabilize the economy.

The basic argument for these government interventions is that markets don't *naturally* provide public goods or handle externalities. These public goods include health and welfare systems, education, roads, research and development, national and domestic security, and a clean environment.

Role of Government

Let's flesh out the basics. First, this topic reviews studies of consumer choice, examines how government stimulates or discourages economic activity, and describes its benefits to a free society. Next, it discusses government regulation and the goals of economic policy. Finally, it describes economic and political competition and discusses taxation and government mistrust.

Utility, Strategy, and Social Decision Rules

William Vickrey (1939) recounts that past studies of consumer choices identified only the rank ordering of various situations in the preferences of an individual or group. Fortunately, when surveys asked individuals questions about their choice, their responses were consistent. From Jeremy Bentham's time to Vickrey's, the underlying basis for measuring functions of welfare economics was the summation of the individual utilities of all society members. Members evaluated desired social states according to the magnitude of this sum.

One of Vickery's postulates preserves this social ordering preference when an individual's taste is unopposed by a contrary taste of another individual. According to him, welfare function ranking is, in each case, a consistent ordering of all feasible choices. A social choice between alternatives is unaffected by removing or adding other options to possible alternative fields.

Public Sector and Economic Growth

Arthur Lewis (1955), a Saint Lucian economist, suggests government behavior plays a crucial role in stimulating or discouraging economic activity. This same catalyst is also present in the conduct of entrepreneurs, parents, scientists, or priests. It's difficult, however, to put their roles in perspective because of political prejudice. The government provides public services like roads, schools, public health, surveys, and research. As a result, they can play a considerable part in developing attitudes favorable to growth instead of promoting perspectives harmful to development. Also, the government sometimes needs to influence the use of resources because price mechanisms don't always yield socially acceptable results.

The distribution of income raises complex problems for less developed countries. Their policy makers endeavor to combine incentives that promote higher equality and saving levels. However, economic growth requires natural differentials in skill, challenging work, education, risk-bearing, and willingness to take on responsibility. Lewis thinks the case for comprehensive production programs in developing countries is valid. Unfortunately, they fall into the realm of central planning. The argument against detailed central planning: It is undemocratic, bureaucratic, inflexible, and subject to error and confusion.

Government production programs need the collaboration of the private sector, which is not always politically feasible. Therefore, public sector programs must properly comprehend what's happening in the private sector. Also, there is a tendency for policy makers to develop programs favoring capital cities with little input from the countryside.

Lewis explains governments of developing economies raise less revenue than developed ones because revenue is harder to collect. In *direct taxation*, it's a problem of technique. Governments should avoid costly taxes when collecting them from large populations. Collecting direct taxes in developing countries is also difficult because of their agricultural base. In some countries, farmers do not trade much of their output. Instead, they only produce enough food and a few manufactured goods for direct consumption. As a result, they distribute only small surpluses in markets. Moreover, if the government taxes subsistence farmers only on money income, they escape taxation.

Countries also have technical difficulties in raising *indirect taxes*. They levy taxes most efficiently when a large part of GDP passes through a few hands. In developed countries, substantial companies produce significant output component channels, making collecting taxes easier.

Governments have a notable effect on economic growth. However, very few governments are corruption-free. For example, they often place obstacles to foreign intercourse, neglect public services, or are excessively laissez-faire. They also exert excessive control, excessively spend, or embark on costly wars. Lewis observes that some countries seem better at picking their way through these opposing dangers than others.

The Role of Government in Free Society

Milton Friedman (1962) suggests the standard objection to a totalitarian society is justifying the *means*. To deny those *outcomes* justify the means is indirectly asserting outcomes aren't the ultimate results. Any outcome attained using the wrong means provides the rationale to halt the process.

It's important to distinguish our day-to-day activities from a general framework within which these customary and legal activities occur. Daily activities are personal actions. The framework is the rules we follow. According to Friedman, the essential role of government in a free society is to provide a process to modify the rules of society to handle differences within the community on the meanings of rules. In addition, it enforces compliance with rules for those otherwise not playing the game.

Friedman feels the need for government arises because absolute freedom is impossible. However attractive anarchy might be as a philosophy, it's not feasible in societies of imperfect individuals. Freedoms conflict, and when they do, a free community must limit our freedom to preserve the freedom of others. Friedman suggests that freedom should be a rational objective for responsible individuals. The necessity to draw a line between responsible individuals and others is inescapable. It means there's an essential ambiguity in our aim of ultimate freedom. Paternalism is unavoidable for those not responsible.

Government Regulation

As Adam Smith thought, it's not from the benevolence of the butcher, brewer, or baker we expect dinner. It's the providers' regard in their pursuit of self-interest. We can't depend on benevolence for dinner, but can we rely on Smith's invisible hand?

Friedman remembers that in the 1960s, there was an explosion in the regulatory activity of the U.S. government. They established at least 21 new agencies in the following decade. Instead of being concerned with specific industries, they covered the waterfront. During the same decade, economic growth in the United States slowed dramatically. Agencies established in response to this regulatory movement imposed high industrial costs long after the industry initially assimilated increasingly detailed and extensive requirements.

In contrast, this government intervention was also subject to the laws of the marketplace, which created economic distortions. Friedman brings up a powerful argument for letting market forces work independently: the difficulty of policy makers imagining outcomes. The only certainty is that no services survive that users don't value highly enough to pay for and pay at prices yielding adequate incomes for the individuals providing the service.

The Goals of Economic Policy

George Stigler (1986) maintains that Western economic policy's first and most ancient goal should be facilitating the highest output of goods and services. The term *maximum output* has evolved to mean deploying, as fully as possible, resources at the disposal of society and deploying these resources as efficiently as possible. Another policy goal should be *economic growth*, where society develops natural resources, accumulates capital, and discovers new products and technologies. These forward-looking activities enjoy a steady rise in income levels relative to the population over time. Lastly, a third goal of economic policy is a *reduction of income inequality*.

Adam Smith (1776) suggests that society should leave economic affairs to private citizens. However, the government does remarkably well if it succeeds in its unavoidable tasks of winning wars, preserving justice, and maintaining various highways of commerce. Smith's economic policies are his belief in the systemic efficiency of natural liberty. The individual allocates resources where they yield the most. In this way, the resources then deliver what's best for society.

Smith's distrust of government drives his strong preference for promoting the activity of the private economy. This distrust stems primarily from the *motives* of the government rather than its *competence*. He feels governments are the creations of organized, articulate, and self-serving groups. These scoundrels were mainly the merchants and manufacturers of his day. Stigler feels mass education and the instinctive reverence for the wisdom of middle-class leaders will ensure democratic governments seldom stray far from the public good.

Economic and Political Competition

Stigler explains that his definition of competition hinges on how much firms can influence the market price. When the influence of the firm is zero, competition is perfect. Competition is usually greater in more extended periods than in short ones.

There's little competition in local governments. But, if any city sets its services or prices at levels where citizens object, they can migrate to more pleasant governments. The more competitive the political system is, the more responsive the design is to the majority's desires. All political systems contain elements of divisions of power. Thus, minorities hold their share of minor offices corresponding to their relative size. Stigler implies that minorities, even when each member acts individually, impose costs on majorities to enforce policies that minorities oppose. Moreover, these costs increase the more significant the minority and the more intense its opposition.

Michael Spence (2011), a Canadian American economist, remembers that in the late 1980s, a group in Washington led by Oliver Williamson developed the *Washington Consensus*. This collection of policies lays out 10 general economic elements critical to successful growth and development. The focus is on economic policy and macroeconomics. Initially, the consensus suggested that society redirect fiscal policy and public spending from small narrow interests to broad-based provisions for progrowth. These provisions include primary education, primary health care, and investment in infrastructure.

Taxation and Mistrust

Abhijit Banerjee and Esther Duflo (2019) think it's unreasonable to expect markets alone to consistently deliver just, acceptable, or efficient outcomes. In a world with skyrocketing social inequality and a winner-take-all atmosphere, the lives of the poor and the rich diverge wildly. The two groups will become hopelessly divided if society allows markets to drive all social outcomes. However, Banerjee and Duflo feel the ultra-rich are not rich enough to finance the entire government. They will resist. Others also need to pay, and the challenge is political. The problem then devolves into the erosion of the legitimacy of government. The public often perceives it as unreliable or worse.

Another reason people are reluctant to support high taxes to receive more services is that citizens are skeptical of government intervention. Yet, government exists in part to solve problems no other institution can tackle. Part of public skepticism is an obsession with government corruption worldwide. But Banerjee and Duflo suggest this view misses the critical point about the source of corruption and the ability to control it. Governments try to do things markets won't touch, thus becoming susceptible to the same shortcomings.

For years, politicians have promised that good things were just around the corner. Unfortunately, this pandering creates an environment where too many people trust no one, least of all, the government. Banerjee and Duflo also think the rich carefully cultivated these anti-government sentiments to avoid attempts to rein in the acquisition of their wealth.

This topic examined how government stimulates or discourages economic activity. It discussed government regulation and frames the goals of economic policy. Finally, it described economic and political competition and discussed taxation and government mistrust. The following section describes its functions.

Government Functions

The government is the largest provider of public services. This topic covers government debt, transportation policy, congestion theory, and regulations.

Government Debt

Vickrey (1939) suggests that in practical terms of finance, policy makers should consider the government's role in the *macroeconomic balance* of economies. For example, one function of government-issued debt is to provide a place where we can invest our accumulated excesses of savings. This excess savings is independent of the levels of our income. The government should actively promote this feature if the government's debt doesn't crowd out private investment. For example, at the beginning of the industrial revolution, policy makers based provisions for retirement on the *family unit* rather than on *individuals*. As a result, individuals only needed to use savings and wealth to create capital assets.

Vickrey recounts that in the 20th century, the public policy for retirement provisions changed. Public and private accumulations providing for old age increased dramatically. Meanwhile, nuclear families gave way to broken families and individuals. Private pension plans also became widespread. As industrial economies matured, and opportunities for profitable investments declined relative to aggregate output. As a result, desired savings and wealth accumulation were higher than formations of capital motivated by profits. The government stepped in and covered the gap.

Government Transportation Pricing

Traffic congestion is an externality that government can manage via pricing. William Vickrey (1939) devoted much of his professional life to advocating congestion pricing in urban transportation. Initially, the policy process begins when policy makers formally present a solution to a transportation problem that is straining cities' budgets. Then, they emphasize the influence of fares on the riding public's usage of the transit system. Vickrey implies political controversies exist over whether fares structures are acceptable to riders or reasonable and equitable to taxpayers. In addition, policy makers need to address ecology, geography, and societal concerns. Finally, it is necessary to ensure the value of produced benefits exceeds the cost of rendering service by as large a margin as possible to achieve optimal utilization.

He thinks government pricing practices of urban *highways* are often irrational, outdated, and conductive to waste. Usage pricing of urban *streets* is nonexistent. State and federal governments' highway taxes and license plate revenue must support highway spending. The pricing of highway services is troublesome during peak hours. Even if urban motorists cover the total cost of urban facilities, usage during rush hour is seriously underpriced.

Vickrey suggests policy makers commonly hold usage pricing of roadways applies to arterial streets and highways but has no application to the usage of access streets. There's little point in levying specific suburban use of side streets in residential areas. Congestion added incrementally is zero, and wear and tear is negligible.

Congestion Theory and Transportation Investment

According to Vickrey, public investment program cycles in transportation begins with investments in *new* routes or provisions for new services under conditions of indivisibility and increasing returns to scale. Then, as investment proceeds, policy makers allocate larger and larger proportions of total investment in transportation to relieve congestion of *existing* routes and expand overall capacity.

There are different types of traffic congestion. *Single interactions* of congestion occur whenever two vehicles approach each other close enough, where one delayed vehicle reduces the possibility of collision. *Multiple interactions* tend to occur at higher levels of traffic density but are below capacity flows. Pure situations of *bottleneck* congestion occur when planners design segments of short routes with fixed capacities that are sufficiently smaller relative to traffic demand than the segments feeding in. Complex conditions of *trigger neck* congestion develop from bottleneck situations when the queue backing up from the bottlenecks interferes with traffic flow, not intending to use the bottleneck facilities. Finally, congestion of the *network and control* results whenever levels reach peak traffic, requiring the application of additional control measures. These measures include formal regulations, including stop signs, routing limitations, traffic lights, train controls, flight patterns, and rules.

Congestion costs, eventually, are density functions of overall flows in transportation for all combined modes and routes. Although some costs contribute less to overall congestion than traffic volume, this condition is present. But, as vehicle interactions increase, accidents per vehicle mile increase. Gradual changes are needed where significant parts of traffic closely compete for alternative routes. This tie-up occurs when traffic bottlenecks one alternative way while the other alternatives are longer and circuitous. As a result, traffic divides to equalize the costs of total traffic per vehicle.

What Regulators Regulate

Stigler (1986) singles out the innumerable actions of regulators. He found these actions provide conclusive proof, not of effective regulation but the desirability of regulator participation. But unfortunately, a plethora of statutes prevents society from evaluating their effectiveness. Therefore, practical tests of economic law should remain independent of the contents of formal rules. He warns that regulatory machinery and government power are potential threats to every industry. One central task in the theory of economic regulation is to explain who receives the benefits of regulation or burdens. It also seeks to determine the form regulation takes.

Stigler maintains that industries primarily seek to acquire their regulation. As a result, policy makers design and operate rules for the benefit of the industries. However, regulated effects are sometimes onerous to the industry, but these regulations are the exception. Critics widely hold two alternative views. The first is policy makers institute regulation primarily for the protection and benefit of the public-at-large or large subclasses. The second view is that political processes defy rational explanations. Politics is imponderable. It's a shifting force that is constant and unpredictable.

Friedman suggests there's an undesirable invisible hand in politics operating in the opposite direction to the invisible hand of Adam Smith. This invisible political hand leads us to promote general and special interests we do not intend to encourage. Bureaucrats haven't necessarily usurped power. They haven't deliberately engaged in any conspiracy to subvert the process of democracy. Instead, circumstances thrust the power on them.

The delegation of different government responsibilities by policy makers often leads to conflicts between bureaucrats. The only solution available is to give power to another set of outside bureaucrats to resolve the dispute. However, the actual problem is a conflict between desirable public objectives.

This topic covered government debt, transportation policy, congestion theory, and regulations. The next topic offers a historical perspective.

Historical Perspective

Society can learn from its mistakes. This section describes U.K. national accounting, studies the geopolitical environment after World War II, notes shifting economic trends, and chronicles post-1960s gloom.

National Accounting in the United Kingdom

Richard Stone (1961), a British economist, explored how U.K. fiscal policy flows into private and public spending channels in a departure from the methodology of the United States. He describes how the United Kingdom measures the channel's consumption spending of individuals, taxes paid, or the amount saved. In addition, he shows how the government measures allocations for defense, education, health services, and other purposes.

Firms never distribute some flows of government income. Instead, these firms profit, but the corporation retains the undistributed part after deducting taxes. The firm saves this undistributed part for expanding capital equipment or building reserves. Stone of the University of Cambridge suggests that economic systems depend on which goods and services the system produces with the ultimate object of satisfying human wants. The U.K. national income accounting divides its production into intermediate and final products.

Socialism in 19th-Century England

Stigler (1986) recounts the transition of public policy in England from pure laissez-faire to collectivism. The change began in the first half of the 19th century and subsided in the era of Margaret Thatcher.

Through the period, shifts in public opinion and adequate electoral power stood behind a change in policy incorrectly attributed to Fabian socialists. The two leading Fabian theoreticians were Bernard Shaw and Sidney Webb. Shaw emphasized that society needed radical economic reform for land rent taxes. Moreover, he expressed deep appreciation of Marx' denunciation of the injustice of capitalism and its pending demise.

Uncertainty After World War II

Evaluating contemporary events differ from examining historical events because policy makers don't know the outcomes the current ones will produce. But, looking back, they can assess the significance of past occurrences and trace the consequences the events brought in their path. At the close of World War II, Hayek (1944) feared what happened in Germany would happen in England and the United States, but the danger wasn't imminent. It wasn't easy to believe they were headed in the same direction, as conditions were still remote from those witnessed in Germany.

There existed the same national organizations developed for defense purposes and retained for the creation of wealth. Moreover, the environment harbored 19th-century contempt for liberalism, bogus realism, and the same fatalistic acceptance of inevitable trends. Hayek suggests the common criticism of classic liberalism by socialists was competition is blind, like justice. Competition is not respectful of people. Participants don't share rewards and penalties in markets according to the merits or demerits of individuals.

Turning Tide

Milton Friedman and Rose Friedman (1979) observed that in the late 1970s, Western governments failed to achieve their proclaimed objectives. This failure produced a widespread reaction against big government. In the United Kingdom, the public response swept Margaret Thatcher into power on a platform of reversing the socialist policies of the Labour party.

The tide of opinion had turned toward the economic freedom and limited government of Adam Smith. Its shift provided well-being to the bulk of the U.K. population. Evidence of the prior socialistic tide cresting was evident in intellectuals' writings, politicians' sentiments, and how people behaved. First, public opinion influenced their behavior. Then, widespread behavior reinforced the belief and played a crucial role in translating it into public policy.

The Friedmans thought the two related ideas of human freedom and economic freedom came to their greatest fruition in the United States. Reforms evolved toward smaller government. They believe society has forgotten the fundamental truth that the greatest threat to human freedom is a concentration of power, whether in the government hands or anyone else. Fortunately, humanity was waking up. Dependence on the freedom of people to control their own lives by their values is the surest way to achieve the total capacity of a great society.

Post-1960s' Gloom

Edmund Phelps (2013), a professor at the University of Pennsylvania and Columbia University, paints a gloomy picture of U.S. economic decline since the 1970s. Deterioration in job satisfaction, employment participation, and relative productivity appeared in his observed data. Examining productivity helps economists understand the reason for this deterioration. There are two types of productivity. The relationship between labor output and hours worked is more common, called *labor productivity*. However, more significant reductions mark underlying slowdowns in the other kind of productivity, which economists describe as output per unit of capital growth or *total productivity*.

Three mechanisms connect the level of employment with the rate of innovation. Directly, a firm raises prices and cuts jobs if it expects reduced competition from threats of new products. Another mechanism connects the level of human capital to prospects of innovation. A third mechanism works through wages and wealth. Increases in labor productivity raise demand for labor. It boosts wages employers are willing to pay and improves employment and prevailing wages in the market.

After World War II, Phelps recounts the consensus was that the United States had reached a golden age. The paternal government provided Social Security, disability benefits, and unemployment insurance. Regulations safeguarded workers, consumers, and their savings. Big corporations offered tenure, and unions fought layoffs and for seniority rights. Then, the golden age passed. Proponents of an increased role of government suggested ways governments should go beyond repairing market failures. For example, political parties solicit group contributions in return for the support of special interests.

This topic offered a historical perspective by describing U.K. national accounting, studying the geopolitical environment after World War II, noting shifting economic trends, and chronicling post-1960s' gloom. Next, the section examined the appropriate role of a government in an economy. It addressed the factors of government intervention, determined their proper functions, and provided a historical perspective. The following section describes a mash-up of political science and economics.

The Political Economy

The political economy is the nexus between sociology, political science, and economics. Social choice theorists study the questions posed in the field by looking at examples, developing general models, and proving theorems. This section discusses social choice, group decision making, and legislation.

Social Choice

The social choice process is how society allocates resources. The primary areas of activity are markets and governments. Each sector carries its strengths and weaknesses. This topic wanders through areas of social choice such as gerrymandering, market mechanisms, and majority rule voting.

Gerrymandering

William Vickrey (1939), a Columbia University professor, suggests the Population Census enables the possibility of cheating in redrawing an electoral district. If society leaves discretion to interested parties, considerable latitude for mischief is present. *Gerrymandering* manipulates an electoral constituency's boundaries to favor one party or class. The remedy limits more extreme manifestations by laying down rules of contiguity and compactness. Vickrey thinks eliminating gerrymandering requires establishing automatic and impersonal methods for redistricting. It's not difficult to develop rules for doing this. These procedures should produce results resembling those from disinterested commissions. If there's no fairness criterion available, it's necessary to resort to the fairness of redrawing the procedures. Policy makers should try to remove the human elements altogether as possible from redistricting processes.

Social Choice

Kenneth Arrow (1951), a professor at Stanford and Harvard, observes that in capitalist democracies, individuals decide their society's choices. They typically use votes to make political decisions. Market mechanisms also make choices, usually economic ones. Alternately in noncapitalist communities, traditional rules sometimes resolve social decisions, such as codes of religion. Other methods, such as dictatorship and convention, have certain definiteness in their formal structure, absent from voting or market mechanisms. For example, there's only one human will involved for choosing in ideal dictatorships.

Utilitarians hold that *measurable satisfaction* is a viable proposition of economic behavior. On the other hand, Arrow and others assume the *interpersonal comparison* of personal utilities has no meaning. Likewise, there's also no relevant meaning for comparing welfare. Instead, Arrow uses models of alternate comparison mechanisms by ordering preference groupings. This method compares bundles of commodities, allowing the individual to consider two or more component alternatives. Each bundle has many desirable components in social states, under certain circumstances or not.

There are distinctions when ordering social states according to our direct consumption called *tastes*. Social scientists call it *order* when an individual lacks *standards of general equity* reflecting social values. Mechanisms of the market consider only the ordering of taste. Everyone's comparison of two alternative social states depends only on commodities received (and labor expended) in the two states. Economists don't simply evaluate actual distributions of welfare in terms of money. Paul Samuelson (1948) thinks such value judgments aren't consistent with any defined ordering of social states.

Arrow makes a case for democracy, arguing that free discussion and expression of opinions are the most suitable techniques for arriving at social ordering. Voting isn't a device where we express *personal interests*. It's where we give our view of the *general will*.

Majority Rule

Friedrich Hayek (1960) defines *classic liberalism* as the broader concern for limiting the coercive power of government, whether democratic or not. Proponents of democracy know only one limit of government: the current majority's opinion. Differences between liberalism and democracy are apparent when identifying their opposites. For democracy, it's authoritarianism; for liberalism, it's totalitarianism. Ironically, neither system excludes the opposite of the other. Democracy can be totalitarian, and authoritarians can act on liberal principles.

Though democracy is a term of praise, it has limitations. Policy makers can extend the boundaries of democracy by widening the eligibility of voters and the range of issues. Still, Hayek suggests it's difficult to regard every extension as an improvement. For example, we have universal suffrage, but the law limits it by age. It excludes criminals, resident foreigners, nonresident citizens, and unique regional or territorial inhabitants. Democratic and liberal traditions agree that majorities should make decisions whenever society requires collective action. However, customs differ in many countries regarding the scope of government action guided by democratic decisions.

Democracy is an essential safeguard of our liberty. The existence of democratic institutions positively affects a general understanding of public affairs. Hayek surmises that the task of the political philosopher is different from expert servants conducting the majority's will. The philosopher must reach beyond and articulate the possibilities and consequences of joint action. This section covered gerrymandering, market mechanisms, and majority rule voting. The next topic analyzes the connection between individuals and group decisions.

Group Decision Making

Studying the influence of collective actions on individuals is helpful. Markets and the government execute these actions. This topic turns to the basics of group thinking, the extent of rational decisions, ownership of the decision, and the need for adopting a *constitution*.

James Buchanan (1962), a George Mason University professor, constructs a theory of collective activity. It involves group actions featuring individual motivation and behavior. For example, we participate in processes where groups decide choices. The problem is we are egoists, selfless, or any combination. Everyone has different aims and purposes for collective action. Moreover, everyone's interests differ for reasons other than ignorance.

This fundamental interdependence of our actions in social choices complicates Buchanan's political choice theory. However, this interdependency is absent in market organizations of economic activity. Nevertheless, his model makes rudimentary predictions concerning the structural characteristics of group decisions. Civil constitutions are at the top of the political process. They position unanimity or complete consensus rules at the ultimate level of decision making where knowledge constrains the decision criterion. All individuals must agree before the decision makers take the appropriate action.

Attainment of consent is a costly process. Recognition of this fact is salient in Buchanan's economic theory of constitutions. He constructs his theory by analyzing individual choices to explain the emergence of a political constitution. However, economic theory can't explain all behavior of humans. For example, some individual buyers pay sellers higher prices than necessary, and some sellers deliberately accept lower prices than buyers are willing to pay.

Adam Smith convinced the public that self-seeking merchant and moneylender activities tend to further everyone's interests in the general economy. Likewise, Buchanan's collectivist theory suggests how similarly concerned members of groups reconcile their interests. Some rationality is present in units of group decision making. They often direct choices toward the achievement of objectives. However, problems arise when evaluating the extent of rationality of group actions.

Economists expect us to be less rational in group choices because of the magnitude of differences in the ownership of the final decision. Responsibility for personal decisions rests squarely on the chooser. However, in the preferences of groups, there is never a precise relationship, even if correctly predicted. Buchanan analyzes problems of individual choice among rules of group decision making. Policy makers evaluate the benefits of group action in terms of cost reductions. Individual participation is costly. Rational people consider this in the accounting of constitutional choices.

Buchanan's analysis suggests it's rational to have constitutions. It is also reasonable for us to choose more than one group decision-making rule under normal circumstances. By concentrating on constitutional problems, Buchanan escapes the need to discuss the comparability of interpersonal utility. He thought only individuals were uncertain about their role in the future processes of the group. On the other hand, decision makers develop the choices of a constitutional rule independent of any specific decision. When drafting constitutions, identifiable self-interests aren't present in their external characteristics. Instead, participation of individual self-interest at this highest level leads them to take positions as representative participants in anticipated successions of group choice.

Buchanan suggests that we establish routines for day-to-day choices. Then, we adopt personal rules dictating our behavior for single decisions. As a result, it requires extra effort only when we break or modify existing laws. Our behaviors confronting political choices shouldn't be different from options describing purely private decisions. The distinction is that it requires more than one decision maker.

This section covered the basics of group thinking, the extent of rational decisions, ownership of the decision, and the need for adopting a constitution. The next topic discusses the decision-making process for the next level down from the constitutional order of decision making in government: legislation.

Legislation

The nature of decisions at the *legislative level* differs from those at the upper constitutional level. This topic delves into the legislative process by examining its range of activity, the social cost of democracy, and the problems with pressure groups.

Individual legislative decisions below constitution making are unrelated in descriptive nature. Rational participants are also aware of the time sequence of political choices. They can gain from the exchange by trading votes on one issue for mutual support for their interest by other participants on other issues. The majority rule allows strong coalitions to secure the benefits of group action without bearing the social costs attributable to them. As a result, the independence criterion for allocating resources between the public and private sectors doesn't exist.

In allocating economic resources between public and private, it's essential to distinguish the ranges of activity the decision makers are contemplating and the extent to which they execute them. As a result, we don't directly choose the size and scope of the public sector. Instead, we first assess the entire organization of the initiative. Then, we choose the rules of decision making. Intuitively, *more* inclusive voting rules produce more stable solutions than *less* inclusive rules.

Buchanan observes that the active promotion of economic interest in large political units occurs in the presence of *special interest* groups. Their success depends on their ability to promote and further the functional interests they represent through political processes. Their emergence to dominant positions is a significant development in the last half-century in the American political scene. He feels these groups severely threaten the premise of the selfless legislative pursuit of public interest. Individuals should be the only meaningful units of decision making. Buchanan's theory centers on this concept because considerations of utility-maximizing motivate individuals. Interest groups exist as something apart from individual members.

This section examined the legislative process by describing its range of activity, the social cost of democracy, and the problems with pressure groups. The section discussed social choice, group decision making, and legislation. The following section searches for helpful lessons for setting public policy.

Political Wisdom

Public policy administration involves subjective judgments, which contrasts with decisions based on mathematics. Nevertheless, a closer look at the philosophy of public policy bears fruit. This section examines the relationship between democracy and freedom, free markets, and socialism.

Democracy and Freedom

Democracy and freedom take on precise meanings when used in combined references. This topic discusses the norms of these terms in political and social activity. It explores political participation, the expansion of economic knowledge, the role of inventions and innovations in technology, and making public policy decisions without all the facts.

Amartya Sen (1999), an Indian-born economist and philosopher who taught and worked in the United States and the United Kingdom, examines the interconnections between *political freedom* and *economic needs*. He argues that forces of economic conditions combine with the urgency of political liberty. On the other hand, antidemocratic opposition argues that granting freedom hampers economic growth. By their nature, poor people usually choose economic needs over freedoms. Interestingly, political emphasis is a Western priority. In contrast, it cuts against the grain of Asian values, which are more disposed toward order and discipline than liberty.

Sen advocates for direct participation in political and social activity. Informed and unregimented forms of values require openness in communication. Moreover, connections between economic needs and political freedoms have constructive aspects. Achievements of democracy depend not only on adopted rules but on the ways citizens embrace opportunities. Political and civil rights are central to generating informed and reflected choice processes. For instance, democracy successfully prevents easily understood disasters, where sympathy takes hold of society.

Sen suggests codes of behavior and their effectiveness vary among developed capitalist economies. Nevertheless, capitalism is successful in enhancing output and raising productivity. The significant challenges capitalism now faces include inequality and the provision of public goods. Sen feels solutions to these problems call for institutions to take society beyond capitalist market economies. Moreover, policy makers have reasons for taking an interest in social justice. Justice is the central concept in identifying the aims and objectives of public policy. However, Sen surmises corruption is a significant obstacle to successful paths of economic progress.

The Experience of the Modern Economy

Edmund Phelps (2013), an American economist, lays out new perspectives on national prosperity. A vibrant society is at the heart of prosperity, engagement, meeting challenges, self-expression, and personal growth. Earning income leads to flourishing but isn't a form of it. He thinks modern economic analysis should begin with an emphasis on original creative ideas. Personal knowledge, uniqueness of information, and each person's imagination frame these ideas. The innovative processes of human experiences should occupy our thoughts.

But in the early stages of human existence, society didn't seek to expand its economic knowledge. In those days, departures from past practices leading to new knowledge and innovations were uncommon. Then, humans desired to experience new opportunities but could not develop new methods and products for society. A turning point occurred during the rise of mercantilism capitalism; merchants invested in transportation. Capitalism became the engine of civilization. Merchants competed with each other in struggles for supply while nations raced to establish colonies. However, they developed what to produce, not the stimulus to create *new* products.

Inventions become *innovations* creating economic knowledge. Phelps observes that most inventors, even headliners, don't train as scientists or are well educated. Instead, designs are born from perceptions of business needs or inspired by what businesses and consumers want. He suggests the dynamism of an economy is a combination of forces and facilities buried deeply under innovation. It's the willingness and capacity to innovate while leaving behind current conditions and obstacles.

It's not practical for economists to measure this dynamism with only economic growth rates. For example, a country with low vigor can still have high growth rates due to high vibrancy. They grow by adopting original products from other economies. Policy makers and commentators don't make distinctions in modern economies. Instead, they view all national economies as virtual machines to produce goods. Phelps characterizes modern economies as ideas. They primarily engage in activities aimed at innovation. Their activities are stages of processes, beginning with new concepts of products and methods.

Hayek (1960) suggests *adaptations* are more predictable than innovations. They don't involve intuitive leaps but are repercussions taking place eventually. They don't go on long if circumstances stop changing. They aren't disruptive but bring closure to disruption. However, most innovations occur while entrepreneurial projects are going on simultaneously. As a result, business is rife with uncertainty, which is a hallmark of a modern economy.

Modern economies foster sustainable output per worker or *productivity growth*. In quantitative terms, modern economic nations go from stationary states to explosive and boundless growth. This upheaval results in favorable movements in real wages, which benefit society. Phelps thinks the economic innovation of countries could be more widespread if potential providers of inventive ideas were free to launch new firms in existing industries. Such free entry permits entrepreneurs to develop and germinate new products for testing. He observes that expanding the firm's role was a crucial development in modern economies. The firms can venture far into the unknown, employ wide assortments of talent, and absorb long loss spells.

Arrow Impossibility Theorem

Eric Maskin was an American economist and mathematician and a professor at Harvard University. Maskin and Sen (2014) considered Arrow's *impossibility theorem* from the standpoint of a public election. Arrow's impossibility theorem involves making decisions without possessing all the required facts. In filling political offices, voting rules are the methods of selecting winners from sets of candidates. The most widely used way is the rule of *plurality* in the United States. Another well-known rule is a rule of a *simple majority*. These two types of voting rules lead to different outcomes. Maskin and Sen examined them using several criteria. These criteria included the properties of Pareto optimality and anonymity. In addition, they use the properties of neutrality, independence of irrelevant alternatives, and decisiveness.

This section discussed the norms of democracy and freedom in political and social activities. It explored political participation, the expansion of economic knowledge, the role of inventions and innovations in technology, and making public policy decisions without all the facts. The next topic analyzes the nature of free markets.

Free Markets

This topic discusses the dynamics of free-market competition, the general level of security, the scope of government, and the intimate connections between economics and politics.

Competition and Nations

Hayek observes no movement of socialism aiming at complete equality ever gained substantial support in history. Not equality in the absolute sense, but more equality. Most people find it disappointing that society doesn't possess satisfactory moral standards to embrace this competitive system dilemma more adequately. We generate standards from regimes of competition that soon disappear after the absence of competition.

Hayek feels the idea of economic security is a vague and ambiguous term. When society regards security in too absolute a sense, the general striving for it becomes its gravest threat. As a result, we all experience limited security. However, free communities can't achieve absolute security for all. Therefore, we shouldn't hand out security as a privilege, except in a few instances, such as judges, where complete independence is essential.

Milton Friedman (1962) suggests nations are collections of individuals, not something over and above them. We are proud of our shared heritage and loyal to common traditions. Still, we should regard government as an instrument with limited scope. Its primary function should be to protect our freedom from foreign enemies and fellow citizens. Beyond this, it should enable us to accomplish more difficult or expensive things together.

Friedman reflects on the role of competitive capitalism. Its purpose is to organize the bulk of economic activity through private enterprises operating in free markets. Comprised of a system of economic freedom, it is a necessary enabler of political liberty. Contrary to many, he is skeptical of the intimate connections between economics and politics. Only specific groupings of political and economic arrangements are possible. For example, societies of socialism can't be democratic to guarantee our freedom.

This topic discussed the dynamics of competition, the general level of security, the scope of government, and the intimate connections between economics and politics. The following section contrasts free markets with socialism.

Socialism

Socialism operates with a more robust political character than capitalism. This prominence exists because the government has a more significant role in allocating resources. This section discusses socialism by examining its nature, providing operational details from a former Soviet planner, and contemplating its popularity.

Economic Control

Hayek observes most central planners run directed economies like a dictatorship. A single expert staff controls complex systems of interrelated activity—the ultimate responsibility and power rest in the hands of a commander-in-chief unfettered by democratic principles. Maintaining economic pursuits means government controls everything unless we declare a specific purpose. Then, when we express this particular purpose, we must get it approved. This approval means government controls everything.

Leonid Kantorovich (1989), a Soviet mathematician and economist, recalls specific peculiarities in the Soviet economy from his role as a central planner, starting with the October Revolution in 1917. At the time, it was the first moment in history that all primary means of production passed into the possession of the people. Detailed planning ranged from specific tasks to individual enterprises for particular periods. Planning on this scale took on unfamiliar problems. They couldn't rely on existing experience and economic theory. He taught at the Novosibirsk State University in Russia.

Stigler sees the massive global expansion of government in the 20th century as the most conspicuous single change in the social organizations of humans. Nations differed widely in the degree they transferred the conduct of economic life to the government. He believed this expansion significantly reduced aggregate output, possibly with a deterioration of moral quality in society. Of course, it is possible to control social development with power, but its use is distasteful to his principles.

An explanation for the popularity of socialism is that it draws the political process toward collectivism. However, it strongly misrepresents the actual preferences of the public. Individuals behave rationally, given the constraints of our political institutions. Socialism views this adherence as nonrational because these institutions become inefficient. Policies of capitalism either benefit the few and slightly injure the majority or slightly benefit the majority and injure the few. Well-financed special groups support most varieties of socialist policies. On the other hand, a large, poorly informed majority is weakly opposed or unaware of these proposals.

This topic discussed socialism by examining its nature, providing operational details from a former Soviet planner, and contemplating its popularity. The section examined the relationship between democracy and freedom, free markets, and socialism, while this chapter discussed the rule of law, surveyed the public sector, studied political economy, and reviewed political wisdom. There is nothing new in our search for the perfect choice of bread loaves, but at least we can see what happens when markets don't perform their function. The next chapter analyzes the value of humans in an economy.

CHAPTER 6

Human Capital

Our journey brings us to an area of centuries-long study by economists stretching back to Adam Smith and Thomas Malthus. Human capital is the economic worth of your experience and skills. This capital includes education, training, intelligence, health, and other things employers and society value, such as loyalty and punctuality.

The concept of human capital recognizes that not all characteristics of individuals are equal. But employers and society can improve the value of that capital by investing in their employees. Moreover, firms perceive human capital as vital because it increases productivity and, thus, profitability. This chapter examines demographic trends, human development, and labor economics.

Demographic Trends

Demographics is the study of a population centered on human factors such as age, race, and sex. In addition, demographic data refers to statistical socioeconomic information. Institutions use demographics to study population characteristics for social purposes, including policy development and market research. Our inquiry in this section discusses population characteristics, minority economics, and a new branch called identity economics.

Population Characteristics

This topic examines the relationship of population growth to capital, exogenous and endogenous factors, population forecasting, and human capital problems.

Trygve Haavelmo (1954), a University of Oslo in Norway professor, suggests that relationships connecting population growth and capital accumulation take various forms. The economic *subsistence level* determines the region's primary consideration of population growth. The available labor force, capital, and expertise determine the *production volume.* According to Gary Becker (1962) from the University of Chicago, human capital concepts are relevant to individuals' and firms' micro-investment in education, training, and other skills and knowledge. They also apply to understanding inequality, economic growth, unemployment, and foreign trade changes.

Becker stresses that researchers have paid little attention to social inequality *within families over generations.* He feels the relationship between incomes or the wealth of parents, children, and later descendants determine inequality. Moreover, Becker felt these inequalities are closely related. For example, a regression of incomes trending away from the mean between parent and child implies large and growing income inequality over time. Conversely, regression toward the average indicates minor and more stable degrees of inequality. Unfortunately, past empirical mobility studies lacked the frameworks or models to interpret their findings. Schumpeter (1942), a Harvard University professor, was the only early prominent economist who considered social mobility between generations.

Human Capital, Fertility, and Economic Growth

Thomas Malthus (1789), an English cleric, scholar, and influential economist, developed formal models of a dynamic growth process where each economy converges toward fixed incomes per capita. Becker's growth model considers this evidence and departs from Malthusian and neoclassical approaches by placing investments in human capital at the center. Becker's analysis implies that rates of return on education and other human capital are higher in developed countries than in undeveloped ones. However, the study of the population is a complex subject.

Some critics believe the world population is growing too rapidly. James Mirrlees (2006) thought commentators arrive at this conclusion too quickly. The growth of the population is a significant problem. But these detractors are hard-pressed to give precise statements explaining their concerns. Consequently, they cannot provide detailed arguments justifying government's intervention.

Debunkers also argue that the current growth rates of the population continue forever. Therefore, the recent growth in birth rates will lead to indescribable disasters. Mirrlees refutes this because these disasters obscure the exact consequences. He counterclaims that birth rates adjust at the right time. Additionally, critics suggest that population growth is problematic when individuals are ignorant of contraception. Therefore, society ought to inform them. Mirrlees accepts this argument, but it is insufficient to establish a rationale for the government to restrict birth rates.

Mirrlees thinks of population policy primarily in terms of the natural course of action affecting the size of the population. His public policy proposals use taxes and subsidies to influence family size. He minimizes the circumstances where the government should tax families to increase their size. On the other hand, public policy arguments for population control rest on the presumption that parents are bad at predicting the future. Therefore, parents do not know what kind of life they create for their children to suffer. If policy makers settle on an optimal policy for population growth, it should include optimal wealth distribution policies. Uncertainty is a feature naturally associated with the decisions on population and families.

The Lucas Model

Robert Solow (1970), an American economist, perceived a yawning intellectual gap when economists suggested circumstances outside the economy determine the growth rates of the population. He feels the growth rates of an economy in the long term are a function of internal factors. Therefore, positioning the theory of economic growth as only influenced by outside factors is unsatisfactory.

There are endogenous elements to the progress of technology. For example, a technology growth is often economically motivated. Entrepreneurs exploit profitable opportunities. But unless reasonable and productive theories exist of endogenous advancement of technology, it is not worth spending time on it.

Solow develops a more elaborate version of Robert Lucas' original attempt to advance beyond standard neoclassical models. Lucas is also an American economist. Lucas modeled *human capital accumulation* as an economically motivated activity. Solow makes an adjustment to Lucas' model to include a voluntary choice of *leisure*. In addition, he tweaks Lucas' model to consider independently allocated leisure time units for each population member.

In American economist Paul Romer's (1994) model, increasing varieties of *intermediate or supply goods* generate economic growth. Solow adapts this same concept to illustrate economic development by integrating human capital accumulation with the concept of voluntary choice of leisure. The model enhancements create an expanding variety of *consumer goods*. Moreover, it achieves this expanding goods assortment through an organized collection of knowledge.

Population and Economic Growth

Simon Kuznets (1973), a Belarus-born American economist and statistician, suggests modern economic growth, as revealed by the experience of developed countries since the late 18th or early 19th century, follows a distinguishable pattern. The data reveals the continuing capacity to supply growing populations with increased volumes of per capita commodities and services. These modern trends of abundance in people and production per capita are not unique growth features. Countries' populations grew and enjoyed rising production per capita even in premodern times. However, the distinctive modern part of growth is *accelerated* growth rates.

In the modern era, economic growth rates are at least five times faster than population growth. In addition, effective use of technology now invites more physical capital and a new range of human skills. The challenges lie in the limited capacity of developing countries' political, legal, cultural, and economic institutions. These institutions need to channel activity in ways to exploit the advantages of their economic backwardness.

Kuznets feels the primary policy question is whether world productive capacity can effectively manage economic activity on its own. This capacity trend features sharp rises in the growth of world populations and concentrations in less-developed countries. In addition, policy makers must consider differences between trends and projections in the short-term and secular fluctuations of production and supply.

He believes available and tested knowledge of technology and known natural resources are adequate for sustaining projected population numbers at moderately rising living standards. However, parts of the world will realize the economic potential of technology, particularly in the less-developed, low-calorie regions, only if political, social, and economic institutions evolve.

Population Forecasting

Clive Granger (1980) focuses on how forecasters generate statistical data in population forecasts. He feels they do not seem to consider how public policy influences population size. This policy component is essential for reliable forecasts for world population and geographical regions. These population forecasts are critical for governments to plan food and energy requirements and organize long-term services. In addition, the estimates are relevant to private firms' long-term investments in infrastructure. Forecasts are long term because significant economic changes do not occur over shorter intervals. However, specific speculations of outcomes suggest that factors affect the size of the population and need careful consideration when forecasting.

Human Capital Problems in Society

Amartya Sen (1999) laments the extensive persistence of hunger in this era of unprecedented prosperity. In the contemporary age, it is a terrible and nasty phenomenon. Famine often visits countries with great severity. Massive endemic hunger causes misery in regions of the world. It debilitates hundreds of millions and kills sizable portions of the population with statistical regularity. Sen feels it is a tragedy that society has come to accept and tolerate this condition as an integral part of life.

Robert Fogel (2000), an American economic historian and scientist, was concerned with the economic prospects of the United States as the new millennium dawned. The critical issues are not how society manages business cycles or whether the economy grows satisfactorily. Instead, the needed reforms should address the urgent *spiritual* needs of this era, both secular and sacred. Spiritual inequality is as great a problem as physical inequality, even more significant. Others worry about issues of egalitarianism by considering the distribution of material goods. However, the primary form of capital is labor skills. Fogel calls this knowledge capital. Realizing the potential in us is not legislated by the government nor provided to the weak by the strong.

Fogel divides U.S. history into four epochs. Each Awakening era lasts about 100 years, including later declining phases. These overlapping periods intersect where champions of one Awakening movement clash with those of the next. The First Great Awakening began and ripened into the American Revolution against the British Crown in the 1730s. The Second Great Awakening began around 1800 and produced the crusade against slavery, culminating in the Civil War. Then, the Third Awakening arose at the end of the 19th century and led to the rise of the welfare state and policies promoting diversity. Finally, the Fourth Awakening began around 1960 and recently entered its political phase. It focuses on spiritual reform. Fogel examines the principal aspects of these cycles and reforms with a more extended treatment of the current religious-political process.

This current Awakening is not merely a social or religious phenomenon. Policy makers usually do not initiate the Awakening movements. Instead, they well up from below. Initially, religious leaders and community activists gave it a voice on the fringes of the establishment. Fogel recounts unsettling cultural advances surfaced in energy production, information retrieval, and communication channels. Disenchantment with changes in technology began emerging in the 1960s.

We want assurances that our children will lead better lives than we led. But unfortunately, the rapid progress in the economy and society causes us to lose our bearings. The persistence of gloom, despite a credible record of achievements, suggests that societal malaise is more moral and psychological than economic.

This topic examined the relationship of population growth to capital, exogenous and endogenous factors, population forecasting, and human capital problems. The following section discusses minority economics.

Minority Economics

Minority economics is the study of minority groups from a social science perspective. This topic features the conditions of African Americans in the United States. It presents an analysis of their cultural conditions in the 1940s by a prominent Swede, Gunnar Myrdal.

American Ideals and the American Conscience

Myrdal (1944), an economist and sociologist, suggests societal conditions intertwine the African American problem in the United States with other social, economic, political, and cultural issues. His study produced a comprehensive perspective on U.S. racial characteristics in the 1940s. He concluded there were no changes in fundamentals in more than a half-century at the time. He observes that African Americans were relative newcomers to the ranks of industrial workers in the North. Thus, they had the least unionization and lowest seniority. Hence, technologically generated unemployment and technological changes affected African Americans the most.

According to Myrdal, there was an African American problem in the United States, and most Americans knew it. It appears in forms and intensities of different regions and among diverse groups of American people. Therefore, Americans need to react politically as citizens and privately as neighbors. He feels the problems of African Americans are problems in the American heart or ethos. It is in that heart that interracial tensions focus. It is there where decisive struggles fester.

Myrdal, a professor at Stockholms Hogskol in Sweden, concentrated on the social conditions in the 1940s but didn't neglect the future. His studies were limited in scope and did not intend to present the complete history of African American problems. Instead, he sought to review generalized aspects of the past. He wanted to understand them and evaluate the significant issues of racial tension.

There is a strong community unity in the United States. Myrdal refers to the declaration of the unity of national values as the American creed. Society associates this creed with America's peculiar brand of nationalism. It furnishes ordinary citizens with a feeling of their American mission in history. Myrdal finds it remarkable that a vast democracy with disparities reached this unanimity of ideals and elevated them into popular perception. The American creed is humanistic liberalism developed in the era of Enlightenment. Myrdal suggests another ideological influencing the American creed is English law. Finally, he observes that the common belief expresses the moralistic attitude in America.

Encountering the African American Problem

To African Americans, the racial problem is critical. Aside from the opportunities for keeping African American problems out of their minds, whites have selfish reasons for submerging these problems below levels of consciousness despite the American creed. When discussing African American problems, everyone is anxious to distance their sources of racial prejudice outside their sphere. However, Myrdal also suggests there are tendencies to incorporate their problems into broader American minority challenges.

On the other hand, unfortunately, a few society members assume our culture cannot assimilate African Americans. In addition to racial challenges, African Americans also have to deal with the complexity of human life. The deeper reasons for the unity of African American struggles are apparent when Myrdal formulates a hypothesis concerning its dynamic causation. This topic focused on the conditions of African Americans in the United States, featuring an analysis of these conditions in the 1940s. The following section explores a relatively new branch, identity economics.

Identity Economics

Individuals contend with outside influences when making economic decisions. To sort through choices, we gravitate toward groups with similar interest. These groups hold common ideas of how to allocate resources. This topic will examine these identified groups' shared ideas and determines the impact on the individual. The discussion includes capitalism and discrimination, women and social change, marriage reform proposals, and identity politics.

Capitalism and Discrimination

Milton Friedman (1962) seems to feel racial or social groups operate under special handicaps associated with the development of capitalism.

He generalizes that pockets of majority discrimination in any society have a monopolistic characteristic. As a result, groups of minorities frequently furnish the most vocal advocates for fundamental changes in capitalist society. Society sometimes tolerates people discriminating against others due to race, religion, or color because they perceive it incurs no cost. However, discriminators will have to pay higher prices for what they buy or receive lower returns for their work because they limit their choices. In other words, those who regard the color of their skin or religion as irrelevant buy things more cheaply.

Women's Agency and Social Change

Sen (1999), a Harvard University professor, recounts society focused on civil rights related to women's *well-being* in the past. However, the emphasis of the agenda of their movement seems to have shifted from their well-being to their *freedom*. The objectives gradually evolved and broadened from this focus on welfare to the role of active women. No longer viewed as passive recipients of welfare-enhancing help, society increasingly perceives women as active agents of change. At first glance, various aspects of the transformation appear diverse and disparate.

Friedman (1962) suggests the perception of our contributions and appropriate entitlements play a crucial role in dividing the joint benefits of family between men and women. As a result, circumstances influencing these perceptions of subsidies and relevant entitlements in public policy have a vital bearing on these divisions.

Marriage Reform

Richard Thaler is a professor at the University of Chicago. Thaler and Sunstein (2008) turn to the institution of *marriage* and explore questions about marriage and same-sex relationships. They present a highly libertarian proposal to protect freedom in marriage, including religious freedom. They hope it will prove acceptable to all sides. Under their proposal, the word *marriage* would no longer appear in any public laws. In addition, the government no longer offers or recognizes marriage licenses at any level. Instead, the government conducts its own business while religious institutions work theirs. The only legal status government confers on couples is *civil unions*. Thaler and Sunstein's primary mantra is that government-sanctioned marriages make it impossible to protect the freedom of religious institutions to proceed as they see fit.

Identity Economics

George Akerlof is a professor at Georgetown University and married to Janet Yellen, Treasury Secretary and former Fed Chair. Akerlof and Kranton (2010) introduce identity and related norms to economics. The branch, at this point, no longer confines itself to questions about consumption. Instead, they consider the wide variety of noneconomic motives. We have beliefs about how we and others are supposed to behave. These norms play essential roles in how economies work. This *taste perception* is vital because norms are potent sources of motivation that affect spontaneous and life-changing decisions.

Identity economics enhances theories of comparative advantage, taste-based choices, and statistical discrimination. For example, Akerlof and Kranton observe employers usually hire men for men's jobs and women for women's jobs. In their models, men are generally unwilling to collaborate with women. Instead, job-specific norms trigger their disinclination. Akerlof and Kranton use identity economics to study work, school, and home. They found identity affects our behavior directly. In addition, our actions often jeopardize the well-being of others, termed *externalities*.

Society often adopts social categories, norms, and ideals of situations as a given. But unfortunately, people and institutions manipulate types, standards, and dreams to their advantage. For example, advertising, the most apparent form of manipulation, induces people to buy more of an advertised product. Akerlof and Kranton believe their pioneering identity economics work is only the beginning to understand these distortions. Their framework themes are self-image, self-realization, situational awareness, identification of in-group versus out-group, self versus other, social structures, power, and differences.

This topic examined an individual's affinity groups with shared ideas, including a discussion on capitalism and discrimination, women and social change, marriage reform proposals, and identity norms. This section took us through a discussion of population characteristics, minority economics, and the new area of identity economics. The following section explores human development.

Human Development

Improving the population's quality makes it more productive and enhances the well-being of its members. This section explores how society can add value by setting policies to fully develop human capital. It includes discussions on health care basics, education, and labor economics.

Health Care Economics

Health care economics studies the economic aspects of providing and managing health care. It traces efficiency, effectiveness, value, and behavior in the production and consumption of health care. The topic includes discussions on health care, government programs, kidney exchanges, and pharmaceuticals.

Economists often credit a seminal article by Kenneth Arrow in 1963 with giving rise to health care economics as a discipline. His theory draws conceptual distinctions between health and other public goods. The differences include extensive intervention of the government, troublesome uncertainty in several dimensions, asymmetric information, barriers to entry, externality, and the presence of a third-party agent.

Arrow explores specific characteristics of health care with a normative approach. He contends that the unique problems of health care economics are adaptations to uncertainty. He found this uncertainty in the incidences of disease treatment efficacy. He insists the subject is the provision of health care, not health science. There are causal factors of health, and health care delivery is only one. Other factors, such as nutrition, shelter, clothing, and sanitation, are more significant at low-income levels.

He explains the scope of health services centers around physicians, private and group practice, hospitals, and public health. He examines the operations of the health care industry and the efficacy of satisfying the needs of society. The uncertainty of health care product quality is more intense than other essential commodities or services. The unusual pricing practices and attitudes of the health profession are well known. Arrow implies that industry objectives to increase returns are disruptive in allocating health resources, particularly in low population density or low-income areas. Also, the most striking departure from competitive behavior is entry restrictions to the field. Friedman (1962) and Kuznets

(1973) argue that these restrictions contribute to the higher incomes of physicians.

Investment in Health

Theodore Schultz (1979) was an American agricultural economist. He suggests that human capital theory should consider your state of personal health as a *supply* of resources. At the same time, the *flows* are augmented health services. We inherit part of the quality of the initial stockpile at birth and absorb additional content. However, the bundle depreciates gradually at increasing rates in later life. Overall, investment in health entails the personal costs of acquisition and maintenance. These investments include childcare, nutrition, clothing, housing, health services, and leisure. On the other hand, the capital flows into health service industries render the benefits of healthy time, work inputs, consumption, and leisure activities.

Improvements in health revealed by longer life spans in low-income countries are the most critical advance in the population's quality in recent years. Moreover, the favorable economic implications of these life-span increases are pervasive. Foremost are the satisfactions people derive from extended life.

Health in the Modern World

Angus Deaton (2013), a British economist and academic, examines the health transitions of society in the modern world. He points out the implications for health advancements in this highly interconnected environment. For example, with faster and cheaper transportation and communication, one country's fitness innovations immediately impact the rest of the world. According to Deaton, in this age of globalization, international inequalities of longevity are shrinking. However, longevity is not the only important aspect of health.

Health is about living, dying, and how healthy people exist when they are alive. One measure of living health is human height. It is a sensitive indicator of undernutrition and the burdens of diseases, especially among children. By 1950, Deaton observed the world's developed countries had completed the most progress in escaping childhood infectious diseases.

In addition, he found that middle-aged and elderly everywhere saw significant reductions in mortality rates after 1950.

Deaton compares developed and developing countries and scrutinizes how the two groups affect one another. Because gathering information on the safety and efficacy of drugs constitutes an international public good, international bodies provide a role in sharing pharmaceutical approval decisions in developed countries.

Proponents for the strict regulation of drugs point to the disasters of premature approvals of the Federal Drug Administration. However, opponents like Friedman (1962) argue that the health burdens of the delays in approving new drugs far exceed the health costs of these well-publicized disasters. Alternatively, he suggests eliminating the regulation of pharmaceuticals. His proposal would feature prescriptions with mandatory labeling systems and letting consumers decide their usage.

Michael Kremer (2002) is an American economist. His view is policy makers should reconceptualize the justification of pharmaceutical regulation. However, if the declared purposes of pharmaceutical rules are the primary reasons for regulation, Friedman's proposal is appealing. Kremer argues that the primary advantages of drug regulation are the incentives created for firms to conduct randomized trials. In addition, researchers have proposed posting information on all public purchases of pharmaceuticals on the Internet. However, posting prices may also facilitate supplier collaboration to maintain high prices.

Consumers, Insurers, and Medicare

Vernon Smith (2008) holds that the primary challenge of public health programs is the reliance on third-party government and employers. The fundamental problem is that A (the doctor) tells B (the patient) what services to buy from A. Then, C (the insurance company) pays A for the services. This process is a nightmare of incentives and explains why health care prices rise faster than other consumer products.

Thaler and Sunstein (2008) thinks the market initiatives for health insurance plans and other private markets need liberal paternalism. Design elements of their choice architecture include understanding the consumers' limitations, assisting them to help themselves, and convincing them that the market serves their interests. For example, they analyzed the Medicare Part D program for drug prescriptions. This program features a variety of drug plan offerings devised by private health care companies. Part D allows consumers decide whether to enroll and which plan to choose. The federal government imposes structure on the plans. For example, they set minimum requirements for coverage and approve all private plans. However, evaluating them with their choice architecture, Thaler and Sunstein feel the existing program suffers from a cumbersome design that impedes good decision making.

Daniel McFadden (2006) is a professor at the University of Southern California and the University of California, Berkley. In a population survey, he discovered an interesting challenge when policy makers introduced the Medicare Part D program. Most Medicare participants had at least adequate knowledge. They intended to enroll despite the complexity of understanding competing program plans. However, low-income, less-educated elderly with poor health were significantly less informed and failed to take advantage of the program. McFadden thinks the Center for Medicare and Medicaid Services (CMS) should have rolled out an aggressive marketing program to identify vulnerable consumers. In addition, the most effective policy should be the default choice of *opt-in* rather than the default choice to *opt-out*. Another method for encouraging participation is using windows of time for enrollment with attractive incentives.

Life-Saving Exchanges

Thaler and Sunstein (2008) propose improvements in kidney distribution for transplants. The price of a kidney is free. However, we can't buy or sell kidneys for transplant, and it's illegal. We can spend money on the costs of hospitals, doctors, and drugs, but the kidney must be a gift by law. The primary source of organs is patients declared brain dead. The major obstacle for boosting donations is the need to receive the consent of surviving family members. In the United States, most states currently use the rule of *explicit consent.*

Integrating Thaler and Sunstein choice architecture would help ensure more organs are available. In their proposal, the government would own the *rights* to a dead body's brains and other parts. Therefore, the government can remove the needed organs without asking permission from anyone. *Presumed consent* is another Thaler and Sunstein proposal. Policy makers would amend laws to assume all citizens' consent. Their proposal allows citizens to register their unwillingness to donate. It preserves the freedom of choice but differs from explicit consent because it shifts the default rules. Alternatively, policy makers can also implement a proposal of mandated choice of consent through a simple addition to programs involving driver's license registrations. Requirements would accompany the renewal of driver's licenses to check a box stating a preference for organ donation. Early results are encouraging in states implementing these changes.

Alvin Roth (2015) studied how matching market design can solve incentives, thickness, congestion, and timing problems. He notes that specific unique markets exist in forms not conforming to conventional notions of markets. He examined the creation of organ exchanges for kidneys. Roth observes that since 1988, the health system has transplanted more than 360,000 kidneys. Unfortunately, the demand for organs exceeds donors. 100,000 people were waiting for a kidney transplant in the United States in 2015. Roth helped design algorithms for the kidney exchange among pairs of donors and patients. A subsequent redesign featured two donors for every patient to increase the chances of a match.

Pharmaceuticals in the Developing World

Developing countries obtain substantial benefits from pharmaceuticals originally developed for developed countries. Michael Kremer (2002) points out that drugs deliver tremendous health benefits to developing countries, but medications are underused or misused. In addition, pharmaceutical research and development on the health challenges specific to developing countries is inadequate. Unfortunately, researchers conduct little research on diseases affecting developing countries, such as malaria and tuberculosis. Kremer explores the policy options for broadening pharmaceutical access and encouraging research and development on products needed in developing countries.

The characteristics of the pharmaceutical industry, differentiated from other sectors, are particularly relevant for developing countries. The industry is unusual in that patent grants provide critical protections for innovators rather than to first-mover or other sources of monopoly power. The regulation of pharmaceuticals and prescription requirements in developed countries facilitates price discrimination among countries by making resale across national borders easier to block.

Historically, the most severe distortions in drug markets in developing countries involve dynamic issues. These countries provide little or no protection for intellectual property rights for pharmaceuticals. The lower incomes of developing countries don't allow firms to recover costs. Therefore, there is little incentive for firms to enter these markets. Kremer considers alternative approaches where firms donate the products to the poorest countries rather than charging the manufacturing cost. This altruistic practice may enhance their firm reputations in the higher-income markets. Also, since individual countries are potentially responsible for market failures within their borders, focusing foreign assistance on delivering global public goods such as pharmaceuticals makes sense.

Death in the Tropics

From Princeton University, Angus Deaton (2013) also explores advances against infectious diseases in developing countries. Improvements in the theory of germs took centuries to evolve in developed countries. However, the developing countries that followed realized the gains more quickly. The introduction of penicillin and other health advances partly created these improvements when they became available during World War II. Unfortunately, this race for immortality cannot continue forever.

Deaton suggests advances in health and public health are not the only relevant issue in developing countries. Better education and higher incomes help, too. In addition, these countries need new cures and medicines if people die of exotic and incurable tropical diseases. Unfortunately, developing countries are often not democratic and not bound to act in the population's best interests. Health care provision and regulation are complex, contentious, and political government functions. Deaton also reminds us funding is a problem. Without educated populations and government capacity, it is difficult or impossible for countries to provide proper health care systems. These capacity needs include effective structures of administration, cadres of educated bureaucrats, statistical methods, and well-defined and enforced legal frameworks.

This section included discussions on health care, government programs, kidney exchanges, and pharmaceuticals in developing countries. The next topic examines education.

Education Economics

The economics of education is a rapidly growing and evolving field applying various economic theories, models, and quantitative methodologies. Researchers use these tools to understand, analyze, and improve the performance of education systems. This topic explores the role of government in school systems, other types of training, and problems in the school systems.

Friedrich Hayek (1960) maintains that competition is a powerful instrument for disseminating knowledge. It demonstrates the usefulness of wisdom to those possessing it. This usefulness leaves no doubt that society must expand knowledge through deliberate efforts. The case for compulsory education up to specific minimum standards rests on the argument that it exposes fewer social risks. Moreover, compulsory education yields more benefits to other society members if the students share detailed basic knowledge and beliefs with the community.

General education is not solely a matter of communicating knowledge. Other obstacles stand in the way. Hayek laments it is troubling that society places the power over the minds of individuals in the hands of a highly centralized and government-dominated education system. He thinks the difficulties of this problem are increasing. Milton Friedman (1962) observes that in today's society, the government or nonprofit institutions primarily pay for and administer general schooling. This situation developed gradually, and took much for granted. Yet, policy makers direct little explicit attention to the reasons for this special treatment.

Policy makers rationalize government intervention in education as providing positive *neighborhood effects*. Neighborhood effects refer to the processes by which various neighborhood conditions influence the well-being of residents collectively or individually. In addition, society holds a paternalistic concern for its children and other irresponsible individuals. Friedman suggests that widening the choice of schooling to parents would improve the situation.

Government institutions have their most significant influence at the primary and secondary school levels. However, they also play a minor role at the higher levels in the United States. Most state and community higher education institutions charge lower tuition fees than private schools can afford to charge. Friedman wants to make capital available for the higher levels on similar terms to human and physical capital investments. His proposal would make limited sums per year available for a set number of years, provided the individuals spend the funds securing training at recognized institutions.

Human Capital Investment

Gary Becker (1962) maintains schooling, computer training courses, health care spending, and lectures on punctuality and honesty virtues are human capital enhancers. They improve health, raise earnings, or add to the literature appreciation of a person. Education and training are the most critical investments in this capital. He demonstrates that the high school and college education in the United States raises an individual's lifetime income. Moreover, this effect occurs even after netting out the cost of school, adjusting for better family backgrounds and the more educated people's more excellent abilities.

Among the observed phenomena are earnings typically increase as we age at decreasing rates. In addition, abler individuals receive more education and training than others. Becker places particular emphasis on broader economic implications. Similar evidence is available from over 100 countries with diverse cultures and economic systems. His analysis of human capital assumes schooling raises earnings and productivity primarily by providing knowledge, skills, and ways of analyzing problems. However, one problem with emphasizing education *credentialism* is that employers do not require information on employee success in schoolwork. Learning and training also occur outside of schools, especially on the job. As a result, college graduates are often unprepared for the labor markets when they leave school.

Training

General training in firms is helpful for society and those firms providing it. On the other hand, economists define *specific training* as training that affects the trainee and contributes to a firm's productivity but is not beneficial to other firms. We also absorb knowledge more effectively if it is presented simultaneously with practical problems. Different circumstances require prolonged specialization.

Becker suggests the most important single determinant in the amount invested in human capital is its profitability or return rate. He evaluates the effects of a college education on earnings and productivity by comparing private and social gains from a college education with those from other capital investments. These comparisons are essential for determining whether there is underinvestment in college education. Socioeconomic gains from education, which society gains as opposed to gains of individuals, differ from private gains because of the differences between social and personal costs and returns. The complete treatment of social return rates on college education involves considering cultural advances and democratic government.

Theodore Schultz (1979) emphasizes that education accounts for improvements in population quality. But in estimating the cost of schooling, economists should include the value of work young children did for their parents. Since schooling is primarily an investment, it is a severe mistake to treat all outlays for schooling as current consumption. This mistake arises from the assumption that schooling is solely a consumer good.

Problems in Schools

Friedman (1962) suggests that education is a significant component of the American Dream. In Puritan New England, authorities quickly established schools, first as church extensions and later as independent institutions administered by secular authorities. Immigrants streaming across the Atlantic thirsted for education in the second half of the 19th century. At first, schools were private, and attendance was strictly voluntary. Increasingly, the government came to play more significant roles, first by contributing to financial support and later by establishing and administering government schools.

Local governments enacted the first compulsory attendance law around 1852, but attendance did not become mandatory nationally until 1918.

As a result, government control was local until well into the 20th century. The standard model was the neighborhood school controlled by a local school board. Then, reform movements got underway, and control shifted away from local jurisdiction to less responsive counties and states, particularly in large cities. As a result, Friedman feels public education now suffers from the sickness of an overgoverned society.

Private market arrangements are more significant at college and university levels than at elementary and secondary levels. Challenges of American higher education, like those in elementary and secondary education, are quality and equality. Choices ease quality problems through competition but exacerbate equality problems. It is eminently desirable for every young man and woman, regardless of parental income, social position, residence, or race to have opportunities to receive higher education.

Kremer (2003), a professor at the University of Chicago, evaluated educational programs in developing countries. They include programs to increase participation in school, provide educational inputs, and reform education. In addition, he extracts education policy lessons for practice. For example, the simplest way to improve school participation is to reduce costs or pay parents for attendance. He studied successful Mexican programs providing cash grants to families conditional on sending their children to school. Education officials expanded these programs and tried them in other parts of Latin America.

Kremer also focuses on policy initiatives in school reform, ranging from decentralizing budget authority to strengthening links between teacher pay and performance. One successful program provides small grants to parent-run school committees to induce them to purchase textbooks.

Thaler and Sunstein (2008) felt most Americans believe children have a right to a good education. However, consensus breaks down when people explore how to achieve this right. Excellent choice architecture does not have to come from wonkish professors with powerful computer algorithms. School choice remains an intensely polarizing issue in American politics. Friedman thought introducing competition was the best way to improve children's schools. If schools compete, kids win. And if schools compete, those with negligible advantages have the most to gain.

Critics of school choice argue that such programs attack the public school systems that help make America a stronger nation.

Alvin Roth (2015), a professor at Stanford University and Harvard University, observes that policy makers sometimes invent solutions in market design, sometimes discover, and often a little of both. Analysts sometimes find solutions to new failures in market design that policy makers pioneered in another market. Public schools differ from private ones because parents do not compete for public schools by offering to pay more. Making this process work well is vitally important. A democracy making free and compulsory education has an enormous collective responsibility to provide its youngest citizens with a top-quality education.

Roth tackles a New York high school placement problem. Kids were getting multiple offers that required administrative time to make and report choices. As a result, numerous requests were gumming up the works and making it congested. So he used an algorithm to ensure children receive just the offer from their top choice. Meanwhile, that simple change frees up recommendations for other kids. In the end, he suggests a computerized clearinghouse.

This topic examined the role of government in school systems, other types of training, and problems in the school systems. The section explored how society can develop human capital. It included discussions on health care, education, and labor economics. The following section explores the economics of labor.

Labor Economics

Labor economics studies the economic behavior of employers and employees in response to changing prices, profits, wages, and working conditions. It seeks to understand the relationship between workers and employers. This section discusses unemployment, collective bargaining, and labor theory.

Unemployment

The labor force is the population segment that provides the human component in producing goods and services. Members of this force either hold down a job or are looking for one. This topic discusses government metrics, types of unemployment, and the changing urban environment.

Unemployment and the Foundations of Aggregate Supply

Paul Samuelson (1948), a professor at MIT, explains aggregate supply describes the relationship between the output of businesses willingly produced and overall prices. The factors underlying aggregate supply are the production output potential determined by the inputs of labor, capital, and natural resources available to the economy. Technology also determines potential from an efficiency angle.

The government gathers monthly unemployment, employment, and labor force statistics in sample population surveys. First, it categorizes people with jobs as *employed*. People without jobs looking for work are *unemployed*. Finally, it considers people without jobs not looking for work *outside the labor force*. According to Samuelson, economists distinguish between unemployment in equilibrium and disequilibrium. Unemployment in equilibrium sometimes happens when people become unemployed voluntarily as they move from job to job or into and out of the labor force. This transitory movement is also called *frictional* unemployment.

On the other hand, disequilibrium unemployment occurs in nonfunctioning macroeconomic labor markets. As a result, qualified people willing to work at prevailing wages cannot find jobs. Two types of disequilibrium are *structural* and *cyclical* unemployment. Structural unemployment arises for workers in regions or industries in persistent slumps because of imbalances in the labor market or high real wages. Cyclical unemployment occurs as firms lay off workers when the economy suffers a downturn.

Friedrich Hayek (1960) observes that employed urban and industrial workers increased relative to the population during the last 200 years. Also, change in technology favors large-scale firms and helps create large new classes of clerical workers. This change assists the growth of the employed segment of the population.

This topic discussed government metrics, types of unemployment, and the changing urban environment. The following section introduces collective bargaining.

Labor Basics

Labor is a significant component of the production process. This topic discusses unions, occupational licenses, job search and markets, and the protection of workers.

Unions

Collective bargaining is the negotiation of wages and other conditions of employment by an organized body of employees. Hayek senses the public policy of labor unions moved from one extreme to the other in little more than a century. Moreover, the movement began when little the unions did was legal. He felt the unions reached a level where they became unique institutions of privilege in his day. The general rules of law are not relevant to them. They became the only important instance where governments failed in their primary function: preventing coercion and violence. Hayek stresses how society permitting the unions to exercise pressure contradicts all principles of freedom under the law. It is primarily the coercion of fellow workers. Whatever true powers of force the unions can wield over employers is the consequence of this primary power of coercing other workers.

Friedman and Friedman (1979) recount state-established commissions of *fair employment practices*. They were tasked with preventing employment discrimination because of race, color, or religion. However, the coercion in the legislation interfered with our freedom to enter voluntary contracts with one another. States also passed *right-to-work* laws. These laws make it illegal to require union membership as a condition of employment.

The principles involved in right-to-work laws are identical to civil rights principles. Both problems interfered with the freedom of employment contracts. In one case, it specified that a firm could not select color or religion as a condition of employment. On the other, the case does not require union membership. Despite the identity of a unifying principle, there is a 100 percent divergence of political views concerning the two laws.

Occupational Licensure

Friedman (1962) thinks overthrowing medieval guild systems was an indispensable early step in expanding freedom in the Western world. It heralded the triumph of liberal ideas, and society widely recognized the unearthed bounty. As a result, by the mid-19th century, we could pursue whatever trade or occupation we wished without permission from the governmental or quasi-governmental authority. However, he feels that there has been a reversal in recent decades. This reversal is the increasing tendency for occupations to restrict individuals from practicing their trade unless licensed by the state. These are restrictions on our freedom to use our resources as we wish.

Licensing is a case where we cannot engage in economic activities except under conditions constituted by state authorities. Similar phenomena are tariffs, fair-trade laws, import quotas, production quotas, and trade union restrictions. The justification embedded in the enabling legislation was to protect the public interest. Unfortunately, however, the pressure on legislatures to license occupations rarely came from mistreated members of the public or, in other ways, abused by members of the profession.

Job Market Signaling

Michael Spence (2011) explores models implicitly illustrating *signaling* in job markets and underlines its interest to economists. He characterizes the problem as a communication challenge. When we face investment decisions under uncertainty, we can only interpret these signals.

Spence looks at markets where signaling takes place. The primary signalers, job seekers, are always present but infrequently participate in markets. As a result, they do not invest capital in acquiring a reputation for signaling. In most job markets, employers are not sure of the productive capabilities of a prospective employee. Nor is this information available to employers immediately after hiring.

The employer signals their expected return in the offered wages. The process assumes we select signals to maximize the differences between proposed salaries and the signaling cost. The cost plays a crucial role in this signaling situation.

Equilibrium Search, Unions, and Competition

Robert Lucas (2002) and Edward Prescott (2002), American economists, examine why workers choose unemployment over employment at a lower wage rate. Offering wages that face workers is like a lottery drawing with a distribution of probabilities. Workers decide to accept the offer or make another drawing by continued search. Distributions of wage rates govern the challenge of worker decisions. They are related to their knowledge of job search outcomes in these distinct markets.

On the other hand, labor mobility influences the distribution of wages over markets. Economists can determine the optimal labor supply behavior and wage distributions in market models. Lucas and Prescott present complete models of job searches of this general type. Their model economy is situated where production and sales of goods occur in spatially distinct markets. As a result, product demand in each market shifts stochastically, driven by shocks independent of job markets.

Friedman and Friedman (1979) observe that the conditions of ordinary workers in economically advanced societies have improved enormously over the past two centuries. Hardly any worker engaged in the same backbreaking labor common centuries ago. The largest remaining group of the labor movement, the worker unions in government, departs from the traditional relationships of employee–employer. These municipal unions do not deal directly with the taxpayers who pay their salaries. Instead, they deal with government officials. There is a loose connection between taxpayers and the officials. These circumstances enable officials and unions to gang up at taxpayers' expense. As a result, people spend other people's money on still other people.

No one protects the classes of workers in firms who have only one employee or who employees are also employers. Individuals effectively having only one employer tend to be highly paid. The Friedmans thought the existence of potential employers provides the most reliable and effective protection for workers. If their employer does not want to pay them, another employer is ready to hire them. The competition for services is the natural protection of workers.

This topic discussed unions, occupational licenses, job search and markets, and the protection of workers. The following section examines labor theory.

Labor Theory

This topic presents advances in labor theory with discussions of transactions in labor markets, the study of life cycles, a theoretical view of unemployment, and analyzing labor in a depression.

Oliver Williamson (1985) implies that organized labor's social systems are identical to monopoly power because neoclassical economics takes institutions as a given entity. Therefore, the cost of transactions approach and labor organizations have essential economic and social ramifications. Williamson applies his theory of cost of transactions to labor organizations.

Labor organizations are a complicated matter, and no single approach describes them. The economics of cost transactions focuses on the organizational aspects of efficiency. Among the potential economic benefits of this approach are determining wages and benefits, productivity enhancements, settlement of disputes, and adequate regard for dignity. First, Williamson evaluates how potential gains vary in this situation and their level of magnitude. Next, he assesses the needs of governance structures for different transactions and their ramifications on union organizations. Finally, he considers the potential hazards of collective organizations.

The transactions of his interest are the recurring type. Transactions in the labor market where there is market value continuity between firm and worker are those where firm-specific conditions of human assets develop. Acquisition of skill is necessary but not enough of a necessity for features of asset specificity to appear.

Unions are the prevailing collective labor organizations in capitalist economies. They allow workers to improve bargains they negotiate involving the disposition of quasi-rent attributable to firm-specific human capital. Williamson suggests that where human assets are nonspecific, the economy does not need specialized governance structures for these labor transactions. Instead, discrete market contracting characterizes the transactions of this type, such as migrant farm labor.

James Heckman (1993), a professor at the University of Chicago, suggests the primary advance in the study of labor supply in the past 50 years was recognizing and interpreting the varieties of distinct labor supply functions. He points out that informed economists should consider allocations of working time over *life cycles*. This more expansive view broadens wages to include current and future values. Also, empirical research focuses on estimating equations of annual hours worked for those working part-time each year.

The weight of available empirical evidence suggests a pattern. First, there is weak or even nonexistent responsiveness to wages. Second, this response applies to the labor supply over life cycles. Third, there's evidence that demand-side variables affect labor supply when holding measured wages constant.

Christopher Pissarides (2000), a Cypriot economist, develops a theory of unemployment by exploring the nature of unemployment in steady states of the economy. He illustrates how he jointly determines wages and unemployment in standard equilibrium models. His central finding is that labor markets match jobs as a decentralized economic activity. As a result, it is uncoordinated, time consuming, and costly for both firms and workers.

Matching functions suggest outcomes of resource investments by firms and workers in the trading process are input functions. These functions are modeling devices to capture the implications of processes of costly labor trading without explicit heterogeneities. Pissarides thinks the usefulness of the matching process depends on its empirical viability and how successfully it captures critical features of the exchange. He aims to show how the matching function derives new and plausible results.

The equilibrium he contemplates is an equilibrium of full rational expectations. The stated aggregate equilibrium is where firms and workers maximize their objective functions. This process is subject to matching and separation technologies, where the flow of workers into unemployment equals the worker flow out of unemployment.

According to Pissarides, a professor at the London School of Economics and the University of Cyprus, job creation and destruction respond to exogenous shocks. In cases of surprises in the business cycle, there is evidence that job destruction rates are even more responsive than rates of job creation. He generalizes his simple model by making job destruction an unknown parameter. It depends on the optimizing actions of firms and workers. Influences of the parameter or policy on unemployment work through job creation and destruction. He contends equilibrium unemployment depends on parameters and is inefficient.

Next, Pissarides introduces policy instruments and studies their effects on model equilibriums. He then develops optimal policy rules to remove inefficiencies. He found search externalities cause them. These policy rules are linear. The model derives them from wage taxes and subsidies for employment or unemployment. First, his approach considers general principles underlying the determination of wages in the presence of public policy. Then, he analyzes the effects of linear policy rules on job creation, job destruction, search intensity, and reservation rules governing decisions on whether to form matches.

Improved contact through the direct intervention of public policy corrects inefficient low intensities of search. However, it does not necessarily improve low reservations of productivity. Therefore, policy makers need to develop other approaches to induce firms and workers to be more choosey about the jobs they create and maintain. An apparent policy having this effect is unemployment compensation. Paying unemployed subsidies would increase reservations of productivity applied to job acceptance decisions and job destruction.

The Labor Factor

Edward Prescott (2006), a professor at Carnegie Mellon University and the Australian National University, feels labor factors are essential in analyzing an economic cycles. Analysts sometimes account for low labor inputs by high marginal tax rates of labor income and consumption. He also shows that other public policies distort labor markets and cause low labor input.

Labor input can also be low because the economy's capital stock is above the constant growth path associated with its current policies. For example, suppose the country is near its continuous growth path, and unexpected policy changes lower the stable growth paths. In that case, labor input falls below its new constant level of growth but then converges upward to this new level.

Prescott thought the productivity of factors is crucial in evaluating prosperity and recession. The differences in total factor productivity largely account for differences in international income. These differences are present even after correcting for the quality of labor input. Productivity shocks are significant contributors to fluctuations in the business cycle.

Dale Mortensen (2003), an American economist and Northwestern University professor, presents a model that does not pay similar workers differently when it embraces the law of one price. He reviews the evidence for the dispersion of wages in two kinds of arguments. First, workers' earnings are statistically associated with the employer's aspects, particularly employer industry and size. He also presents a simple theory of wage dispersion with static one-period structures. The essential feature is that workers have only partial information about employment opportunities.

Banerjee and Duflo (2019), both from MIT, perceive the increasing sophistication of robots and the progress of artificial intelligence generate considerable anxiety in the labor force. We stress out about what happens to our societies if only the fortunate have exciting jobs and everyone else has either no work or has a horrible job. Inequality may balloon as a result. Moreover, Banerjee and Duflo worry that modern technologies such as artificial intelligence, robots, and automation generally destroy more jobs than they create. This transition makes workers obsolete and causes the wages share of GDP to dwindle.

This topic presented advances in labor theory with discussions of transactions in labor markets, the study of life cycles, a theoretical view of unemployment, and analyzing labor in a depression. The section discussed unemployment, collective bargaining, and labor theory. The chapter examined demographic trends, human development, and labor economics. Human capital is an area the public usually doesn't consider, but it has gained relevance in economic sciences. It provides another clue in our hunt to locate the process for choosing bread loaves. The next chapter begins to string together the pieces of the puzzle we have uncovered.

CHAPTER 7

Domestic Big Picture

The human capital component in the last chapter was the final missing piece in the economic puzzle revealed. Now, we can combine the elements and consider the economy as a whole. Macroeconomics analyzes the structure of an overall economy with its markets and other institutions. This chapter examines these general operations and discusses economic cycles, developing public policy, and macroeconomic theory.

Economic Cycles

Economic cycles result from existing conditions along with changes in relationships between supply and demand in the market of goods and services. These changes upset the economic equilibrium. However, the economy eventually restores this equilibrium with constant rhythms of time depending on consumer demand. This section examines economic cycles. The discussion includes dynamic cycles, forecasting, and a history of economic cycles.

Dynamic Cycles

Economic cycles come in a variety of shapes and sizes. This topic describes the types of movement, the different lengths with their characteristics, and a subset—business cycles. It also depicts noncyclical shocks to equilibrium and the computational experiment approach.

Types of Movements

In the 1930s, neoclassical economists did little to verify their theoretical results of empirical observations with statistics. Ragnar Frisch (1965) from the University of Oslo in Norway thought this neglect was due to the inadequate quality of available data. As a result, economists didn't develop a neoclassical theory with data verification in mind. Now, contemporary macroeconomic theory derives its concepts from empirical data, and in turn, theory dictates new measures. Robert Lucas (2002) suggests that neoclassical economists should use a business cycle approach.

While Edward Prescott (2002) supports everything Frisch proposes, he takes issue with how economists and policy makers should interact. For example, Frisch thought it should be a democratic process. In contrast, Prescott feels economists should educate noneconomic savvy individuals and let them evaluate macroeconomic policy rules.

Jan Tinbergen was a Dutch economist and one of the first Nobel winners. Tinbergen and Polak (1942), suggest the objective of analyzing economic dynamic cycles should be to describe and explain the magnitude of fluctuations. These magnitudes are variable. Cyclical variables and their movement are often complicated. Tinbergen and Polak also make a distinction between *systemic* and *random* movements of economic growth. With systemic movement, variables represent one value following another according to a pattern. However, in random movement, all design is absent in arriving at successive values.

There are distinct types of systemic movement, including *steady monotonic* and *periodic*. One difference between steady monotonic and periodic movements is essential. In the case of monotones, the movement never reverses direction. The simplest type of monotonic movement is a straight line. This line rises or falls with the horizontal line as the intermediate case. For this straight line, the difference in two successive levels of units is always the same.

On the other hand, periodic movement patterns repeat themselves after certain time lapses. The cycle *damps* periodic movements when each successive fluctuation has less significant magnitude than the preceding cycle. Conversely, economists sometimes call trends showing explosive movements *antidamping*. Purely regular changes are *undamped*. Tinbergen and Polak surmise that most economic activities of a phenomenon are much more complicated than the simple movements discussed above. Nevertheless, actual economic series approximate any one elementary movement.

Two movements of different data series may have connections. Movements are entirely independent, but they usually exist in a particular relationship. Often no precise relationship exists but has an approximation. Researchers call these *stochastic relationships*.

Long-Run Developments

Tinbergen and Polak explore movements occurring over centuries to determine their relationship to economic development. For example, the world population increased rapidly over the last two centuries due to reduced mortality rates. However, growth rates then slowed because of the emergence of birth control in the latter part of the period. The behavior of other population curves based on marriage, fertility, and mortality rates aren't as simple. Still, in their early stages, these different curves approximated the primary population growth curve.

Tinbergen and Polak suggest *interruptions* occasionally occur in the regular patterns presented above. These interruptions occur before the preceding tendencies of the period resume. In addition, certain other events have as primary consequences not temporary but lasting economic changes.

Cyclical Movements

Business cycle movements (versus economic cycles) have additional periodic characteristics. Economists measure them in terms of GDP. They make distinctions among these trends by noting the differences in length. Most business cycles are irregular, making measuring their degree of damping difficult. However, researchers haven't observe significant damping because business cycles repeat themselves with roughly the same amplitudes. Cycles have natural tendencies of damping, but new disturbance factors continually keep them from showing a steady pattern.

Seasonal fluctuations caused by changes in natural or conventional seasons are the most essential shorter rhythmic fluctuations. The economy feels the natural influences of seasons most strongly in areas with direct contact with nature, such as agriculture.

Noncyclical Shocks to Equilibrium

Trygve Haavelmo (1954) facetiously characterizes precise, simple models of economic growth as belonging to the world of fiction. Nobody expects them to depict the accurate facts they aim to explain. However, if exact models are of practical value, they provide reasonable interpretations of their deviations. For example, he points out that stochastic processes are time-indexed sets of random variables. If the indexes use integer values, they are *discrete* processes. However, they are continuous processes if the indexes use *continuous ranges* of real values.

Stochastic modeling presents data and predicts outcomes to account for unpredictability or randomness. These events are shocks to the model unaccounted for, like wars, technological changes, or political regime changes. Regarding the relationship between war and inflation, Haavelmo observes that countries can fight wars, particularly minor ones, without significant effects of inflation. However, shortages of specific commodities usually characterize an extended period of war.

Business Cycle Fluctuations

Haavelmo surmises business cycle phenomena occur in different countries in divergent forms and periods. Therefore, separations between trend and cyclical movements offer considerable analysis advantages. However, business cycles are complicated, so economists can't satisfactorily describe them with single principles or economic features. This challenge makes it difficult to render a comprehensive picture of business cycles. Nonetheless, Haavelmo seeks explanations for fluctuations in GDP analysis. Economists consider this money stream the product of the money supply's size and *velocity* (turnover). Therefore, growth possibilities of the money supply during economic booms provide opportunities for expanding the flow of payments.

There are *time lags* between changes in income and corresponding changes in consumption. As for capital investment, evaluating these type of lags are essential for understanding cyclical mechanisms. For specific income categories, certain time lapses occur before income becomes available for spending. Also, causes of seasonal lags include spending on travel in the summer and buying Christmas presents in December. Specific lengths of contracts stabilize spending. In addition, there's psychological inertia in most people. Only slowly do they acknowledge their higher income and adapt their spending.

Business Cycles and Aggregate Demand

Paul Samuelson (1948) ties business cycles to aggregate demand. He describes business cycles or fluctuations using GDP, income, and employment swings. Widespread expansion and contractions in economic sectors delineate them. They occur in all advanced market economies. He suggests that most business cycles occur when shifts in aggregate demand change GDP, employment, and prices. These transitions occur when changes in spending by consumers, businesses, or governments affect total expenditures relative to the production capacity of the economy.

Declines in aggregate demand lead to recessions or even depressions. Conversely, upturns in economic activity could generate surges of inflation. Samuelson distinguishes expansion phases and peaks from recessions and troughs. Theories of business cycles differ in their emphasis on external and internal causes. For example, ancient societies suffered when failures in harvest produced famines. In other times, excessive spending by the government and reliance on money creation to support this fiscal policy lead to runaway inflation.

According to Haavelmo, prices and quantities in smaller isolated markets also illustrate cyclical fluctuations. These effects are different from general business cycles. For example, industry patterns of residential construction result from price mechanisms described as disturbances. In actual life, data change continuously, and shocks constantly affect economic systems. These shocks are broad-based. Economists legitimately consider them a series of random variables. Economic fluctuations, particularly cyclical ones, are pure successions of arbitrary changes.

Maurice Allais (1997), a French physicist and economist, develops the *X factor* representing the physical influences of exogenous time series. He rejects theories of mathematical change that ignore chance, uncertainty, and probability. Instead, he examines the structures of fluctuations. At first, they are incomprehensible such as sunspots or stock market quotes. However, these fluctuations present periodic features; therefore, such systems correspond to almost regular functions. Furthermore, Allais felt independent circumstances typically distribute successive values of periodic functions.

The Computational Experiment Approach

Finn Kydland (2006), a University of California, Santa Barbara professor, recounts that recurrent above-trend output and employment fluctuations in business cycles puzzled economists for a long time. Understanding business cycles requires the development of methods to understand the economic behavior of uncertain dynamics. Kydland and Prescott (1996) also recounted that economists formerly viewed business fluctuations as *deviations from theories* before developing these methods. However, after creating upgraded models, researchers extensively used computational methods to examine business cycles.

In the 1970s, the common assumption was that *monetary shocks* were behind cyclical components. On the other hand, neoclassical models emphasized different factors, primarily growth in productivity and input. They accounted for component movements of change eventually. Kydland (2006) also felt early views suggested that technological development fluctuations produced economic changes but were unlikely to play many roles in aggregates. However, during the 1980s, technology shocks renewed interest in them as a significant source of fluctuations. After that, the business cycle theory treated cycles of growth and technology as integrated, not as two-component sums driven by varied factors.

When conducting experiments, the first step is to compute the decision rules of equilibrium. Kydland and Prescott (1996) became more confident they could study the contributions of the vitality of technology. For example, they built model economies to trace all fluctuations to technology shocks. Researchers need to establish theoretical relationships to specify the willingness of people to substitute *consumption* and *leisure*. Next, Kydland and Prescott evaluated models of other researchers involving efficiency structures of wages and money supply over the years.

Kydland and Prescott originally developed a methodology to study business cycles. The critical fact of business cycles is that two thirds of the fluctuations account for labor input variations and one-third for total factor productivity. However, no apparent candidates for high labor supply explained the economic contraction in 1999. Their methodology is also useful for studying other phenomena, such as the stock market valuation. Their alternate models produce equilibriums when corporate market values are similar to production assets' value.

This section described the types of movement, the different lengths with their characteristics, and business cycles. It also discussed noncyclical shocks to equilibrium and the computational experiment approach. The next topic highlights economic forecasting.

Forecasting

Researchers forecast future economic cycles. This topic describes the most fruitful type: business cycle forecasting. It discusses its users, examines various kinds of projections, looks at anticipation surveys, and points out the types of indicators.

Clive Granger (1980) was a professor at the University of Nottingham and the University of California, San Diego. He points out that management and economics are decision sciences concerned with sensible decision making and its effects. Any decision forms an opinion about what will occur in the future, thus forecasts. Major consumers of forecasts are government officials at the federal, state, and local levels. Upper-level business management also uses projections. Finally, situations in our daily lives require personal forecasts.

There are various types of projections, each requiring different approaches. The further in the future the time horizon, the less accurate they become because significant errors are likely to occur. Estimates of the *one-time event* use relevant information but are difficult or expensive to prepare.

Granger explains that forecasters translate aspects of society and the economy into numerical form. For example, time series appear to hold smoothly increasing components. After plotting historical data on charts, analysts often select curves to fit the data. Granger observes that when statisticians first studied time series, the limited number of data series available for any practical value contained cyclical components. As a result, the complete process of analyzing the time series was lengthy and costly.

Economists define the subjective survey data of *anticipations* as asking participants about their plans for future spending, labor needs, or other resource requirements. An indirect way of obtaining related *attitudinal* data is by asking households or firms how satisfied they are with present economic conditions.

Because decision makers watch for *turning points* in economic activity, they focus on predicting them. Decision makers measure economic conditions and turning points using systematic methods. They integrate the patterns they find to make predictions for the future. The National Bureau for Economic Research assembles groups of experts to plot GDP, industrial production, and other indexes to develop *leading indicators*, such as the stock market. Economists anticipate a series of leading indicators to turn before the aggregate economy. A second economic set of *coincidental* indicators responds simultaneously with aggregate economic measures, such as industrial production. Data sources release them quicker than others, adding value. Finally, *lagging* indicators denote a series reacting slowly to changes in general economic directions, such as unemployment rates.

This topic described business cycle forecasting. It discussed its users, examined various kinds of projections, looked at anticipation surveys, and pointed out the types of indicators. The following section provides historical context.

Cycle History

We can learn by studying the past. Computers have simplified the handling of data used to analyze past economic cycles. This section investigates money supply trends since the Civil War and the 2008 financial crisis.

Friedman and Schwartz (1963) examined the money supply of the U.S. economy from data back to 1867. Their study marks the beginning of the ongoing U.S. government studies of estimates of state banks. Money supply plays a crucial role in U.S. economic and political developments. For the first time, estimates of money supply constructed by Friedman and Schwartz provide a continuous series covering more than nine decades. The most notable feature is its solid upward trend in growth.

Policy makers believed state-chartered banks were shortly going out of business when Congress passed the National Banking Act of 1863. The financial aftermath of the Civil War dominated the greenback period from 1867 to 1879. For domestic payments, gold was simply a commodity like any other. Following the war, there was a period of rapid growth in banking volume. This growth produced a sharp rise in the ratio of deposits to currency. However, state taxes on banknotes created economic

deterrents to their circulation. Friedman and Schwartz contend conflicting trends came to a head in the bank panic of 1907. The Federal Reserve
System (Fed) began operations soon after. This event heralded a significant historical U.S. monetary watershed.

Rapid increases in money supply during World War I and after
occurred when the Fed provided an inflationary engine of war funding.
The rest of the 1920s were a high tide of the Fed and the money supply.
Unfortunately, this era ended abruptly in 1929, with the downturn in
the stock market ushering in the Great Depression. By the bank holiday
in 1933, the money supply had shrunk by a third, and panic was more
severe. Ironically, the Fed possessed ample power throughout the contraction to fix the monetary deflation by pumping up the money supply and
preventing the banking collapse, but it didn't do it. As a result, significant
changes in banking structures and monetary systems resulted in the Great
Depression. Congress reorganized the Fed with more centralized power
given to Washington and less to district banks.

Legacies of the Great Recession

Michael Spence (2011) recalls the run-up to the monetary crisis of 2008.
It featured the excessive leverage of financial institutions and households,
inflating asset bubbles in stock markets and real estate. The bubbles eventually collapsed and left damaged balance sheets. The policy fixes in the
aftermath resulted in higher savings rates creating demand shortfalls and
an uptick in unemployment. He wonders whether the combined fiscal
and monetary stimulus was the right way to stabilize the U.S. economy.
On the other hand, at the height of the crisis, fiscal stimulus and massive
financial liquidity injections eased effects and prevented credit squeezes.

According to Spence, the best way to use the government's fiscal deficits
and debt is to address income distribution issues, particularly unemployment, without discouraging work incentives. In addition, policy makers
should encourage capital investment in the supply-side and reform the
public sector to support growth in the longer term.

Economic governance refers to institutional and procedural systems
established to achieve a nation's objectives in the economic field. Analysis
of economic governance evaluates the institutional processes supporting

economic activity and transactions. For example, protecting property rights, enforcing contracts, and taking collective action to provide appropriate physical and organizational infrastructure help achieve these processes' objectives.

This topic investigated money supply trends since the Civil War and the 2008 financial crisis. The section examined economic cycles, including discussions on dynamic cycles, forecasting, and a history of economic cycles. The following section discusses public policy.

Managing the Economy

Society can harness an economy to help it bring well-being to its members. Policy makers are responsible for allocating public resources. This section examines the economic policy-making process. It discusses economic governance and monetary and fiscal policy.

Governance

The government administers the laws of society. This topic outlines economists' tasks, describes the government's activities, and presents a policy framework. In addition, it discusses the creation of money, examines a theory of rational expectations, and debates the mix of fiscal and monetary policy.

Tasks for Economists

During the 1993 U.S. budget talks, William Vickrey (1939) stressed that the immediate goal of public policy was to boost the economy rapidly to the point of full employment and keep it there. He suggests there should be at least as many job openings as individuals seeking employment. This condition has favorable consequences for production levels. It also reduces the budgetary drain of government transfers for unemployment insurance and welfare benefits. In addition, full employment eases tensions over cutbacks in defense, race relations, free trade, and immigration. Finally, this upgrade of labor tends to raise wages and lift low-skilled workers' esteem.

Vickrey felt economists should adopt altruism. He proposes various supply-side measures to promote capital investment, but the ones actually adopted seem unusually weak compared to available actions. Moreover, policy makers ignore other more effective measures on the supply side for economic stimulation and improving capital investment allocation due to political unpopularity. Even if carried forward more vigorously than advocated, supply-side measures will likely fall short of causing rapid growth toward full employment. The Phillips curve, which relates inflation to levels of unemployment, provides economists a tool to understand these relationships.

Activities of the Government

Jan Tinbergen was a researcher at the Dutch statistical office. Tinbergen and Polak (1942) suggest that public policy should focus on the economic activity of the government. Policy makers should not worry about the actions of individuals, enterprises, and labor unions. They should test the effectiveness of existing policies by comparing economic development under these policies with what would have happened without them. This comparison implies that commentators shouldn't simply observe what outcomes occur after introducing an approach and attribute it to the policy.

Tinbergen and Polak explore setting policy for trends and business cycles. For example, the economy can achieve a desired production volume and maximize it using all production factors. Therefore, the policy should avoid involuntary idleness in aspects of production. Hours worked should approximate what policy makers require from the labor force. They should grant workers the flexibility to choose longer hours for higher wages, or shorter hours for lower wages. Tinbergen and Polak also felt maintaining stable levels of prices is essential. Substantial changes in either direction are undesirable. Volatile changes lead to significant wealth for specific segments and large losses for others. Levels of wages equate to labor productivity and other production factors.

Policy Objectives Framework

Theodore Schultz (1979), a University of Chicago professor, thinks policy objectives should contain economic content focusing on the means or facilitating processes. However, policy makers should keep in mind economic activity influences value far up the scale of ultimate outcomes. Economists believe that if governments participate too actively and directly, it reduces the freedom of action of firms and households. Countries give high priority to international trade problems among issues of policy. In Schultz's day, developed countries had to deal with mass unemployment. Wasteful use of resources also ranked high in public surveys. Another significant policy challenge pertains to economic inequality. One way to identify issues is to recognize that problems arise from *imperfections* in allocating existing resources. The principal policy objective is to achieve significant economic efficiencies.

Creation of Money

Merton Miller was a professor at the University of Chicago. Miller and Upton (1974) explain that only a tiny portion of the money supply is government-supplied fiat money in modern economics. Fiat money has no intrinsic value but has exchange value because society accepts it. Instead, the private sector creates the bulk of the money supply. They illustrate that this process based on bank deposits that doesn't necessarily arise from deposits of physical money. Instead, the bank creates the money by generating a borrower's liability and crediting the cash to the borrower's account. The private sector also uses this double-posting process to make purchases or settle debts.

Rational Expectation

Thomas Sargent (1986), an American economist, recalls that concepts of *rational expectation* transformed the macroeconomic theory during the 1970s. This transformation happened because policy makers previously ignored readily available information which could improve liquidity decisions. Keynesian consumption, investment, and rules of money demand only planted the technical seeds. The transformation's consequence is that now society slowly appreciates the relevance of day-to-day macroeconomics. This growing understanding applies new concepts and language.

Policy makers often coordinate monetary and fiscal policies because governments face the constraints of budgets. Economists construct *econometric models* to provide quantitative advice on the effects of alternative economic policy. In addition, policy makers borrow from game theory to understand the dynamics of their policy choices. Dynamic games or solutions equilibriums are collections of dominance structures and strategies. For example, in Nash equilibriums, each player takes the other player's approach as given and beyond their influence. The need for quarterbacks and receivers to coordinate their roles reflects this interdependence in football. It's also reflected in the problems of coordination facing monetary and fiscal authorities.

According to Sargent of New York University, inflation taxes aren't legal taxes paid to governments. Instead, in the context of rational expectations, inflation occurs at higher rates than initially expected when the government departs from its initial policy. Inflation nonetheless acts as the functional equivalent of a tax by reducing the intrinsic value of demand. Therefore, the responsibilities of monetary and fiscal authorities need to be restricted. Society can accomplish this goal through legislation. Sargent thinks the policies can achieve superior outcomes if they accept this consideration. Finally, he presents his choices for monetary jurisdiction within an extremely monetarist model.

The Monetary and Fiscal Policy Mix

Supply-side economic policy is concerned with the growth of production capacity. However, James Tobin's (1997) focus on demand-side economics analyzes economic management via fiscal policy. In the 1980s, Tobin thought the economic power of producing goods and services wasn't a binding constraint on real output. Instead, monetary policy lowers or raises interest rates. It also expands and restricts demand through the floating regimes of currency exchanges. Tobin's proposed policy mix makes distinctions between the combined stimulus administered by the two policy sources and their relative contribution.

Potential GDP is what market economies is capable of producing, with households and businesses making most decisions affecting allocations of prices and resources. Tobin relates potential output to the full employment of labor in Keynesian theory. Gaps of deflationary demand show up in shortfalls of actual production but not in prices. The relationship of William Phillips from New Zealand and his Phillips curve blurred distinctions of Keynesian inflation in sensible ways. Economists came to understand that inflation of prices affects inflation of wages.

John Maynard Keynes was a British economist. He explicitly described monetary economies where markets set nominal prices, a significant difference between Keynesian and neoclassical economics. The classic and Keynesian models' differences are apparent when analysts focus on longer intervals and *anticipated* inflation. This type of inflation contrasts with *unanticipated* inflation. As a result, neoclassical economies eventually adopt new growth paths, with unemployment reduced to natural levels. On the other hand, Keynesian models fall back to a stationary trade-off.

Neoclassical economics is a theory of real or relative prices. It involves multilateral barter. Tobin suggests that there is a nonaccelerating inflation rate of unemployment (NAIRU) at any given time that is uncertain and floating. Therefore, the theory implies no durable trade-off between unemployment and inflation. This principle undermines the Phillips curve. Whether it's constant or a function of the unemployment rate, the uncertain location of NAIRU is an independent source of policy trade-off. Tobin implies NAIRU is not a precise number.

This topic listed economists' tasks, described the government's activities and presented a policy framework. In addition, it discussed the creation of money, examined a theory of rational expectations, and debated the mix of fiscal and monetary policy. The following section discusses monetary policy.

Monetary Policy

Monetary policy refers to the government's efforts to control the money supply. It tries to influence its volume growth and velocity (turnover). This topic describes its operation, monetary theorists, and quantity theory. It also presents a monetary policy framework, describes the microeconomic foundations for the demand for money, and prescribes a cure for inflation.

Monetary Policy and the Economy

According to Paul Samuelson (1948), the Fed conducts its policy through changes in a crucial overnight interest rate called the *federal funds rate*. This short-term rate is the rate banks charge each other for exchanging excess reserves above the required ones at the Fed. The Fed influences the federal funds rate by exercising control over money market instruments, primarily through open market operations. Economists measure inflation rates by monitoring the changes in price indexes from one period to another. The primary price indexes are the consumer price index (CPI), personal consumption expenditures (PCE), and the GDP deflator.

Monetary Theorists and the Quantity Theory

Lawrence Klein's (1943) econometric models focus on levels and swings of several factors. They include interest rates, deregulation, new introductions of credit instruments, and similar developments. *Monetarists* assume money supply turnover is a constant. Therefore, the primary effects of interest rates are on the cost of borrowing or final demand. There are monetarist and rational expectations theorists who think similarly. *Rational expectations theorists* think that fiscal policy has no natural effect on aggregates because decisions in the private sector neutralize whatever public policy makers do. Debates about monetarism, supply-side economics, and rational expectations impact the structures of economic models.

Klein, a professor at the University of Pennsylvania, examines aspects of the empirical quantity theory on long-term equilibriums. *Quantity theory*, the essential principle in macroeconomics, suggests levels of prices are proportional to the money supply. The quantity theory equation is MV = PT (money supply times velocity equals price multiplied by transactions or GDP). Its reasoning sustains Friedman's assertion that increases in the money supply always cause inflation.

The Monetary Framework

Friedrich Hayek (1960) observes that experiences of the last century taught society that a stable monetary system was necessary. However, compared with the preceding century, policy makers in this period still monkeyed with the money supply. He suggests the primary economic threat is inflation when the government controls monetary policy. Economists deliberately advocate a continuous upward movement of the general level of prices. Also, inflation and deflation can be local or sectional phenomena. The case against the discretion of monetary policy isn't quite the same as against control using the coercive powers of government. Nevertheless, Hayek doesn't wish to weaken the case for any arrangement forcing authorities to do the right thing.

Before the 1960s, Friedman (1962) thought full employment and economic growth became the primary excuse for widening the government's economic intervention. On the other hand, free-market critics felt it inherently unstable that private free enterprises were the culprit. Friedman found these arguments misleading. He felt government mismanagement produced the Great Depression rather than any inherent instability of the private economy. For example, from 1930 to 1931, the Fed managed monetary policy so ineptly that it converted a moderate contraction into a significant catastrophe.

Governance

A Canadian economist, Robert Mundell (1964) introduced supply conditions into the Keynesian system and integrated it with income and interest determination theory. He limits generalizations to four different cases. Mundell developed the version of the Keynesian system made famous by John Hicks (1939) but used a more complex apparatus. He thought Hicks's analysis was unsophisticated because it didn't explicitly account for aggregate supply conditions. With both wages and prices flexible, nominal money supply doesn't make any difference to equilibriums of real systems.

Mundell suggests there is only one level of money supply yielding full-employment equilibrium with a given level of wages. However, other price rigidities arise from monopoly, cartel, or government control arrangements. Keynes was active in the 1930s and assumed rigid wages, no growth, and closed economies. As a result, pessimistic expectations dominate his model in the short run. However, from 1940 to 1971, the global economy experienced the most significant sustained growth period, in contrast to weak demand in Keynes' conditions.

The changing economic, environmental, and psychological policy orientations made Keynes' general theory obsolete. Mundell provides an alternate theory with the basic concept of a growing global economy composed of interacting national economies. The primary significance of public debt rests on the effects of capitalization of future income streams.

The Microeconomic Foundations for the Demand of Money

Miller and Upton (1974) suggest that the money supply is the medium that affects most economic activities. Government policies concerning money creation are significant in sequences of boom and bust that plague modern industrial economies. However, there's a dispute over how important a contributing factor it is. Miller and Upton work through simple numerical examples of household cash management, using money as a medium in all exchanges. Empirical evidence suggests real balances of per capita cash grow at the same rate as real spending per capita over extended periods.

Miller and Upton evaluate what determines the value of real money. The value of money declines when quantities of money units increase. The problem with Keynes' general theory regarding how we form inflation expectations is a significant unsolved macroeconomic problem. They suggest inflation is the same as excise taxes levied on cash holders at rates equal to the money supply growth. It applies to all members of society. Citizens also believe fairness requires progressive taxes. The rich should pay more significant proportions of income than the poor.

The Cure for Inflation

Friedman (1962) thought the legal-tender qualities of the currency imply governments accept pieces of paper to discharge the debt of taxes due itself. Courts regard them as discharging debts stated in dollars. Private persons accept them because they are confident others will. Friedman feels inflation is a disease. Economists offer a cure for inflation, but slowing money supply growth is hard to implement due to its adverse effect on economic growth. The challenge is conjuring up the political will to take the necessary measures. Moreover, the side effects of the initially slower money supply growth, such as potential recession, are painful.

Mundell (1971) shows how to stop inflation. Monetary authorities should determine the desired nominal level of the money supply. Therefore, controlling inflation involves changes in the growth of the money supply. However, it's evident that abruptly ending the money supply's growth isn't the right policy. Instead, he thinks nominal interest rates should rise less than inflation rates, so real interest rates fall during inflation. Mundell integrates inflationary effects into his model in the short term, intermediate term, and long term.

James Tobin (1997), a professor at Harvard and Yale Universities, recalls Friedman's monetarism provoked hot debates on the conduct of monetary policy from the 1950s to the 1970s. Monetarists wanted central banks to stop explicitly setting interest rate levels. Instead, the central banks should target the money supply's growth. Monetarist proposals differ in time horizons over which policy makers fix the growth rate of the money supply. Friedman advocates setting it permanently. In practice, the Fed reconsiders numerical targets for growth in money supply when it meets eight times a year and reports to Congress twice yearly.

This topic described monetary policy operation, monetary theorists, and quantity theory. It also presented a monetary policy framework, described the microeconomic foundations for the demand for money, and provided a cure for inflation. The following section discusses fiscal policy.

Fiscal Policy

Fiscal policy uses government spending and taxation to influence the economy. This topic examines taxation problems, growth limits, and the passing of the Keynesian revolution.

The Problem of Progressive Rates of Taxation

According to William Vickrey (1939), progressive rate taxation imposes rates that vary more than a fixed proportion of a tax base. This arrangement exists because it conforms with popular concepts of the ability to pay. Economists measure the progression rate by how tax burdens vary with income.

Unfortunately, it's an imperfect and misleading measure of the ability to pay. Policy makers often agree on the baseline against which they measure the progression. However, measuring each degree of progression in tax structures or deciding on patterns of tax progression remains challenging.

The standard measure of tax progression compares degrees of inequality in selected base distributions after deducting the tax burdens. Any strictly adhered pattern of progression implies high marginal rates at the top of the schedules, leads to severe inequalities, and distorts incentives. Complex political forces impinging on formulating a progressive tax system produce administrative monstrosities. It isn't effectively progressive or equitable. It doesn't maintain economic efficiency. While society wants to remedy inequality situations, political prospects aren't bright.

Can We Grow Faster?

While faster national output and GDP growth are desirable, James Tobin (1997) thinks it doesn't mean they're feasible. Some fiscal policy prescriptions for progrowth stress incentives to produce. They typically *augment the purchasing power* of households and business firms. Another economist school loyal to the supply-side doctrines of Reaganomics urges *tax-cutting* as the centerpiece of macroeconomic policy. These proponents appeal to the effects of labor incentives. Faced with lower marginal tax rates, individuals work more hours per week.

Tobin suggests that using fiscal policies as instruments of macroeconomic stabilization faded because Keynesian advocates overplayed their hands. Tobin recalls that from 1962 to 1964, when JFK first considered and recommended cutting taxes, the economy was recovering from the 1959–1960 recession. Moreover, Reagan's tax cut took effect in the depths of the worst recession since World War II. The 1980s were a period of recession recovery, bringing unemployment back down. The prosperity of workers also rose during this time because of the demand-side stimulus. George H.W. Bush repeated Reagan's income tax cut as his presidential campaign's central economic and fiscal issue. Unfortunately, voters didn't take him seriously.

This topic examined taxation problems, growth limits, and the Keynesian revolution's passing. The section explored economic policy making by discussing economic governance and monetary and fiscal policy. In contrast, the following section discusses macroeconomic theory.

Macroeconomic Theory

Macroeconomics deals with the aggregate economy's performance, structure, and behavior. This focus contrasts with microeconomics, which focuses on individual actors' choices. A macroeconomic theory explains how supply and demand interact dynamically in an economy with multiple markets. The approach identifies a precise set of circumstances under which equilibrium prices will likely achieve stability. This section discusses general equilibrium, neoclassical economic growth, and transformation methods.

General Equilibrium

Economists determine the general equilibrium by analyzing how aggregate supply and demand interact. Keynesians assume it occurs in a steady state, while neoclassicists suggest the form is dynamic. This topic discusses utility and preference and diminishing marginal utility.

Utility and Preference

John Hicks (1939), who lectured at the London School of Economics and Cambridge University, worked with Alfred Marshall's pure theory of consumer demand, the principal work of his day. It assumes that consumers derive utility or satisfaction from their purchases. This utility is a synonym for our welfare. Economists interpret it as a measure of personal happiness. More functionally, it summarizes what guides our choice. Economists use it for constructing choice models of individuals. Individuals make decisions to maximize this utility.

Rejected is diminishing marginal utility because it has no clear sense. Hicks's law of market conduct deals with consumer reactions to changes in market conditions. When we distribute spending between more than two goods, indifference models lose their simplicity. On the other hand, Hicks tries to find a precise meaning for our wants. He demonstrates it when prices vary, affecting decisions of buying and selling. Objects bought and sold don't have to be consumer goods, or they need not all be consumer goods.

Neoclassical Economic Growth

James Meade (1961), a British economist and a professor at the London School of Economics and the University of Cambridge, explores how simple classical economic systems behave during *equilibrium growth*. He observes procedures of variable change over time instead of comparing two static positions as in prior methods. Reasons economies grow:

- His method removes net savings from current income, so the capital base of production increases.
- Working populations are growing.
- The progress of technology allows given amounts of resources to produce more output as time passes.

One of two types of goods in classic economies, *consumer goods* satisfy all ultimate human needs for food, clothing, and shelter. The economy also uses *capital goods* as factors of production, facilitating the production of other consumer goods or the output of capital goods. Meade wants to observe this system's growth through time while the existing capital base grows, the size of the working population increases, and the progress of technology raises productivity. In Meade's model, central monetary authorities set interest rates at levels to preserve constant living costs.

Adjustments in nominal wages per worker and nominal rent per acre of land achieve full labor employment, and land are available at any moment. Wages per worker are always low enough to incentivize entrepreneurs to employ available labor forces. Meade examines primary factors determining growth rates of real income per capita:

- GDP growth and living standard growth rates tend to increase at any point in economic development.
- The nature of the progress of technology increases productivity.

- The elasticities of the substitution of factors are high. These elasticities tend to increase the importance of those factors proliferating and raising GDP growth.

Miller and Upton (1974) concede macroeconomic theory is abstract in its approach to economic questions. However, this abstraction doesn't mean irrelevance. On the contrary, the issues macroeconomics addresses are real and vital. For example, they examine determinants of living standards and the effects of government monetary and fiscal policies. Their emphasis on abstraction represents a belief learned about significant economic problems by stripping away detail and clutter of institutions, which often confuse primary issues.

Models of neoclassical economic growth eventually replaced the older Malthusian models. These new models manage the two general classes of factors better than the simpler models of Malthus. For example, one set of models relates to differences in living standards among countries. The term *neoclassical* applies to models taking full employment of resources as a natural economic state when prices and wages are flexible. Miller and Upton examine models based on the research of Robert Solow in the 1950s.

A neoclassical growth model uses human labor as one of two inputs in production functions. The second factor of production is no longer land but capital. They define it as a productive resource where production increases supply. Since it involves two factors growing over time, neoclassical models are more difficult to describe than simple Malthusian ones. Nevertheless, the models found the key results in the capital-to-labor ratios. Mechanisms to bring about the use of available resources of capital then become straightforward. The problem is finding the quantity of money to use at any rental (interest) rate for individual entrepreneurs.

In market economies, processes determining capital interest rates and a given allocation of base capital of a firm are the exact price mechanisms governing any other commodity or service prices and quantities. Prices change until quantity demanded equals quantity supplied. In practice, these adjustments involve thousands of individual transactions in different markets. With capital goods, there are also complicated arrangements of contracts.

Modern technology changes are slow but show steady improvement in the long term rather than abrupt lurches following a breakthrough. For example, Robert Fulton invented the steamboat in 1809. He assumed society would immediately adopt it and limit wind power exclusively to pleasure regattas. Instead, steam displaced sail gradually, beginning in the most effective areas, such as inland waterways. Then, it caught on in areas where speed generated a premium, such as mail and passenger traffic. Finally, 100 years after the invention, commerce used steam for oceanic cargo transportation.

Ongoing processes of innovative technology are like continued population growth. Miller and Upton treat technological change as a trend governed by forces outside the economic model. This trend increases the adequate supply of labor in the same way that growth in population increases the actual labor pool. The neoclassical model implies that an economy's growth rate depends on savings. However, saving rates are essential though they cause short- and long-term effects on income and consumption per capita levels.

Miller and Upton examine primary influences on the behavior of savings of individual households. Keynes argues that neoclassical theory is deficient because it considers full employment of resources as the only stable economic equilibrium. Keynes' monetary theory primarily attempts to unify the treatment of employment to full employment. He wanted his function to imply proportions of saved income increased and portions of consumed income decreased when income increased.

Miller and Upton point out that studies of long-range history show no systematic evidence for saving to increase relative to income. This finding assumes income increases and society gets more affluent. Keynes' *propensity to consume* underestimated actual spending levels after World War II. Friedman and Modigliani developed the currently accepted theory of the function of *lifecycle consumption* in the 1950s. Both avoided any reliance on psychological tendencies to save or spend. Instead, their models assume individuals have no wage income in the first 20 years of life. Then, they consume less than their wage income each year during their working years. After retirement, income is curtailed while consumption continues. This pattern reminds us that saving and consumption patterns involve more than blind psychological urges of thrift and unthinking mechanical responses to changes in the level of current income. We make economic choices.

One difference between this life cycle and Keynes' theories is that consumption depends on wealth and age, not simply current income. In addition, modern economies typically have the government removing considerable productive resources from the private sector through taxes. However, the government provides other services, such as national defense, in response to demands expressed through various public services.

Miller and Upton extend their model to the public sector but omit determining the proper size of government. Raising income taxes from capital and lowering tax burdens on wage income have the immediate benefit of increasing consumption for the public. They are dismayed at the trade-offs between consuming now and consuming later. They find it deplorable. Policy makers proceed as if there are no adverse consequences for future consumption levels.

Neoclassical Growth Theory

Paul Romer is a New York University professor and a former chief economist of the World Bank. Evans, Honkapohja, and Romer (1998) recount a great deal of historical analysis addressing the performance of the U.K. and U.S. economies at the turn of the 19th century. Observers pointed to the *abundance of U.S. natural resources* as an early advantage. More recently, scholarship concludes that the quantity of resources also interacts with *scale to create supply*. For example, the United States started as an importer of European technology. Still, distinctive U.S. technologies emerged by the first decades of the 19th century. Moreover, the United States possessed efficient transportation and commercial infrastructures early on, linking most citizens into a truly national market. These large markets, with homogeneous consumers, encouraged firms to incur the cost of design and setup required for long production runs of standardized goods constructed with interchangeable parts.

Scale acts through larger markets for both consumer and capital goods. The same motivations enable investments needed to take advantage of other natural resources. Evans, Honkapohja, and Romer extend scale effects to the rise of new institutions such as the U.S. Geological

Survey, private universities, large multidivisional firms, and specialized research laboratories.

Allais's Contribution to Economic Science

Maurice Allais's (1997) dominant approach is a synthesis of ideas. First, in one comprehensive view, he wants to combine a study of natural and monetary economic phenomena. Second, he associates the analysis of efficiency conditions with income distribution. Third, he tries to link theoretical analysis with applied sciences. Fourth, he seeks to relate economics to other social sciences of psychology, sociology, political science, and history. Finally, he believes in this synthesized concept and its close connections between theoretical and applied economics.

Allais's contribution to economic science includes a theory of maximum efficiency in general equilibrium, with the economic foundations of calculus. Another contribution is the theory of intertemporal processes. It seeks maximum capitalistic efficiency. In his work on intertemporal processes, he analyzes the influences of indirect production processes' characteristics on GDP levels. In addition, Allais sought alternatives to the expected utility theory.

In monetary theory, his experience shows that neither economic efficiency nor equitable income distribution existed in countries with an unstable money supply. He bases his monetary dynamics theory on several elements. First, it involved fundamental equations of monetary dynamics. Second, it also implicated functions of heredity and relativism. These functions are demand for money, money supply, and rates of forgetfulness and psychological interest. Third, his theory rests on guiding ideas applicable to social sciences. Finally, his results show that irrespective of frameworks of institutions, we react mechanically to similar sequences of complex events in the same ways.

Methods of Transformation

Edward Prescott (2002) ponders the recent revolution in macroeconomics. Its transformation of methodology reshaped how economists conduct science. Before the change, the study of macroeconomics was separate from the rest of economics. Macroeconomics progressed from searching for a theory to deriving theoretical implications. It involves people making decisions based on what they think will happen. What actually happens depends on their expectations and judgments. Concepts of equilibrium are dynamic and core to modern macroeconomics.

Prescott introduces growth models of single sectors where granular people independently decide how much income they consume and save. They also choose how much of their time to allocate to markets. Time is the most precious resource we possess. He suggests that macroeconomic models were systems of mathematical equations before the transformation. These systems determined outcomes for given values of variables, including current policy actions, predetermined variables of a variable, and any stochastic shock values. The older models evaluated each equation of the system with sets of a parameter. A fundamental assumption was that the equations were invariant to public policy.

The models after transformation are dynamic, fully articulated model economies in general equilibrium. Preferences describe what model individuals choose from their given sets. The models organized tastes and technology from the empirical data in comprehensive structures approaching general equilibrium.

This section discussed general equilibrium, neoclassical economic growth, and transformation methods, while the chapter discussed economic cycles, developing public policy, and macroeconomic theory. Combining the elements we have encountered gets us a little closer to figuring out which bread loaf to buy. The next chapter introduces modernization, starting with a section on agricultural economics.

CHAPTER 8

Modernization

Our journey brings us to a point where it's helpful to derive lessons from successful economies and apply them to less fortunate ones. *Modernization* in economics refers to the process where an economy reaches a level of activity that efficiently allocates resources. It is not a general era but a stage in a particular economy. Economies develop at different speeds—largely independent of one another.

A *developing* country with less efficient resource allocation is usually highly dependent on agriculture. This reliance involves our most basic need: nutrition. Minimizing this dependency is the first step on the path to higher development. This chapter explores the field of economic modernization. Most developing countries have a dominant agricultural base. Therefore, the chapter opens with an examination of agricultural economics. A discussion follows on growth theory and the challenges it creates.

Agricultural Economics

Agricultural economics analyzes resource allocation, distribution, and the use of commodities employed and produced by farming. This section examines public and private agricultural economics. It treats farming as a social institution, describes the farm labor transition, and makes policy suggestions.

Agricultural economics started as a subset of economics, dealing with land usage. It focused on maximizing crop yields while maintaining a healthy soil ecosystem. Throughout the 20th century, the discipline expanded. As a result, the current scope of the field is much broader.

Today, agricultural economics includes various applied areas that overlap with conventional economics. For example, agrarian economists contributed substantially to mainstream economics, econometrics, development economics, and environmental economics. As John Maynard Keynes (1936) points out, the most critical distinction in agriculture is that fluctuations respond to seasons rather than general commerce. He describes fluctuations in agriculture in terms of large harvests and how this distorts pricing mechanisms and alters planning functions.

Farming as a Social Institution

Theodore Schultz (1949) explored the state of the institution of the American family farm in the late 1940s. He formulated essential principles, rules, and procedures for achieving meaningful policy objectives. But unfortunately, it's challenging because existing public policy objectives were usually vague. He portrays the family farm as an entrepreneurial firm. In agricultural economic analysis, the farm is a self-contained enterprise. It's a decision-making unit for production, vested with entrepreneurial features. Schultz's farm production theory involves the organization and management of the farm combined with land, labor, and capital. Schultz (1979) suggests that worldwide farmers focus on costs, returns, and risks. Within their small individual, allocative domain, they are fine-tuned entrepreneurs. Unfortunately, they are adjusting so subtly that experts do not recognize how efficient they are.

Schultz observes that most people in the world are poor. If society understands the economics of being poor, it can comprehend the essence of developmental economics. The world's poor people derive their well being from agriculture. Agriculture in developing countries has the potential economic ability to produce enough food for their still-growing population. However, the decisive factor in improving the welfare of poor people is improving the population's *quality*.

Schultz suggests two intellectual mistakes mar the work of agricultural economists. One mistake is the presumption that standard economic theory is inadequate for understanding low-income countries. New, separate approaches are needed. Also, a widely held view is that the world has a fixed land area suitable for growing food. Schultz disagrees and feels space, energy, and cropland don't foreordain the future of society. Instead, the evolution of human intelligence to use the land efficiently decides it.

This topic introduced Schultz's view of farming as an entrepreneurial firm and suggested agricultural economists make two intellectual mistakes. The following section is about farm labor migration to nonfarm sectors.

Farm Labor Transition

The agricultural work force has been declining over time. This decline occurs because it requires, in absolute terms, less human effort to produce all the farm products demanded by the global economy. As a result, farming needs fewer workers, even with full farm employment, high incomes, and significant exports in the general economy. This section looks at the labor migration out of farm employment.

Fuller employment and freer trade diminish the farming labor, the farm population's size, and the relative proportion of agricultural production and farm income of national GDP. As a result, evaluating land, labor, and capital return rates are more critical compared to other economic sectors.

Shultz laments policy makers grossly neglected farm policy development after World War II. This neglect negatively impacted the finances of agriculture though there was some progress in on-farm management. Demand for farm products expanded more than policy makers expected. Fundamental changes in national employment triggered these shifts. Therefore, farm prices tracked broader economic employment levels, wage levels, wage structures, and other factors.

Farmers with access to *outside* capital were more likely to obtain enough capital to establish a successful farm by renting rather than borrowing to own the land. Unless measures of financial reform alter these lending policies of credit institutions enough to offset the effects of shrinking sizes of farms entirely through ownership, the results are net losses of income. One alternative is to adjust the credit facilities to compensate for rationing capital losses when farmers borrow funds.

Agricultural Public Policy

Schultz thinks agriculture became considerably disadvantaged in the national general economies' modern development and operation. However, in the 1940s, steadfast public support surfaced for achieving well being equality for the agricultural population. This support suggested that policy makers weave *equality* of agricultural incomes into their loosely formulated policy aims. The challenge was to figure out whether policy makers could segment this element of equality into meaningful components.

This topic discusses agricultural public policy by framing the problem, addressing agriculture's stability, analyzing agricultural program effects on the economy, and describing the connection between agriculture and natural resources.

Personal income performs essential socioeconomic functions. Ideal accounting models suggest that increasing an economy's potential total output should cause a change in the allocation of resources. Schultz proposes advanced metrics that researchers can tailor to measure income levels generated in agriculture. The primary problem is that an excess labor supply burdens agriculture. At the same time, the supply of farm products grew more rapidly than demand exacerbating the problem, the opposite of Malthusian propositions.

Schultz implies the two significant difficulties of agriculture policy are its short- and long-term inefficiency. Studies find that agriculture productivity levels are 25 to 50 percent below general economic levels. Evidence suggests this waste is immense, primarily embedded in the millions of farm people's use of time, energy, and natural resources. However, there are a few isolated farming sectors that use resources better than most nonagriculture industries.

The Economic Stability of Agriculture

Trygve Haavelmo (1954) observes cycles of agriculture run independently of the general business cycle. Agricultural cycles have unique triggers. For instance, prices are low if there's an abundant supply of hogs. Consumers aren't prepared to eat more than normal quantities of pork. Low prices influence farmers decisions, but they don't affect them right away. Raising pigs takes time, plus there are psychological lags for the farmers in spotting changing conditions in the market. Once there's recognition of the abundance and low prices, they trim their herd. Then, after about a year and a half, low supplies of hogs appear because the farmers had a disincentive to raise more. This condition leads to high hog prices without a lag. These higher prices eventually lead to higher supplies of hogs in another year and a half.

The chief characteristic of this micro cycle is that prices and quantities move in opposite directions. This mechanism is present in most agricultural markets. Low crop prices still prevail at new planting times in the following years. Schultz (1949) suggests that economists should seek explanations for the tendencies toward this two-year price cycle. Lessening the instability of farm income should become a primary policy aim in the United States.

On the supply side, Schultz focused on the importance of farm technology progress to measure the effects of production changes. The farm problem isn't a food problem. It's an incentive problem. While in constant disequilibrium, unfortunately, contemporary economists emphasize market gluts, chronic shortages, and low farm prices. Instead, Schultz contends that public policy for agriculture should have the primary goal of the best distribution of the labor force, emphasizing reducing the excess supply of agricultural labor. Proposals should also seek improvements in the state of the art technology. On the one hand, international trade extends and enlarges the economic capacity to adjust to secular developments. But, on the other hand, difficulties also occur in differential effects in income elasticity among various farm products. Elasticity refers to the sensitivity of demand quantity to changes in price.

The primary effect of fluctuations in general business cycles on agriculture is that *food prices* correlate closely to these cycles. Therefore, Schulz proposes a compensatory system of price payments to farmers during recessions. Economists define this payment as the difference between market prices when farmers sell their products and prerecession prices. The procedure involves claims on government spending during a recession. These income transfers should be strictly countercyclical in design and independent of agricultural supply and demand. They shouldn't induce inconsistent decisions of agriculture production with long-run requirements and also not clog trade channels.

Economic Effects of Agricultural Programs

Schultz recalls that the United Nations embraced public policies for food and agriculture after World War II. Their emphasis in food policy was on nutrition benefits and acute food shortages. It also held a strong orientation toward general population welfare and progressive leadership.

The U.S. agricultural segment that emerged from the war was enlarged and competitively robust. However, these market conditions channeled agriculture into price policies unfavorable to foreign trade and adverse to any necessary adjustments. Meanwhile, the state department hatched a different global plan to achieve conditions favorable to multilateral trade. As a result, the United States drifted into concealed dumping policies, especially in farm products. International economic relations at the time were sufficiently disorganized to provide relief. Meanwhile, the United States remained committed to ineffective prewar policies for setting farm prices.

Schultz explored criteria for developing action programs, administrative machinery for economic effects, and assessing results. For example, government control of crop production is artificial, and storage policies aren't effective ways to supplement the farmer's income. Also, policies for loans have a more significant economic impact.

Friedrich Hayek (1960) observes that increased urban and industrial populations are always associated with developed countries' growth in wealth and civilization. However, this growth decreased the proportions and absolute numbers of the agricultural population. In addition, technological advances increase the productivity of human effort in food production. As a result, agriculture needs fewer workers to supply the more significant needs of the population.

Overall growth rates in the global general population is declining. Positive changes in income per capita reflect further advances in technology. However, though population increases cause proportional increases in demand for food, consumers spend less of their additional income on increased food consumption.

Unfortunately, the increase in farm productivity clashes with this inelastic demand. Therefore, if those engaged in agriculture want to maintain their average income, their numbers must decrease. Suppose such a redistribution of labor between agriculture and other occupations occurs. In that case, there's no reason agriculture shouldn't derive benefits from economic advances in the long term. But, if the agricultural population is large, the decline, while it proceeds, is bound to operate to its disadvantage. Hayek thinks the more significant the reluctance of farmers to shift to other occupations, the more influential the differences in income levels during transitions.

However, when public equality policy delays this adjustment, the problem is steadily compounded. The challenge of the agricultural population suffers from deliberate policy acts. The pain grew so large that equalizing productivity requires impractical shifts in a limited time. Most experts and sensible people in the West understand that agriculture policy's primary problem is to remove the government from control systems and restore market operations.

This topic discussed agricultural public policy, addressed agriculture's stability, and analyzed agricultural programs' economic effects. The section examined public agricultural economics by treating farming as a social institution, explaining the outgoing farm labor transition, and making public policy suggestions. The following section introduces growth theory.

Growth Theory

An economic concept highlighted by Adam Smith suggests that unlimited human wants foster ever-increasing productivity. This notion underpins growth or development theory. It means that real GDP per capita will perpetually increase, driven by the profit pursuits of people. We can apply lessons from successful economies to help developing countries modernize by harnessing these pursuits. This section introduces growth theory by describing its basics, recounts the evolution of its body of knowledge, and discusses economic development's mechanics.

Growth/Development Basics

The economic process of modernization is the path a developing nation trods in its evolution to a developed state. The ultimate milestone is where the balanced allocation of resources can provide its citizens with well-being. This section provides an overview of growth or development theory. It discusses the core of modern growth theory, examines the global economic picture, and explores long-range concepts of economic development theory.

Economic Growth

Paul Samuelson (1948) suggests that the analysis of fundamental economic growth should examine factors leading to potential output growth in the *long term*. Growth in output per capita should be an essential government objective because it's associated with rising real incomes and living standards. He thinks capital accumulation with a complementary labor force should form the core of modern growth theory in neoclassical growth models. This approach uses a tool known as *aggregate production functions* to relate inputs and technology to total potential GDP.

According to Samuelson, proportional output per worker sometimes increases (labor intensity) without changes in technology and innovation. This condition occurs because diminishing returns of capital don't match increases in capital per worker. Hence, expanding capital lowers capital return rates while raising real wages. Changes in technology increase the producible output for given sets of input. In addition, these changes push the aggregate functions of production upward, making more output available with the same infusion of labor and capital. A branch of growth theory seeks to uncover the processes generating technological changes. Samuelson analyzed economic growth trends in the 20th and 21st centuries. These significant trends are consistent with neoclassical growth models and augmented by technological advances.

Theory of Evolutionary Dissimilarities

Trygve Haavelmo (1954) examined the global economic picture through international statistics and finds striking economic dissimilarities among nations. There were regions where millions starved, and lacking tools hampered productivity. In other places, books and magazines flooded society, while in still others, illiterates were in the majority. Haavelmo suggests economies need efficient planning for practical operations. He analyzes their public policies by clarifying basic principles.

Haavelmo discerned the guiding principles of the individuals responsible for directing the economic policy of their respective countries. He found the underlying reasoning underwhelming and sought more concrete answers in social science. Unfortunately, theories regarding the nature of long-range economic developments weren't abundant in the economic literature in the 1950s. Therefore, Haavelmo selected several variables to analyze. They include regional indexes of the total output of production, sizes of the regional population, indexes of total accumulated capital and education, and indexes of the level of technical knowledge.

Long-range concepts of economic development theory base their foundation on functions of production. Haavelmo evaluated the productivity growth and population time paths in his production function. Dynamic models, even those with influences of random shock, have deterministic properties. Haavelmo's primary emphasis in his simple treatment of economic growth models is their formal properties. He distinguishes the structural parameters of the model and those describing the system's initial conditions.

This section provided an overview of growth or development theory. It discussed the core of modern growth theory, examined the global economic picture, and explored long-range concepts of economic development theory. The next topic introduces several growth theories.

Theory of Economic Growth

Growth theorists search developed countries for successful recipes for resource allocation. This topic traces the evolution of the branch. It debates the presence of inside and outside factors, explores the expansion of fundamental freedom, and suggests prosperity and depression are relative concepts.

Arthur Lewis (1955), a professor at Princeton University, focuses on expansion in *output per capita*. He is concerned with its growth rate, not distribution. His interest isn't primarily product demand but goosing production while tempering consumption. This output growth per capita is a supply-side issue and depends on available natural resources and human behavior. Lewis believes the natural resources of climate, fresh water, fertile soil, valuable minerals, and a topography facilitating transportation are essential. However, he mainly pays close attention to human behavior and is concerned with natural resources only as they affect this human behavior.

He conducts his inquiry into human actions at various levels. He employs this approach because there are causes of proximate growth and causes of the causes. For example, his first cause is reducing costs in the system, either by reducing the cost of production or by increasing yield through inputs of effort. Secondly, there's an increase in knowledge and its applications. This process has occurred throughout human history. However, more rapid growth in output in recent centuries was associated with a more rapid accumulation of knowledge and production applications. Lastly, growth depends on increasing capital or other resources per capita.

Lewis concludes that growth is the result of human effort. However, societies widely differ in how vigorously members seek out and exploit opportunities. People make unequal efforts to acquire wealth if their *attitude* toward action differs. Social conventions and taboos restrict opportunity in blatant ways. Lewis evaluates the scope that community institutions offer to promote economic growth efforts. He realized people wouldn't make an effort unless the institutions assured them of the fruits of their labor. Contrarily, some romantic philosophers suggest humans are creatures who only work for the pleasure of creative effort.

Lewis, like Hayek and Sen, thought the growth of income per capita in developed countries is rightly associated with the growth of economic freedom. Therefore, he examines obstacles to institutional liberty. He notes that we don't necessarily take the most reasonable road to economic development. Lewis suggests attitudes and institutions may favor growth but often must counter cultural doctrines. For example, primitive societies widely practice the concept of family unity. In contrast, in modern Western societies, middle- and upper-class women fight battles to obtain the right to work.

Extensions of commerce and specialization are also vital parts of economic growth. Lewis shows that economic exchange stimulates specialization because the division of labor depends on the extent of markets. The larger the markets, the greater the potential for specialization. Every community has sections of the population specializing in producing manufactured articles as independent producers. Production on a small scale, whether in homes or small workshops, will best survive in industries with no standardized mass demand.

Lewis also examines the accumulation and application of knowledge. He suggests there are always gaps between what experts know on how to do things efficiently and what ordinary people do. The learning growth rate in literate, prescientific societies depends on philosophical attitudes. The Renaissance stimulated the growth of knowledge in every field. So it is profitable and advantageous if society accepts new knowledge from the experts and applies it to production.

Lewis considers the relationships between resources, population, and output. For example, there's no empirical evidence of birth rates rising with economic growth. He also contends that governments sometimes need to influence the usage of resources because price mechanisms give results that are not always socially acceptable.

An MIT professor, Robert Solow (1970), surveys macroeconomic growth theories. He suggests they might have simple frameworks but are capable of surprising elaboration. For example, real output per capita constantly grows over extended periods. On the other hand, real capital stocks grow at constant rates to *exceed* the growth rates of labor input. Moreover, growth rates of real output and capital goods stocks tend to grow at about the same rate, so capital-to-output ratios show no systematic trends. Finally, output per capita growth rates differ from country to country.

Solow also perceived growth in the money supply isn't constant in growing economies in the long term. He tackled further applications of growth theory by examining public investment. He develops growth theories regarding the endogenous growth of the 1980s, including contributions from Paul Romer. They conclude that growth rates of consumption per capita, output per capita, and capital per capita are equal to exogenous growth rates of technology. This conclusion assumes progressive rates of labor-augmenting technology.

Solow provided road maps for the landscape of contemporary growth theory. In the days before inexpensive computing, there weren't effective ways to study paths of nonsteady states. Once comprehensive approaches, and not just stable conditions become the primary objectives of growth theory, broader and deeper economic issues surface.

Romer's (1994) theory distinguishes itself from neoclassical growth by emphasizing that economic growth also results from internal systems. Endogenous growth implies output is growing faster than exogenous factors alone. This emphasis contrasts with Solow's exogenous-only technology effects. Furthermore, Romer uncovers that economies' choices in private and public sectors cause variances in growth rates across countries. Finally, he explores whether the income of different countries per capita converges. On Robert Lucas's model, he cites the failure of cross-country convergence.

Romer observes enough evidence to reject all earlier growth models in the 1950s through the 1970s. He feels the economics profession changed how they viewed international trade, development, economic growth, and economic geography. Paul Krugman (1995), a *New York Times* columnist and a professor at the City University of New York, investigates the evolution of concepts in development theory and economic geography. He found a circularity exists. Economists find opportunities where countries experience self-reinforcing behavior of industrialization. At the same time, it can also be a condition where there is a failure to industrialize enough. This irregular movement of goods changes the geography of market potential, typically reinforcing or not, the advantages of already-favored locations. His main point is that solutions can be found in economic geography and developmental economics, which mainstream economists ignore. They are unwilling to consider what they can't formalize (Donald Rumsfeld's unknown unknowns).

Like Hayek and Lewis, Amartya Sen (1999) suggests that economic development also expands people's basic freedoms. This focus on human freedoms contrasts with narrower development views, such as associating the narrative with growth in GDP. Of course, growth in GDP is essential for expanding the privileges enjoyed by members of society. But freedom also depends on other determinants, such as social and economic arrangements. Still, other factors are political and civil rights.

Sen suggests that people in the world suffer from various unfreedoms. If development is to occur, policy makers must remove significant sources of unfreedom like poverty and tyranny. Once they mitigate these sources, they should treat individual freedoms as basic building blocks. Sen's evaluative approach concentrates on empirical data and a more traditional analysis of practical ethics and economic policy. These instrumental freedoms directly enhance the capabilities of people, but they also supplement and reinforce one another. For example, poor economies have less money to spend on health care and education.

The Growth Model and an Accounting Framework

Edward Prescott (2002) thinks economic prosperity and depression are relative concepts. He looks at the significant international differences among developed industrial countries and the changes in these differences over time. These countries all have healthy market economies and well-educated populations. However, variations in aggregate output per working-age person are significant. He uses available measures of factor input to identify changes in policy or policy differences that give rise to prosperity or depression.

The two critical elements of Prescott's growth theory models are the aggregate production functions of stand-in firms and the utility of stand-in households. Technology is a central element of his thinking. Capital factors depend on how policy makers tax them and the nature of distortions in capital markets. Productivity is the key factor. Economists can also use growth theory to study secular growth and fluctuations in business cycles.

This topic traced the evolution of growth theory. It debated the presence of inside and outside factors, explored the expansion of fundamental freedom, and suggested that prosperity and depression are relative concepts. The following section takes a look at the underlying operations of economic development.

Mechanics of Economic Development

Growth theory has many moving parts due to its complexity. This topic explores the more subtle details of growth theory. It features constructing models, discussing the accumulated knowledge of human capital, and synthesizing other economists' transition models.

A University of Chicago professor, Robert Lucas (2002) examined the original development theory describing industrialized economic behavior. Then, he attempted to adapt the modern growth approach to obtain a cohesive grasp of rich and poor economies in a world of vast differences in income and growth rates. First, he uses theoretical methods in a series of mathematically explicit models. Then, Lucas reconstructs them to exhibit certain observed behaviors. These behaviors include sustained income growth, sustained or increasing inequality, episodes of trade-related development, and demographical transitions.

Lucas examines economic development problems to account for observed patterns across countries and time, income levels, and growth rates per capita. He follows Solow's neoclassical model and considers two new adaptations to incorporate the effects on human capital. First, he focuses on technology and abstracts from demographic economics to take population as given. Second, Lucas formalizes the thinking of decisions of individuals to acquire knowledge and the consequences on productivity of the decision.

Lucas suggests that the primary growth engine of economic knowledge is the *accumulated knowledge* of human capital. This accumulation occurs in schools, research organizations, and factories. For society to sustain such learning, workers and managers must continue to take on new tasks. Lucas also thinks real production per capita in a world constantly evolves. Models forecasting the next century predict that, eventually, all nations will join the industrial revolution. It assumes people are alike. Their behavior differences are primarily due to differences in resources at their disposal.

Both classical and modern production theories succeed in accounting for the central features of the contemporary behavior of production and population. By introducing fertility decisions into growth theory, Lucas views the industrial revolution and associated fertility level reductions, known as *demographic transitions*, as various aspects of single economic events. He examined the evidence underlying the scenario he studied and suggested using the term, the *industrial revolution*, to refer to the onset of sustained income growth per capita. The most striking feature of his thinking is aggregating types of behavior.

Asymmetric Equilibria of Steady States

The central theme of Lucas' models is that worker incomes in steady states are determined independently of technology or levels of population and resources. Despite awareness of the importance of physical and human capital accumulation, classical economists lacked methods to observe how its possibility affects equilibrium values.

Lars Peter Hansen et al. (1995) and Edward Prescott (2002) provide an alternative explanation of transitions from Malthusian economic states to perpetually growing ones. In their approach, the economy initially produces goods with land and labor using technology without any growth engine. There are also fertility relationships linking population to production levels per capita. If land-use technology is the only one operating, the economy remains in a steady state called Malthusian. Hansen and Prescott postulate a second technology using labor but not land. It improves at exogenously given rates like Solow's.

Lucas' (2002) point of departure assumes the existence of two production technologies. His model produces goods with these technologies, one using labor and land and the other using skilled labor only. Lucas tries to imagine economic environments consistent with the facts of both classical and modern economic theories that economists designed them to explain.

However, the industrial revolution isn't exclusively an event of technology. Depending on where such inventions occur, they induce essential shifts within the relative power of different societies. The histories of politics and the military are tales of conflict over how economies distribute this share of power. Lucas argues that incorporating the decision of fertility into growth theories sharpens the thinking of economists on the kinds of growth in human capital essential to increase income.

Lucas synthesizes transition models from other economists where land per capita and human capital levels are states' variables. The onset of the industrial revolution also generated an improved understanding of its gradual diffusion of development. Like Krugman, he feels geography is part of the reason for the diffusion. Lucas suggests that population growth attains an upper bound at a point where it either remains steady or declines. However, there are few theoretical models relating the growth rate of the population to the growth rate of knowledge.

This topic explored the finer points of a growth theory. It featured constructing models, discussion the accumulated knowledge of human capital, and synthesizing other economists' transition models. The section introduced growth theory by describing its basics, recounting the evolution of its body of knowledge, and explores economic development's mechanics. The following section addresses what could go wrong with growth theory.

Problems of Growth

Recipes for modernizing a developing country may look good on paper, but factors on the ground sometimes hinder progress. Let's investigate some of these obstacles. This section examines the shortfalls. It identifies development obstacles, analyzes historical growth patterns, and presents competing views of growth.

Development Obstacles

Capital Formation

Simon Kuznets (1973) of Yale University examines the quantitative aspects of capital formation. He analyzed the global conditions of capital from 1850 to 1970. Whether economists judge these ratios of formations of capital as high or low depends on the criteria used. This topic describes sources and trends of capital formation, analyzes changes in modern economic growth theory, and discusses the world's widespread hunger, undernourishment, and periodic famines.

A significant source of economic growth is the magnitude of capital formation embodied by technological changes. Proportions of capital formation to GDP rose significantly during the modern era of economic growth in many countries. Kuznets doesn't accept that economists *require* high ratios of capital formation because some successful countries maintain low and constant ratios of capital formation.

Trends in the structures of domestic capital formation aren't easy to identify. For example, there are wide divergences in incremental capital ratios to output. Moreover, international differences in these ratios aren't reducible to differences in industry structures. Kuznets detects a gradual rise in capital ratios to GDP in most countries through the period studied. However, capital formation percentages were significantly lower from 1850 to 1970 than in the modern period.

Changes in Modern Economic Growth

Kuznets suggests economic growth represents the build-up of capacity to supply increasingly diverse economic goods to its population in the long term. Advancing technology may be a source of economic growth but sometimes only a potential one and not a necessary condition for equilibrium. Moreover, the progress of technology and its pace differ over the centuries and among the world's regions.

The primary characteristic of modern economic growth is the high production growth rates per capita in developed countries. Kuznets contends that the transformation rates in these economies' structures were high. Developed countries reach out to the rest of the world, thus making for one world. However, *economic performance* only limits the spread of modern economic growth. These characteristics are interrelated. The mass application of technological innovations is closely related to the further progress of science. In turn, it generates the basis for advances in other technology.

The changes in living standards exhibited by urbanization involve various costs and returns. Unfortunately, these factors are not included in existing economic measurements such as GDP and are therefore unobservable. The structural differences represent the shift of the relative sector shares in the economy. It was apparent to Kuznets that given the complexity of modern society, there is a need to develop a new quantitative measure to captures the essential aspects of economic performance meaningfully.

Kuznets observes rich nations produce a high volume of economic goods relative to their population size. This abundance exists because the quantities of physical assets approximate the level of control over the production of goods. The long-term production level per capita measure is still the most reasonable criterion of national wealth and poverty. However, some nations, particularly smaller ones, show sustained elevated production levels per capita because nature richly endowed them with the natural resources desired by others.

Gaps appear between developed nations and poor, less-developed nations. The significance of aggregates and structure gaps depends on the magnitude and number of societies at either end of the comparison, called the *population base*.

Famines and Other Crises

Amartya Sen (1999) noted that the world has widespread hunger, undernourishment, and frequent famines. Tacit pessimism often dominates the international reactions to these miseries. Unfortunately, there's little factual basis for this pessimism of assuming that nature can fix hunger and deprivation. He is mainly concerned with the transitory nature of famines and other transient crises. They may or may not include open starvation but involve sudden outbreaks of extreme poverty in a significant population segments.

Moreover, hunger isn't related only to food production and the expansion of agriculture. The political economy of causation and prevention of famine also involves institutions and organizations. Sen analyzes the economics of these institutions for their ability to prevent starvation. How the economic process distributes the total food supply between separate groups within the country is crucially important, even when opportunities for international trade are absent.

Democracy has a role in preventing famines. The causal connection between democracy and famines' nonoccurrence isn't hard to see. For example, since the economic reforms of 1979, official Chinese pronouncements have provided ample justification for the importance of financial incentives. Sen feels this preventive role of democracy fits nicely into the demand for protective security. He thinks economic development challenges include eliminating persistent endemic deprivation and preventing sudden severe poverty.

This topic described sources and trends of capital formation, analyzed changes in modern economic growth theory, and discussed the world's widespread hunger, undernourishment, and recurring famines. The following section analyzes historical patterns of growth.

Historical Patterns of Growth

Michael Spence (2011) at New York University examines the development of the Industrial Revolution. This section introduces Spence's views on growth theory. Then, it discerns a pattern of shifted social behavior after World War II. Finally, it suggests ways to understand high growth in the developing world.

Up to 1750, economic growth was negligible everywhere. By modern standards, there existed a small, commercially oriented middle class. Then, around 1750, England headed out on a new industrial revolution course. Per capita incomes began to rise. Sustained growth accelerated for the first time in history. The pattern spread rapidly in the 19th century to continental Europe and the United States, Canada, Australia, and New Zealand.

By 1950, the average incomes of people in these countries increased 20 times. Applying science and technology to production, coordination, communication, management, and institutional innovation drove this new growth. Changes in governance and how politics and government interacted with the economy also contributed to this growth. However, outside this group of nations, the prior years' simple patterns of stagnant economic behavior continued.

Spence recounts that this mixed pattern of global behavior shifted again after World War II. Finally, after two centuries of divergence, patterns of high-speed convergence have taken over. Advanced countries grew at high rates in the immediate postwar period, thanks mainly to successful recoveries after the war among the victorious and defeated. A few developing countries also grew at high speeds. People, human capital, and knowledge formed the basis for sustainable wealth creation.

In addition to economics, Spence suggests a broader range of social issues generates faster growth in developing countries. Countries spend extended periods in a mode of no growth or low growth. Global governance needs to catch up to the levels of economic interdependence. It's labor productivity that determines personal incomes in a market economy. Over time, productivity gains happen when policy makers add capital and market incentives.

Spence suggests one way to understand high growth in the developing world is to look at the successful cases where economies achieve sustained high growth. Then, determine what they have in common. For example, a rapidly expanding modernization and expansion period began post–World War II. The Global Agreement on Tariffs and Trade of 1947 hatched this growing openness. It removed barriers to trade policy.

Spence implies that the practical aspects of growth and development are physical and measurable. However, parallel processes of accumulating intangible assets and capabilities and how they interact also exist. Moreover, the vast global market enables developing countries to specialize in producing what they can do proficiently.

Spence explains that the worldwide economy divides goods and services into tradables and nontradables. One country produces tradables another consumes, such as electronics, autos, and industrial machinery. However, a country must domestically produce the nontradable goods it needs while specializing in providing tradables where they have a competitive advantage. The government's primary role is facilitating structural change by investing in human capital, protecting people in transitions through income support, and providing access to essential services.

The nongovernment sector is the most critical driver of the internal dynamics that sustain high growth. The supporting role of government is to foster an environment where the private sector is profitable. This dynamic cuts loose competitive dynamics. Sustainable development requires markets to provide price signals, develop incentives, and guide the allocation of resources. Unfortunately, Schumpeter's process of creative destruction may be chaotic, but it is effective, especially at high growth rates.

Spence thinks it's a strategic mistake to safeguard people by protecting their employers. However, older workers present a unique problem in a rapidly changing economy. Education and infrastructure are principal investments in the public sector's needs to support growth. He suggests education is an investment to create public benefits and private returns. Unfortunately, economists observe widespread underinvestment in education in poorer developing countries.

Spence suggests that economic freedom and inclusiveness are closely related. However, economic freedom isn't the same thing as democracy. He believes success in economic performance has attributes. Government should be competent. Spence laments that most developing countries haven't yet achieved sustained growth patterns. A sustained lack of progress in a world where the majority is experiencing expanding opportunity has problematic consequences. In addition, he associates security challenges with the persistent lack of growth.

In developing countries, social lethargy translates the immediate demand of day-to-day life into political pressures. Dysfunctional governance is a different source of failure. Many poorer and lower-growth countries are small. Spence recalls that during the 2008 crisis, it was apparent that significant multinational efforts were needed to stimulate economic contractions. The problem was the leakages of capital flows. The result was neither fully noncooperative outcomes nor fully cooperative ones.

Industrial countries experienced bouts of severe financial instability in the 2008 crisis. Ironically, some developing countries formerly considered more vulnerable during the same period stayed remarkably resilient. Technology contributed to the solution. The penetration of mobile cell phones is high in many developing countries and is rising in the rest. In achieving connectivity in the developing world, cell phones solved the communication and lack of infrastructure problems. It's hard to overstate the economic importance of this trend. Payments, savings, and credit become accessible to a broader group.

This section introduced Spence's views on growth theory. Next, it discerned a shift in social behavior after World War II. Finally, it suggested ways to understand high growth in the developing world. The following topic introduces competing views of growth theory.

Competing Views of Growth

Economists don't always agree on the proper way to apply growth theory. This topic presents the views of several economists with varying opinions. It suggests global convergence is like a single firm subject to diminishing returns laws. Some economists compare different economies rather than individual firms or people. The topic also discusses why the economy doesn't always smoothly deliver resources to their most productive use.

Abhijit Banerjee and Esther Duflo (2019) contemplate the sustainability of economic growth. Continuous growth over a long time is unprecedented, but that doesn't mean it can happen again. Fortunately, the incentives for innovation are at all-time highs. The number of countries leading booms of technology is expanding. Growth can explode again, fueled by another industrial revolution. Artificial intelligence can power economic development, even teaching us to write better legal briefs and tell better jokes.

Banerjee and Duflo think the existing measure of GDP doesn't do an adequate job of gauging well-being. For instance, the cost of providing social media has little connection with the well-being it generates. Ironically, a slowdown in measured productivity growth coincided with the explosion of social media. The dilemma is that economists can't determine how much economic value to assign these free products. They try to develop this value by estimating people's willingness to pay. They attempt to measure hours of browsing instead of working and earning money.

Solow (1970) suggests that growth eventually slows because people start saving earlier in their life cycle. This slowing generates more money to invest and makes more capital available per worker. However, it lessens the need for workers and lowers the return on capital investment, discouraging savings. His theory implies growth will likely slow down after a fast phase, following dramatic transformations. On the other hand, Solow's concept of convergence involves countries' scarce capital and abundant labor. They should grow faster because they haven't yet reached their collective balanced growth. These countries can prosper by improving the balance between work and capital. As a result, one expects the process to reduce differences in GDP per worker across countries over time. Poorer countries eventually catch up with their more affluent counterparts.

Solow predicts that GDP growth rates per capita among rich countries will not differ once the global economy reaches balanced growth. The only differences come from total factor productivity. For rich countries, this growth is about the same. Finally, Solow determines what drove technology upgrading in countries already at the forefront. This process may apply to countries already on balanced growth paths but might not work for ones where capital is scarce.

Paul Romer (1996) thinks of global convergence as a single firm subject to diminishing returns laws. To undo the Solow effect assumes an economy with more capital also has a more productive capital base. Romer argues that Silicon Valley firms use less traditional physical capital and more human capital. This shift toward human capital features a different specialized skill set than conventional manufacturing. These tech firms hire clever employees hoping they'll produce brilliant and marketable ideas.

Because Solow's and Romer's theories operate at levels of entire economies, Banerjee and Duflo (2019) compare different economies rather than individual firms or people. This comparison is always challenging because economies tend to differ in many ways. For example, growth in a specific country region is more evolved than average national development because it cannibalizes growth from the rest of the economy. It draws away capital, skills, and labor from other areas. It's hoped the benefits of the gains in the more developed regions offset the costs of the losses to the other areas. Nevertheless, growth in developing countries is essential for most economists and entrepreneurs because of its implication for human welfare.

The Smoothness of Resource Production

In growth theories, economists assume the economy smoothly delivers resources to their most productive use. Therefore when growth fails, the lack of adoption of available technologies isn't just a problem for poor households. Some firms have more employees than they need, while others cannot hire enough. Unfortunately, society breeds this misallocation into the national culture. For instance, in slower economies, owners like leaving their children a running business and prefer to avoid the risk of outside control associated with external financing.

Growth seems to slow down as countries reach certain income levels per capita. Nevertheless, many critical successes of the last few decades directly result from a policy focused on outcomes, even in some developing countries. Banerjee and Duflo think that policy makers should focus on outcomes. They should place a strong emphasis on the well-being of the poorest. It offers the chance to change millions of lives more profoundly than finding recipes for the small increases in growth in rich countries.

This topic presented the views of several economists. It suggested global convergence is like a single firm subject to diminishing returns laws. Some economists compared different economies rather than individual firms or people. The topic also discussed why the economy doesn't always smoothly deliver resources to their most productive use. The section examined what could go wrong. It identified development obstacles, analyzed historical growth patterns, and presented competing views of growth. This chapter explored the field of economic modernization and opened with a section on agriculture economics. A discussion followed on growth theory and the challenges it creates. Because bread is essential to life, this chapter clarifies the processes happening in all economies but doesn't contribute much to loaf choice. The next chapter introduces international economics.

CHAPTER 9

International Economics

In the last chapter, we looked at how developing nations transition to developed ones. One feature in the previous few decades has been the explosion of globalization. This chapter looks at both types of countries and how they interact globally. It discusses global trade, international finance, and world public policy.

Global Trade

Nations exchange goods, services, and capital in international trade. Trading globally exposes consumers and countries to goods and services unavailable or more expensive domestically. This section analyzes trade models, focuses on factor movement, and weighs in on interregional activities.

Trade Models

Economists construct trade models to illustrate how international trade occurs in simple cases between two countries and a one-product market. First, they base the models on each country's separate supply and demand functions. Next, the researchers identify domestic equilibrium prices and quantities for a given product market in these two countries. Finally, differences between domestic prices play a role in determining the direction of trade flow. In this topic, our laureates present their trade models. It describes the dynamics of these models and forms helpful conclusions.

Interregional Trade Conditions

Bertil Ohlin (1933), a Swedish economist and politician, developed a theory of international trade in harmony with the mutual-interdependence pricing theory. His approach falls outside the classical labor theory of value. Moreover, he demonstrates that international trade theory is only one part of the *general location theory*. General location theory considers the geographic aspects of pricing. Ohlin develops certain fundamentals of this location theory as background for international trade theory. He also examines local differences in the supply of factors of production within each country.

Ohlin analyzes the movements of domestic and external production factors, particularly product activity. In addition, he explores the various mechanisms of international trade and global capital trends under conditions of fixed rates of foreign exchange. He stresses that understanding the *geographical* distribution of factors of production is essential. Ohlin establishes a doctrine of one-market theory. The dimension of space is vital in economic life because natural conditions confine aspects of production to specific localities and relocate only with difficulty. A region, in some respects, is a unit requiring economies of scale to differentiate it from other areas. There are also interregional differences in the endowment of production factors. Regions manifest these differences in relative prices of raw materials and factor prices as conditions of trade.

Interdependence of Regions

Ohlin, a professor at the Stockholm School of Economics, presents the interdependence of prices of goods and production factors in each trading region by painting a simple picture of the price mechanisms. The total requirements of each element in all industries determine the supply of this factor. Commodity prices are equal to the cost of production obtained by multiplying the quantity of each required factor by its price. As a result, rich regions export goods cheaper than other regions and import the rest.

Regions, like individuals, reap certain advantages from *specialization*. Each area has a limited supply of production factors and usually cannot produce everything it wants efficiently at home. Some effects on trade are due to economies of large-scale production. Ohlin applies the theory of interregional trade to the particular case where regions are different countries. Nations are the most significant type of region because national borders have more distinctive characteristics than borders within countries, and harbor a community of mutual interest.

Obstacles such as the cost of transportation reduce trade. Ohlin addresses the relative cost of transporting goods at various stages of production from the point of view of *production locations*. The *transportation facilities* of different nations also influence international trade. Countries with good transportation facilities in the interior and possessing plenty of resources produce copious quantities of goods and also have significant foreign exchange. On the other hand, countries located far from outside sources and markets of raw materials primarily export easily transportable goods.

What's important for goods in the earlier stages of production isn't only natural resources but efficient transportation facilities. The character of industry and trade depends on these facilities, supplies of factors, and other essential elements. Ohlin thinks of countries as groups of locations. The controlling details for the site of industry and international trade on the demand side are the tastes of individuals and the desire for ownership of the factors of production.

He suggests that the monetary mechanism is the primary difference between domestic and international capital movements. Capital moves only in goods and services but is not freely mobile geographically. Moreover, the monetary instrument varies with the monetary system's organization and central banks' habits and traditions regarding credit policy.

International Relations

Arthur Lewis (1955) thinks a country's level of participation in international trade depends on several factors. It is partly resources, partly the barriers it places in business, and partly its stage of economic development. Also, the causes of international migration are numerous and not all associated with economic growth. For example, some large migrations of history avoided famine and hunger.

Samuelson (1948) demonstrates that free trade raises GDP. There is more to go around for everybody. However, presenting anything definitive about commerce by comparing countries is difficult because growth and inequality depend on many elements. In his view, there's a unique wage for every worker with the same skills. However, Banerjee and Duflo (2019) differ from Samuelson. To them, labor markets are sticky because wages rarely fall at the same rate they rise. Given this stickiness, countries hunker down when negative news arrives from greater competition abroad. They hope the problem disappears on its own instead of embracing it and allocating resources to their best use.

Other trade barriers include the unwillingness of importers to do business with unknown manufacturers due to the uncertainty of the transaction. On the other hand, the value of a brand name of large manufacturers wards off competition and reduces importers risk. This outsized role of reputation means international trade isn't only about reasonable prices, innovative ideas, low tariffs, and cheap transportation. Banerjee and Duflo suggest continued gains from trade depend primarily on how much a nation imports and the extent to which tariffs, cost of transportation, and the other costs of trading internationally influence these imports. On the other hand, if the product desirability remains unchanged even as prices change, the importing country likes what they buy abroad, and trade increases welfare.

International trade is much more critical for smaller and poorer countries. This condition exists because skills and capital in these countries are often scarce. Poor domestic integration also makes economies sticky. Conversely, international trade gains are small for a large economy like the United States.

Samuelson suggests any solution to labor force dislocations affected by changes in trade patterns involves limiting the number of affected workers. Countries can assist them by helping them relocate, switch jobs, or find a way to receive better wages. Contrary to other economists, Banerjee and Duflo seem to think policy makers should *subsidize firms* adversely affected by trade. For instance, they can reduce payroll taxes in some specific areas. However, their proposal has practical difficulties. Banerjee and Duflo feel society needs to squarely address the pain, along with helping workers change locations. Other economists take for granted that they can quickly move to new jobs or locations.

In this topic, several economists presented trade models. Then, it described the dynamics of these models and formed helpful conclusions. The following section describes the movements of the factors of production.

Factor Movements

Factor Movements and Commodity Movements

Bertil Ohlin (1933) stresses that the obstacles to the movement of interregional *production factors* vary with the type of region under consideration. Natural resources are immobile. The stimulus to ensure laborers and capitalists overcome relocation obstacles is primarily the need to raise prices. The policy makers can also determine the catalyst necessary to overcome the difficulties. Therefore, it's clear that different workers and different units of capital can meet the challenges of differing magnitudes. The trade volume depends on the absolute amount of production in various regions. This topic describes factor and commodity movements, discusses the location of industry, and analyzes transportation facilities.

Ohlin distinguishes production locations between producers who produce the raw materials in one place and those that finish the product in another. Therefore, the site of the industry to create a finished product depends on the relative transferability of raw materials and finished goods. First, he examines the location of industries producing raw materials and their markets. It gets more complicated with several resource markets and products with similar raw material sources. If raw materials prices are equal at all locations, the case is simple. However, the cost of raw materials may differ at various sources. Ohlin argues that even if all sources of raw materials have equal quality, the demand for some may be greater than for others.

The location of consumer markets is also essential. Areas often have exceptionally close associations with related sites where transportation lines converge. In addition, these activity centers offer good transportation facilities for manufacturing. Economies of large scale are essential in the transportation industries, no less than in production in a narrow sense.

Ohlin suggests that the movement of labor and capital also influences transportation relationships, just as transportation lines adapt to traffic demand. Improving transportation facilities that producers route through concentrations of economic activity, where they're already favorable, attracts additional population and production.

He maintains that everything depends on everything else in economic life. Differences in the local costs and supplies of production factors affect the locations of production factors and interregional trade within countries. This relationship is similar to international differences affecting foreign commerce. The raw materials factor of production moves quickly between some regions and with great difficulty between others. Therefore, Ohlin divides areas depending on the economic problem under analysis.

This section described factor and commodity movements, studied the location of industry, and analyzed transportation facilities. The following topic explores interregional activities.

Interregional Activities

Trygve Haavelmo (1954) examines the characteristics of economic interactions in networks of regions. First, there's a possible natural competition for a share of limited resources. However, there are other ways of acquiring goods and services than production and peaceful trade sources. An essential type of trade is exchanging knowledge, ideas, and ideologies. Measuring levels of education and expertise and comparing these data to each region is complex. Education is contagious. The receptiveness of an area to the intensity of education depends strongly on the level of education already existing. It also depends on the level of material wealth.

Haavelmo emphasizes that the causes of large migrations are complex. Therefore, in arriving at an economic theory of migration, Haavelmo considers the economic conditions in various regions and the thought processes of the economic reasoning of prospective emigrants.

Banerjee and Duflo (2019) suggest migration pervades the politics of the United States and Europe by the way it disturbs the balance of the local labor force. They think this emphasis is overblown and present data supporting their view. Furthermore, they feel it's racial alarmism, driven by intermingling a fear of race and myths of purity. The only valid reason for a disconnect is economics. Millions of potential migrants can earn more if they find a way to get to the West.

But unfortunately, the West perceives the arrival of immigrants as driving down wages in destination countries and making everyone worse off. However, Banerjee and Duflo contend that this argument is also wrong. There's no credible evidence that low-skilled immigrants hurt the domestic population due to the structure of job markets. On the contrary, it makes everyone better off.

Wage differences among the regions aren't crucial because many could make the move but don't. While living standards in parts of the world are below Western standards, they exist at levels where it is tolerable, and inhabitants aren't anxious to leave. So, it's not enough to compare the earnings of migrants with those remaining at home. Abundant evidence supports the notions of significant episodes of immigration that lift the prospects of whole domestic economies with minor effects on negative wages. This principle is that supply and demand structures accommodate the influx.

Another stabilizing reason is that migrants increase the demand for domestic labor, which slows the mechanization process. Employers reorganize production following influxes of migrants by creating new roles for native groups with low skills. Without foreign connections, the attractions of the home country go beyond creature comforts. Banerjee and Duflo suggest migration is a plunge into the unknown. The actual migration crisis isn't that there's too much international migration.

The section analyzed trade models, focused on factor movement, and weighed in on interregional activities. The following section describes international finance.

International Finance

Before the collapse of the 1944 Bretton Woods Agreement in 1973, the global currency system was a combination of *fixed and adjustable pegs*. Governments would interfere with trade flows to manipulate exchange rates. As a result, international trade was not efficient. Currently, the global system features *free-floating rates* with minimal trade interference. Let's investigate the characteristics and history of the two systems. This section explores international finance. It discusses financial globalization, suggests growth policies, and recounts currency crises.

Basics of International Finance

In national accounting, Paul Samuelson (1948) characterizes exports as credit items while imports are debits. More generally, credit items are transactions to increase a country's holdings of foreign currencies. Conversely, debit items are ones to reduce the holding of foreign currencies. One significant component of the balance of payments is the *current account*. It includes merchandise trade, services, investment income, and transfers. The other account is the *financial account* consisting of changes in the official reserves of the government and private sectors. The fundamental rule of balance-of-payments is that the sums of both these accounts nets to zero.

International trade and finance introduces a new element to a domestic economy: exposure to different national currencies. Relative prices or foreign exchange rates link them. So, for example, when Americans import Japanese goods, they must pay Japanese yen. The interaction of these supplies and demands determines the foreign exchange rate. Samuelson thinks of a fall in the market price of a currency as depreciation, and an increase is an appreciation. According to the theory of purchase power parity of exchange rates, rates tend to move with changes in relative prices in different countries.

The Market for Foreign Exchange

Fabozzi et al. (2013) review the spot market for exchange rates and hedging foreign exchange risk markets. They define an exchange rate as two parties exchanging the amount of one currency for another currency. Exchange rates are free to float in developed countries and some developing ones. By custom, exchange markets typically quote an exchange rate in the home currency (except yen/dollar). According to the *purchasing power parity* relationship, the exchange rate between two countries is proportional to domestic prices and inversely proportional to prices in the foreign market.

Fabozzi et al. (2013) note that the foreign exchange market is an over-the-counter market dominated by large international banks. A cash stream denominated in a foreign currency exposes an investor or issuer to foreign exchange risk. There are instruments that borrowers and investors use to hedge against adverse movements of foreign exchange rates, such as currency options and futures. They are similar to other derivatives and use currency exchange rates as their notional value.

Financial Globalization

This topic discusses Milton Friedman's thoughts on the threat of losing economic freedom through trade and his tirade against currency controls.

Despite its technical character and forbidding complexity, Milton Friedman (1962) thought the subject of international monetary arrangements could be a severe threat to economic freedom. His observations suggest that imposing straightforward *foreign exchange controls* is the most effective way to convert a market economy into an authoritarian economic society. Unfortunately, this step leads to rationing imports and controlling domestic production in never-ending spirals.

The U.S. residents and their government seek to buy foreign currencies with dollars to purchase goods and services in other countries. At the same time, foreigners want to acquire dollars with foreign currencies for corresponding purposes. As a result, Friedman maintains that markets force down domestic prices relative to foreign prices. The lower U.S. prices and increased foreign prices make U.S. goods more attractive to foreigners, thereby boosting the number of dollars foreigners want to buy. Moreover, in countries with pegged exchange rates, exchange rates change through devaluation or appreciation by the government.

In the past, governments manipulated exchange rates to administer their domestic public policies. Friedman feels straightforward controls are the worst choice from almost any point of view and certainly the most destructive of a free society. Instead of any clear policy, policy makers allowed the international community to rely on controls in one form or another.

Globalization is a trendy term used to explain the trends of the world trade associated with revolutions in electronics, computers, and communication. Friedman suggests globalization proceeds faster in finance, where digital revolutions are more applicable than physical trade.

This topic discussed the threat of losing economic freedom through trade and railed against currency controls. The following section analyzes global financial policies.

Financial Growth Policies

The next topic discusses global financial growth policies. It examines primary policy goals, investigates liquidity access to global capital markets, and draws implications of liquidity shortages. Tobin (1997) thinks rapid economic growth should be the primary goal of the people of Asia, Africa, and Latin America. However, the price for this faster growth is a temporary obstacle to domestic consumption growth. To restrain domestic consumption and stimulate savings, he proposes reducing the demand for luxury consumption in their society. He also suggests these countries adopt a transaction tax on spot currency trades to stabilize markets and discourage speculation. Although first introduced by Keynes to slow growth, Tobin was later associated with this concept (the Tobin tax) by a magazine writer.

Tobin also advocates limiting risks in foreign exchanges by making exchange rates more flexible, either through floating outright or around widened bands of frequently adjusted parities. Fixed exchange rates in their usual form, adjustable pegs, are alarming for most countries. He couldn't understand why policy makers didn't put this post-Bretton Woods floating policy into place sooner.

The problem was central banks using fixed exchange rates with adjustable pegs often run into trouble with domestic monetary policy. Tobin thinks the challenge with adjustable pegs is that policy makers arbitrarily adjust them, enabling private speculation for the event when this adjustment occurs. An alternative is *dollarization* or using the U.S. dollar instead of their national currency for stability. However, the downside of this policy is that the United States does not consider the satellite countries' economic conditions when making their domestic public policy. This obliviousness causes friction in the satellites' economies to fester. Another alternative is setting up a currency board requiring 100 percent of reserves in a hard currency such as the U.S. dollar against the monetary base of the local currency.

Tobin thinks developing countries should foster financial reform and create regulatory institutions. These actions would support modern national financial systems and independent currencies without direct connection to another currency. Moreover, the globalization of financial markets makes essential contributions to the economic progress of developing and emerging countries.

Developing economies made great strides in liberalization and globalization in recent years. This transformation was especially evident with the Asian tigers, who integrated policy reforms into their financial systems, markets, and institutions. However, short-run speculators influenced their currency exchange markets like other capital markets. This source of uncertainty disrupted their trade flow. This speculation is a big problem in currency markets where most transactions are short term and reverse positions within a week.

In the 1980s, Tobin believed the global economy punished Asian countries during their currency crises for offenses they didn't commit. The instability made it too easy for banks, governments, businesses, and speculators to buy and sell huge blocks of a country's currency in panicky moments. His takeaway from the Asian meltdown is that global policy makers must find ways to make the currency exchange system less volatile. Instituting his Tobin tax would be one way to dampen exchange activity. However, he acknowledges that implementing a transaction tax impairs liquidity.

Liquidity Provision With Access to Global Capital Markets

Bengt Holmström and Jean Tirole (2011) model an open economy featuring free access to the global markets of goods and financial instruments. They develop valuable perspectives on worldwide events and current concerns involving global imbalances. They also address savings/insurance instrument shortages in small countries like Thailand. These instruments play a significant role, given the characteristics of modern markets of their enormous scope and depth of liquidity.

International markets often can't provide all of a country's liquidity needs because borrowers have to repay foreign investments and obligations with their internationally pledgeable income. Therefore, the amount of pledgeable income constrains the liquidity a borrower can access. The problem isn't that the international markets have limited instruments for transporting wealth from one period to another or securing insurance across states of nature. Instead, the country seeking insurance can't produce enough tradable goods to pay them back.

Implications of a Liquidity Shortage

Holmström and Tirole examine how firms with access to international financial markets enrich and modify aggregate liquidity shortages.

They look at how the corporate sector, the domestic government, and the global financial markets ideally share the supply of liquidity. Unlike private investors, the International Monetary Fund (IMF) has a significant capacity for monitoring sovereign government finances and holds leverage over them. Sovereign risk is the potential for a nation's government to default on its debt by failing to make its interest or principal payments. Moreover, the IMF can go beyond orthodox interventions and offer a variety of liquidity facilities to help countries and their institutions in trouble. As a result, the role played by the IMF differs from that played by a national treasury or central bank.

This topic discussed financial growth policies. It examined primary policy goals, investigated liquidity access to global capital markets, and drew implications of liquidity shortages. The next sector recounts a historic currency crisis.

Currency Crises

Exchange Rates and the International Financial System

Holmström and Tirole recall that after World War II, countries created a group of international economic institutions to organize the global system of trade and finance. Under this Bretton Woods system, countries pegged their currencies to the dollar and gold. This system provided fixed but adjustable rates of exchange. When the Bretton Woods system collapsed in 1973, today's hybrid system replaced it. Currently, virtually all large- and medium-sized countries have flexible exchange rates.

Holmström and Tirole highlight that an open economy operating with flexible exchange rates often uses *monetary policy* for domestic macroeconomic stabilization, working independently of other countries. For example, a domestic decline in money supply leads to higher interest rates that attract foreign capital and financial flows. These flows lead to a rise in the exchange rate. In the longer run, operating in the global marketplace provides new constraints and opportunities for countries to improve their economic growth.

Besides promoting high savings and investment, Holmstrom and Tirole suggest countries can increase their growth through a wide array of policies and institutions besides promoting high savings and investment.

The common wisdom is significant trade deficits indicate that deindustrialization is occurring.

The section described international finance by discussing financial globalization, suggesting growth policies, and recounting currency crises. The following section discusses world public policy.

World Public Policy

Robert Mundell (1971), a professor at Columbia University, suggests that economic theory and economic policy are mutual complements. This relationship exists because the development of relevant theory improves policy making. The increasing importance of policy decisions raises the significance of marginal utility theory. Analysts commonly argue there was a decline in the international coordination of policies by governments managing the global payments system. Imbalances emerge when individual governments pursue divergent macroeconomic policies. Countries initiate this shift away from coordinating balance-of-payments financing and other approaches to limit the direct consequences of their actions on their domestic conditions.

However, in the 1990s, the end of the Cold War shifted focus to the growing importance of economics in U.S. foreign affairs. As a result, there is now a parallel shift toward coordinating monetary and fiscal policies, which is crucial for domestic politics and economics. This section discusses world economic policy. It describes the global monetary theory, surveys the worldwide economy, and examines international governance.

Global Monetary Theory

Foreign currency exchanges complicate global monetary policy. This topic discusses global policy, including international liquidity and inflation, the conditions of world monetary equilibrium in models, and the ideal structure for a world bank.

Mundell suggests a policy becomes ineffective when its underlying theory is more obsolete than necessary. The approach also gets backward when policy makers develop their ad hoc theories or rely on the luck of intuition to fit the outdated policy. Problems crop up unexpectedly.

Mundell thinks the mark of a mature science is its ability to contribute solutions quickly. For this purpose, economic science has a reservoir of models capable of rapidly converting to practical uses. Thus, it's helpful to have on-hand models of economic depression even though the world may be in a state of inflation. Likewise, growth models can bear fruit even if the world is regressing. Thus, this process provides a valuable mathematician/empiricist bridge.

International Liquidity and Inflation

Mundell reviews the decisions of world monetary policy makers at the IMF that created a new unit of international money. The IMF holds official accounts of Special Drawing Rights (SDRs) as units of value for each country. Countries should create new money only during a shortage of liquidity. In these times of liquidity scarcity, countries behave like fiscal budget deficit countries and follow restrained monetary policies. The goal of international policy is to stabilize world prices and employment.

According to Mundell, the proper moment for introducing new liquidity is after the global economy feels the pain and reverses its expectations. In an integrated international monetary system, new monetary assets have a more significant impact on the international distribution of liquidity shortages than their magnitude.

Mundell examines the conditions of world monetary equilibrium in a comprehensive bicountry model. It links inflation, interest rates, money stocks, rates of credit expansion, and the balance of payments in a growing world. He found that for a given rate of credit creation in each country, the growth rates of transactions and output determine the balance of payments. As a result, domestic growth creates a need to increase the money supply, reducing spending below income. A central bank automatically creates the additional money supply when it intervenes in the exchange market to prevent the appreciation of its currency. They do this by buying foreign currency, which depreciates the home currency. A central bank also purchases domestic assets. It satisfies growth-induced increases in desired cash to avoid unnecessary foreign reserve accumulations.

Other central banks pursue different policies. For example, the public may determine the quantity of money it wants to hold and how the supply increases. Mundell realizes the policies of various countries aren't symmetrical concerning one another. Only domestic considerations constrain U.S. monetary authorities in governing their monetary policy. Mundell develops the optimum structure of a world central bank. He derives optimal proportions of hard and soft money for the international system. In central banking, the theory seems far more complicated because every approach has an immediate application to policy.

His goal is to maximize real income. Income includes the services of money. Therefore, startup central banks usually begin with high reserve ratios to GDP, which commands trust. In contrast, a central bank doesn't earn trust when it chaotically manages its affairs. It is subject to withdrawal at the slightest disturbance. Trust has many dimensions. Trust in the value of assets is a question of degree. When countries make the institutional commitment to form a world central bank, they imply a fair degree of confidence. Therefore, this growth of confidence allows for a fractional reserve system that is not 100 percent backed.

This topic discussed global policy, including international liquidity and inflation, the conditions of world monetary equilibrium in a model, and the ideal structure for a world bank. The following section surveys the global economy.

Global Economy

This section traces the development of trade relations since World War II. Spence recounts the world needed a new international trade system. After World War II, leaders established the United Nations (UN) in 1945 and the General Agreement on Tariffs and Trade (GATT) in 1947. The UN created GATT to reduce tariffs. Its sole focus was postwar recovery of the industrialized economies while ignoring the developing nations. Fortunately the foreign trade benefits soon spilled over into the larger developing group and became a vast, though not complete, success.

The World Trade Organization (WTO) evolved from GATT when most countries, including many developing countries, became members in the 1990s. This inclusion reflected developing countries' growing size, power, and influence. Moreover, it made sure it represented the interests of smaller and poorer nations in governing world trade. The colonial system disappeared as the global economy emerged in the postwar period. Old colonies became new countries. The economic juggernaut, once confined to a few developed countries in the last two centuries, spread to most of the world.

The cost of things change, and there are limits to substituting capital for labor. Exchange rates are prices. In an open economy, they're actual prices. The country's imports also become cheaper and cheaper relative to domestic goods and services, though economists can't easily explains why. Spence suggests that for many years leading up to the currency crisis of Asia in the late 1990s, the conventional wisdom was that market forces set exchange rates without government intervention.

At that point, things changed. Developing countries managed their exchange rates to ensure their export sector remained competitive in global markets. But managing currency isn't risk-free. Until the 1990s' crisis, economists thought the balancing act in developing economies was associated with managing the exchange rates a domestic issue of growth and development.

World policy makers build GATT and WTO on the principle that the global system requires a rules-based approach. Spence recalls the Doha round of negotiations in 2001. This round was complex in scope, leading to difficulty in reaching a final agreement. Nevertheless, the developing countries continued to manage their currencies independently, maintain control of inbound and outbound capital flows, and acquire a growing set of foreign currency assets as reserves. Spence thought it's increasingly apparent there are limits to globalization in a nation-centric government structure. However, the basic open economy, high investment, and savings growth strategies will continue to work.

China several times floated the idea of a super-sovereign currency via SDRs at the IMF. However, for a fully global system to continue to develop, it needs enhanced coordinated oversight with objectives that are not purely national. Through its initial period of growth starting in 1978, China balanced its savings and investment. Then in 2005, the pattern shifted. The rapid increase in their trade surplus became an unwelcome surprise to Chinese leaders.

This section traced the development of international trade relations since World War II. The next topic analyzes global governance.

Global Governance

Global governance refers to the coordination of government policies in the international economy. This topic recounts the Great Recession worldwide, evaluates the G20 as an effective forum, and explores what happens when things go wrong.

Spence recalls policy makers reset the global economy after the Great Recession monetary crisis of 2008. However, consequential breakdowns had occurred in multiple jurisdictions in the lead-up to the problem, and many factors contributed to it. When global policy makers gathered in 2008, they realized other countries replicated their national-oriented narratives. There was also a multicountry effort by the G20 to arrest the economic collapse using massive fiscal and monetary policy stimulus.

After a while, national and regional considerations started to dominate policy making again after the reset. Spence suggests the crisis demonstrates that the globalized world has reached a peak level of international connectivity. However, the condition exceeded the boundary of national policies and the usefulness of global architecture. In retrospect, it became apparent to Spence that the world ran a hybrid system with different de facto rules and practices for advanced and developing countries. Nevertheless, managing changes and growth in complex transitions serves them well.

The G20 and Global Growth

Spence thinks the G20 should address the reform of coordinated financial regulations and restore the rebalancing of global demand. In addition, major developing economies should be more accountable for their increased global responsibilities. Restoring balance to the global economy and maintaining it requires structural changes in many economies. The run-up to the 2008 crisis and the subsequent crisis management process hold essential lessons.

The G20, a mixed group of advanced and developing countries, has assumed responsibility for setting priorities in the global economy. However, Spence feels the G20 fails in the mission for increased growth, but not because of disagreements. The most crucial single economy is the United States, where things are not perfect. Its education system has many solid segments but has widespread problems with efficiency and effectiveness. In addition, fiscal policy requires a long-term balance between the trade-off of short-term stimulus and the costs of the risk of sovereign debt.

China weathered the Great Recession better than most countries by reacting quickly to the collapse of foreign demand with domestic stimulus. The result was a rapid transition to high growth over the following decade. Spence feels their challenge is transitioning to middle-income status in China's internal growth and development. Lowering elevated levels of savings relative to investment reduces surpluses in the current trade account.

With future growth rates approaching China, India operates on a tried and tested model of an open economy. Their challenges are significant but well understood by their political leaders and policy makers. An unusual feature of India is its high ratio of services to income. Spence also explores how Brazil grew at a 7 percent pace for 25 years after World War II. Then, economic slowdowns started to occur accompanied by political regime changes shifting from democracy to military dictatorship and back.

After World War II, Spence recounts Europe began economic and political integration processes requiring a century to complete. As a result, the scope and depth of their global economic interdependency ran well ahead of international governance structures. Economies are the domains for the pursuit of the self-interest of individuals. Europe's economy remains self-interested but hasn't unified its political systems.

This topic recounted the Great Recession worldwide, discussed the G20 as an effective forum, and described what happens when things go wrong. The section discussed world economic policy. It described global monetary theory, surveyed the worldwide economy, and examined international governance. This chapter looked at developing and developed countries and how they interact globally. It discussed global trade, described international finance, and suggested world public policy. However, many goods and services, mainly services, are not involved in international commerce such as haircuts and sushi. The same is true for a loaf of bread. The next chapter discusses social justice.

CHAPTER 10

Social Justice

While globalization improved the lives of millions, other challenges exist. We live and thrive in a world where each individual is unique. This environment requires accommodations for these differences. However, there are many different approaches to tackle the problem. As a result, the proposed solutions to society's challenges vary widely.

Let's apply the concepts explored in this story to these seemingly intractable problems. This chapter looks at some of the unsolved economic questions facing our world. Our journey takes us through the social justice jungle by addressing inequality, income redistribution, and climate change issues.

Nature of Inequality

Friedrich Hayek (1960) felt the aim of the struggle for liberty is equality before law. This extension of the equality principles to *rules for moral and social conduct* is the primary expression of the democratic spirit. It's doing the most to make the inequalities that liberty produces inoffensive. However, equality of general rules of law and conduct is the only kind conducive to liberty. Moreover, it's the only equality secured without destroying liberty. This section explores the nature of inequality. It discusses equal opportunity, modern egalitarianism, and the scope of the problem.

Equal Opportunity

This topic on equal opportunity provides a definition for equality, suggests endless varieties of human nature, and debates conditional equality.

Equality and Merit

Hayek thought liberty had nothing to do with any other sort of equality. Unfortunately, it's bound to produce inequality in many respects.

This outcome is the necessary result and part of the justification of our liberty. It's not because it assumes people are equal or attempts to make them equal. On the contrary, the argument for freedom demands that the government *treat* everybody equally. This argument recognizes that we are different. However, it insists these individual differences do not justify the government treating us differently.

Hayek argues that the human species' endless varieties of human nature are a particular fact. If the differences aren't significant, then freedom isn't necessary. Economic inequality isn't an evil to justify using discriminatory coercion or privilege as a remedy. No individual or group of individuals can determine the potential of other humans. However, Hayek believes in certain similarities between all humans.

Society has evolving preferences to express the desire to secure conditional equality. Moreover, most people do not object to the bare facts of inequality. On the contrary, they regard it as natural; the system shouldn't reward anybody more than they deserve for this pain and effort. Hayek also argues that membership in a community or nation entitles us to the general wealth of the groups to which we belong. This demand conflicts with the desire to base distributions on personal merit. There's no merit to being born into a community. Likewise, there's no apparent reason the joint efforts of any group members should give these members a separate claim to the group's wealth.

Culture and Human Rights

Amartya Sen (1999) observes current society acknowledges human rights rhetoric more widely than in the past. The language of national and international communications reflects shifts in priorities and emphasis. It has also become an essential part of the literature on economic development. However, Sen feels this apparent victory of human rights coexists with a natural skepticism about the depth and coherence of this approach. He laments the problem is that human rights activists confound the consequences of legal systems. Another line of their attack concerns the form ethics and politics of human rights take. Finally, Sen contemplates the authoritarian lines of reasoning found in Asian culture, which often receives indirect backing from the West.

This topic on the equal opportunity provided a definition, suggested endless varieties of human nature, and debated conditional equality. Finally, it noted society acknowledges human rights rhetoric more widely. The following section investigates the current status of modern egalitarianism.

Modern Egalitarianism

This topic summarizes the egalitarian views of our laureates. First, it describes the components of egalitarianism. Next, it assesses the extent of income redistribution. Finally, it points out severe defects in the theory and expresses distrust of using utility theory in policy making.

Robert Fogel (2000), a professor at the University of Chicago, suggests his Fourth Great Awakening's current epochal movement features technological changes which disrupt prevailing culture. This unraveling evolved from repeated efforts to adapt institutions to radically new modes of production and consumption. Adhering institutions to the accelerating permutations in the past two centuries was prolonged and increasingly complex. The activists creating new reform agendas portray individuals clinging to their old ways as enemies of progress.

According to Fogel, modern egalitarianism has three components. First, it starts with the conviction that society is better off if the rich transfer income to the poor. Second, proponents believe the government is the proper instrument to redistribute it. Third, progress requires developing and implementing public policies and various institutions to execute these redistributions. For example, increasing the opportunity of the labor force to be directly employed by federal, state, and local governments and instituting unemployment insurance should enhance job security. However, Fogel seems to think the capacity to turn the government into a hiring agency isn't a good idea. Promoting greater equality in resource distribution doesn't mean achieving improved welfare as envisioned by the reformers.

Fogel adopts Angus Deaton's (2013) assessment of the extent of income redistribution. Redistribution should theoretically provide overall welfare gains, attributing them to egalitarian reforms. However, at issue is determining alternative measurements, identifying complex interactions between policies, and assessing them retrospectively. Deaton feels the record of the 20th century contrasted sharply with the two preceding centuries. Back then, circumstances convinced the Social Gospel movements' leaders that intervention was indispensable for advancing significant egalitarian outcomes.

Fogel examines the proper role played by the government. He evaluates current issues regarding improving living standards and their implication for measuring inequality. For example, it's often argued that income transfers from the households at the top of income distributions to those at the bottom are self-defeating. The reforms are never fully implemented because old and new waves of egalitarian reformers tend to misunderstand each other's concerns. At the same time, leaders of the prior Third Awakening missed the relevance of *personal responsibility* as a critical element in their struggles.

Fogel recounts that the situation arrayed the two mighty egalitarians' camps against each other. He suggests that postmodern patterns have evolved into a pilgrimage for self-realization and the desire to find deeper meanings in life. This quest contrasts with the endless accumulations of consumer durable goods. Current inequality issues in the United States didn't arise from the shocks of rapid urbanization alone. The emerging crises also paid homage to the changing nature and distribution of work and leisure. Changes in industry structure, the use of time, organization of work, and consumption structure all give rise to new sets of egalitarian issues, some material and some spiritual.

Fogel feels it's only been in the past century the social process launched rich nations of the world onto a plane previously contemplated by the dreamers. Although material assistance is essential for overcoming spiritual isolation, policy makers don't correctly target spiritual aid.

James Mirrlees (2006), a professor at Oxford University and the University of Cambridge, found severe defects in this approach. For example, many economic transactions occur between individual agents or firms with effective monopolies on at least one market side. Another defect is the need to have rigid distributions of assets to people before the reformers claim the resulting equilibrium is satisfactory. Finally, taxation is a complicated function of income. Mirrlees' tax models are only one situation with asymmetric information between a principal (government) and an agent (the consumer).

Mirrlees believes the Arrow–Debreu classic frameworks for welfare economics are unsatisfactory in situations with imperfect and unreliable information. The government's policies and the policies it should adopt depend on consumer information, what they do, and what they are. However, the welfare theorems' asset redistribution requires information the government can't obtain.

Utilitarianism implies a society of individuals holds similar values. Because we are not wholly identical, we shouldn't desire equal utility or levels of satisfaction. Mirrlees feels utilitarians shouldn't rely on the utility functions they believe governs economic policy, even if they have the power to do so. Instead, he evaluates how equilibriums implement welfare optimums when taking advantage of production economies of scale. Arrow (1951) points out it's optimal for producers with similar technologies to do different things when pursuing economies of scale.

This topic summarized the egalitarian views of several economists. First, it described the components of egalitarianism. Next, it assessed the extent of income redistribution. Finally, it pointed out severe defects in the theory and expressed distrust of using utility theory in policy making. The following section presents competing views of egalitarianism for the future.

Stormy Weather

Economists don't always agree on how society should fix its problems. This topic summarizes the outlook of equal opportunity. On the one hand, it presents a foreboding picture of the world, its divisive direction, and rules for preventing further deterioration. On the other hand, the section paints a rosy picture where this is the best of times, and society has crafted ways to fix the rough spots.

Joseph Stiglitz (2012), an American New Keynesian economist, thinks an ominous chapter in market economies emerged from the 2008 Great Recession. It appears as a large and expanding cloud of inequality. It weakened the economic sustainability of the American social framework at the margins. He examined the scope of inequality in the United States. He wondered how it affects the lives of millions in diverse ways. He laments society is becoming more divided and no longer the land of opportunity.

Inequality in America didn't just spontaneously happen. It is an artifact of society. Stiglitz's thesis is that even though market forces help plant the degree of inequality, government policies shaped those market forces. The conventional wisdom is that flexible and accessible labor markets contribute to economic strength. However, the government acted out contrasting roles in the inequality of the 1970s and 1980s. Stiglitz feels politics is a battleground for fights over how to divide the national economic pie. Unfortunately, the irony is that the wealthy seek to manipulate political systems. They welcome unequal outcomes.

Stiglitz, a former chief economist for the World Bank and chairman of the Council of Economic Advisors, contends that the United States should lead in creating the rules of the game. His central argument is that the popular models best describing the income determination at the top don't base their structure on an *individual's contribution* to society. Society needs more robust and more effectively enforced competition laws. Creating a more level playing field and ending the race to the bottom should temper the harmful effects of globalization. In addition, society needs to support workers' and citizens' collective action. Finally, significant political reforms need to occur. Stiglitz' normative vision of humanity is a society where the gaps between the haves and the have-nots narrow. It's where there's a sense of shared destiny and shared commitment to opportunity and fairness.

The Well-Being of the World

In contrast, Angus Deaton (2013) thought life was better now than at any other time in history. More people are affluent, and fewer people live in dire poverty. However, he feels the world is still unequal. Unfortunately, inequality is often the consequence of progress. Deaton points out that not everyone gets rich simultaneously and receives immediate access to the latest life-saving measures. However, inequalities, in turn, affect progress.

Progress in health has been as impressive as progress in wealth. But, this progress expanded inequalities. Inequality influences the invention process, sometimes favorably and sometimes unfavorably. Sen argues there are many different views regarding what society should make equal. Instead, Deaton's arguments emphasize what inequality does, whether inequality helps or hurts, and whether it matters what kind of inequality society discusses.

Deaton contemplates the material well-being, that policy makers typically measure by income and amounts of money we spend or save. Instead, he uses well-being to refer to everything favorable for a person living a good life. It isn't a single quantity like temperature; it's multifaceted. Deaton also thinks our hunter-gatherer ancestry shapes human equality. Evaluating how hunter-gatherers organize depended on where they live and their local environments. As a result, equal sharing was necessary because most groups didn't or couldn't store food.

Deaton, like Stiglitz, thinks the last dozen decades showed a particularly marked contrast between the material well-being of most people and those at the top. For example, while economists comment positively about equal opportunity, they do not penalize people for success due to challenging work. Initially, they used world market prices to make living cost comparisons. However, Deaton thinks purchase power parity (PPP) comparisons are better than market exchange rates. PPP measures consumption in local prices versus world prices. As a result, the gap in measuring well-being narrows.

But, to Deaton and other economists, why some countries proliferate, and some grow slowly remains a mystery. Moreover, he laments that a billion people still live in material poverty. Developed countries try to help close these gaps by donating foreign aid, but its local distribution often leads to local corruption. One solution is requiring recipient governments to demonstrate commitment to sound public policies. In addition, it's essential that individuals in donor countries more effectively understand the problems in distributing aid.

The most compelling cases for reducing funding distortions are those countries where foreign aid is a large share of GDP and accounts for all government spending. Aid could be effective, but recipient governments often misdirect it rendering it ineffective. Moreover, large inflows of foreign aid often change recipient politics for the worse.

This topic summarized the outlook of equal opportunity. It presented a foreboding picture of the world and contrasted it with a rosy picture. The section explored the nature of inequality. Finally, it discussed the spirit of equal opportunity, modern egalitarianism, and the scope of the problem. The following section analyzes income redistribution.

Income Redistribution

The proper policy for redistributing income lies at the heart of politics' liberal/conservative divide. Solutions are difficult to agree on because fairness is a subjective concept with a different meanings for different people. In addition, other agendas get thrown into the debate of redistribution. This section discusses income redistribution. It examines optimal taxation principles, positions income redistribution as a social goal, and debates Social Security's (SS) merits.

Optimal Taxation

This topic discusses the need for fair taxation and describes optimal tax structures. Mirrlees (2006) thinks progressive-rate income taxation is an important policy instrument in any economic system where society values equality. Even in highly socialist economies, where the government employs all workers, the shadow prices of highly skilled labor are higher than the disposable income available to laborers. Therefore, policy makers developing redistributive policies usually base progressive-rate taxation on a person's income. Of course, economists can argue that society should base its tax on its potential to earn income. Still, personal income is the most natural and reliable measure. However, like Deaton, Mirrlees objects to policy makers using comprehensive equality programs of social income utilities because it would discourage unpleasant work.

Mirrlees points out the general properties of optimum income tax schedules and the rules that govern them. They are dependent on complicated processes. For example, it isn't possible to state a universally accepted reason why marginal tax rates should be higher for high-income, low-income, or intermediate-income groups.

Distribution of Income

Economists consider many factors when analyzing the distribution of income. This topic makes a case for it being a social goal and the tendency for some activists to propose steep tax structure progressions. It also makes a case for not assuming society will find an optimal solution.

Milton Friedman (1962) was from the University of Chicago. He suggests the central element in developing collectivist sentiment in this century, at least in Western countries, is the belief that income equality is a social goal. Consequently, there is a degree of willingness to use the arm of the government to promote it. The ethical principle used to justify income distribution in free-market societies is to reward each member according to what individuals and the assets they possess produce. However, the successful application of this principle implicitly depends on the government's action.

Property rights are matters of law and social convention. Payments corresponding to production are necessary to achieve proper treatment of equality. Friedman illustrates the dilemma when one individual may prefer a routine job with time off for basking in the sun to more exacting jobs paying higher salaries. It's essential to distinguish between personal endowments, property inequality, and inherited and acquired wealth inequalities. However, this distinction is unsustainable. Wages aren't primarily distributive but allocative according to the effort. This allocation effect is present when they correspond to their value in production in market societies.

According to Friedman, humanitarians' and egalitarians' sentiments help produce steeply progressive tax structures on individual income. Friedman ponders these measures and points out how different their actual effects are from those intended.

False Expectations

James Tobin (1997) recalls that following the collapse of the Soviet Union, the West expected excommunist countries to prosper under free-market capitalism. Instead, their disastrous economic system pinned Soviet citizens' living standards far below their Western neighbors. In Russia, workers and other productive inputs required substantial restructuring. During the Soviet era, they had transitioned from producing essential activities to providing activities of social value. Massive rationalization is both a current necessity and a future hope.

It's a fallacy to expect reorganization to occur independently, much less quickly enough to satisfy impatient public aspirations. It doesn't happen even in Western countries with well-established capitalist and democratic institutions. Developed capitalist economies contain immense varieties of markets. Yet, in the euphoria of the Soviet breakup, Tobin felt Western advisers often forgot that ideologically pure systems of free markets don't win economic victories on their own. Instead, policy makers achieve it with mixed economies where governments play substantial and crucial roles.

The topic presented a case for making income distribution a social goal and discussed steep tax structure progressions. However, it also assumed society won't always find an optimal solution. The following section discusses SS.

Social Security

Social Security represents a central U.S. policy for redistributing income. This topic discusses the policy implications of SS, recounts the realization that CPI overstates inflation, and presents proposals for privatizing SS.

Friedrich Hayek (1960) contends there should be some provision for those people threatened by the extremes of poverty or starvation due to circumstances beyond their control. Society should accept this provision as a duty of the community. In the early modern period, the local orientation of the arrangements to supply this public assistance became inadequate. Hayek explains this condition happened when the growth of the large city and increased individual mobility dissolved old neighborhood ties.

Then, policy makers organized this provision of services nationally and created special agencies to administer them. Society offered this public assistance to those requiring protection against acts of desperation on the needy. The quantity of relief should exceed a subsistence level to keep recipients alive and in good health. Up to this point, even the most consistent defenders of liberty begrudgingly accepted justification for the whole SS apparatus. The primary reason for compulsory membership in SS presumes a unitary organization's greater efficiency and administrative convenience.

Hayek laments that the SS system's unnecessary complexity and consequent incomprehensibility, created for democracy, spawned a fundamental problem. It's a paradox that the government claims its superiority in an economic area where new, more effective private institutions emerge through a gradual evolutionary process not out of design.

The most important branch of SS before World War II was unemployment insurance. This insurance has since become unimportant. Hayek thinks the difficulties social insurance faces are the consequence of design. Society universally accepts income redistribution by progressive taxation as just. However, Hayek objects after evaluating redistribution and progressive taxation. He seems to think that there are no clear principles anchoring policy once society abandons beliefs of exacting the same income proportions from all individuals.

Initially, those advocating progressive-rate taxation during the latter part of the 19th century stressed they only wanted to achieve the equality of sacrifice but not redistribution of income. One explanation offered supporting progressive tax rates was that society couldn't fund an expansion in public spending without resorting to steep progressions.

Hayek expresses sorrow that circumstances soon proved these virtuous assurances of progressive taxes were false. Moreover, it's sometimes contended that *proportional* taxation is as arbitrary as *progressive* taxation. Nevertheless, society widely accepts progressive taxation because most people think an adequate income is the only legitimate and socially desirable reward.

Eventually, economists concluded that CPI was not the best measure of inflation. Then, in 1995, the Boskin Commission found that its correction could contribute to complex fiscal and political problems. As a result, the CPI was in the spotlight of politics and statistics, primarily because of its use in indexing the benefits of SS.

Tobin argues for an index purposely built for SS because of the unique spending patterns of retirees. He proposes an upgrade to improve changes over time in the prices of representative market baskets bought in cash transactions. The improvement should also recognize the contributions of nonmarket changes in physical and social environments to consumer satisfaction, welfare, well-being, and quality of life. Allowing for the quality changes arising from new products or modifying existing ones is the most challenging task confronting the designer of an index.

Privatizing Social Security

Thaler and Sunstein (2008) were intrigued when Sweden launched a plan to privatize its SS system in 2000. They thought Sweden's officials meant well in some aspects of their choice of architecture but made at least one crucial mistake. This mistake led its citizens to choose ineffective portfolios. The program presents participants with combinations of unfettered money management competitors and many fund choices. A better mix of nudges would have helped. By evaluating why this happened, they learned a lot about reforming our SS.

Thaler and Sunstein felt the Swedish plan should have adopted a middle ground where the program selects defaults but encourages participant choice. Unfortunately, the government and private funds stopped advertising after an initial enrollment period. As a result, enrollment plummeted. They also thought the fundamental problem is that government planners don't always select the best choice of architecture. It is better to design a program with a comprehensive combination of funds. Experts should begin by choosing effective default funds and then guiding participants through processes of simplified fund selection.

This topic discussed the policy implications of SS, recounted the realization CPI overstates inflation, and presented proposals for privatizing SS. The section discussed income redistribution. It examined optimal taxation principles, discussed the merits of positioning income redistribution as a social goal, and debated the merits of SS. The following section discusses the economics of climate change.

Climate Change

The economics of climate change refers to the study of the economic costs and benefits of climate change and the impact of actions to limit its effects. Participants in the climate change debate, from academia to government to nongovernmental organizations, have increasingly used economic evaluations to determine the costs of addressing climate change. This is because climate change disrupts seasonal weather patterns in the long term affecting the global economy. Since 1880, the average temperature has risen around 1° Celsius, or 1.9° Fahrenheit. That's faster than at any other time in the Earth's history. This section discusses the economics of climate change. It discusses the basics of climate change, analyzes pragmatic mitigation proposals, and describes international policy coordination.

Clearing the Air

This topic presents the basics of climate change economics. It recounts past global policy initiatives and acknowledges that society has finally recognized the significant risks of climate change. It describes how researchers use baseline scenarios, analyze the perils of the ocean, and study the link between climate change and economics.

Thaler and Sunstein (2008) recall governments worldwide took aggressive steps to protect the environment in the past. The government used significant resources to act over concerns with pollution in the air and water, pesticides, the spread of toxic chemicals, and the loss of endangered species. A range of international agreements controls the environment. In recent years, the focus shifted to global problems of the environment, including the depletion of the ozone layer. Now the public attention focus is on climate change. They wonder whether their behavior nudges of choice architecture could help reduce the *greenhouse gases* (GHG) affecting ozone depletion.

Governments seeking to protect the environment by controlling the harmful effects of pollution venture well beyond nudges. Typically, regulators choose command- and control regulations and reject free choice and markets. However, it is appropriate for the government to fix the problem by realigning markets when they severely distort incentives. For example, one proposal imposes taxes or penalties on those polluting the environment. In climate change, taxes on GHG are a simple example. Another cap-and-trade approach requires those polluting to hold rights to spoil specific amounts. Thaler and Sunstein think getting the prices right is critical but realize these approaches are politically tricky.

The Challenge of Climate Change and Developing Country Growth

Michael Spence (2011) suggests global warming is the most complex challenge to global governance in recent years. He opines that after many years of research, most people finally recognize the significant risks of climate change. However, some skeptics claim society suppresses the full range of scientific knowledge, causing an overstatement of the problem. Others admit there is a warming problem but think it's too soon to comprehend the scope of the problem.

Climate change supporters endeavor to persuade society to transition from acknowledging the problem to doing something about it. But, according to Spence, this next phase is a massive challenge because devising strategies for the long term requires society to expend enormous inputs of science, technology, and capital.

High-growth developing countries include more than half of the world's population. One way to mitigate the climate problem is to limit the growth of these developing countries, but this is morally indefensible. Spence feels the only way to establish a global agreement on mitigation strategies is to start with a shared understanding of what the corrective path envisions. Effective plans must recognize different starting points for each developed country regarding per capita emissions. In addition, developing countries need to remove energy subsidies and create incentives for energy efficiency.

First Encounters of the Public

An American economist, William Nordhaus (2013) also observes that climate change is getting much attention. However, people disagree about whether it is accurate, necessary, or human. He feels global warming significantly threatens humans and the natural world. He suggests economic growth produces unintended but perilous climate and earth systems changes. These changes will lead to unforeseeable and dangerous consequences. Nordhaus ponders the science, economics, and politics involved and the steps necessary to undo what society sowed. He suggests climate science is a dynamic field. Fortunately, earth scientists developed the essential elements of the field over the last century and firmly established them.

Natural sources drove past climate changes varying from ice-free to snowbound Earth. The current primary concern is not air temperature but the effect of temperature on human and natural systems. Nordhaus works with the explanation that there are several alternate strategies for slowing climate change. The most promising is the *mitigation or reduction of emissions of GHG.*

Global warming is a particularly tricky challenge because it is global. Nordhaus' comprehensive picture of future climate change requires projections of the economy and its energy use. Researchers calculate these variables and parameters in computerized models. Models of integrated assessment are comprehensive models including climate, other aspects of science, and the economics of climate change.

According to Nordhaus, a professor at Yale University, agriculture is the most sensitive to the climate of all major sectors. Therefore, scientists expect the farms to feel the impacts of climate change the most. However, the extent of climate change and the size of the damage and severity on sectors like farming depend primarily on the pace of global economic growth over the next century. Therefore, researchers use a *baseline scenario* to project economic growth, emissions, and climate change without emissions reductions or other climate change policies.

For example, in the fourth Intergovernmental Panel on Climate Change Assessment Report in 2007, the authors ironically project the potential of global *food production to increase* with local increases in the mean temperature range of 1° to 3° Celsius. However, the report projects frequent increases in droughts and floods to affect crop production negatively, especially in low-latitude subsistence sectors. It's striking to Nordhaus how this scientific evidence summary contrasts with popular rhetoric.

Ocean Perils

The impacts on agriculture and health are primarily unfavorable, mainly if policy makers poorly manage them. However, Nordhaus thinks the expected risks are within the range of economic shocks experienced regularly. Moreover, while impacts on farming and health should arrive quickly, sea levels will rise slowly over centuries. This slow swell is because oceans have risen slowly since the last ice age. A significant component of the rising sea level is melting ice from glaciers and ice caps, but estimates are highly uncertain. Nordhaus suggests this uncertainty is because the oceans always rose and fell over Earth's geological history. About 4 percent of the world's population and output are in regions at or below 10 meters (33 feet). However, the vulnerability of a region is determined not only by elevation. Flooding poses significant risks, even for higher elevations, in areas subject to hurricanes or intense storms.

Among Nordhaus' themes is linking climate damage to economics. Additionally, he points out essential distinctions between managed systems and unmanageable systems. Circumstances increasingly insulate the market economies of high-income countries from the vicissitudes of climate and other natural disturbances. Economists have labored for many years to estimate the aggregate damage of climate change. The estimates of the impacts of climate change presented by Nordhaus represent the state of the art.

The topic recounted past global policy initiatives and acknowledged how society has finally recognized the significant risks of climate change. It described how researchers use baseline scenarios, analyzed the perils of the ocean, and studied the link between climate change and economics. The following section discusses the pragmatic steps to mitigate the effects of climate change.

Pragmatic Mitigation

Nordhaus thinks mitigation is the only real solution in the long run to reverse the accumulation of GHGs. Mitigation consists of reducing the emissions and atmospheric concentrations of CO_2. In addition, there are other long-lived GHGs, such as methane. In terms of fossil fuels, burning coal emits 10 times more CO_2 than petroleum and 5 times more than natural gas in emissions per dollar. This topic discusses the pragmatic steps to mitigate the effects of climate change. It looks at the promising areas of policy change, debates the balance of costs and damages, and discusses the market mechanisms for determining prices.

Nordhaus suggests public policies for climate change should encourage modifying lifestyles by curbing carbon-intensive activities, producing goods and services with low-carbon or no-carbon technologies, and burning fossil fuels but removing CO_2 after combustion. He acknowledges that effective and efficient policies affect billions of people's and governments' decisions worldwide. The *cost* of reducing CO_2 is an essential topic in the economics of climate change.

Nordhaus feels sensible climate change policy targets require balancing abatement costs with climate change damages, a cost–benefit analysis. Then, he applies this analysis to evaluate different targets for slowing climate change. But unfortunately, the cost–benefit study incorporates strange and singular elements, such as tipping points, abrupt changes in climate, sharp discontinuities, and catastrophes. As a result, critics of the cost–benefit analysis argue it's inappropriate to evaluate decisions on climate change.

Setting simple targets for temperature is insufficient in a world of competing goals. Nations want to ensure they're not subsidizing undeserving countries or feeding corrupt dictators with green policies that are excuses for skimming greenbacks. Nordhaus suggests climate change policy is a tale of two sciences. Designing effective policies to control climate change also requires social sciences. The choices of individuals need consideration, too.

The most critical element for mitigating the effects of climate change is developing an efficient market mechanism for determining carbon prices. The best way to accomplish this is placing a price on the emissions of CO_2. People think energy and climate policy are isolated from overall economic policy, but there's an essential economic connection. A carbon tax is the nearest thing to a perfect tax. Moreover, Nordhaus contends that the carbon tax substantially benefits public health by reducing harmful emissions, particularly those associated with burning coal.

This topic discussed the pragmatic steps to mitigate the effects of climate change. It analyzed the hopeful areas of policy change, debated the balance of costs and damages, and discussed the market mechanisms for determining prices. The following section explores suggestions for the coordination of global policy.

International Policy Coordination

Effective policies for global warming should be international. Nordhaus suggests global warming is an unusual economic phenomenon known as a *worldwide externality*. A global externality differs from other economic activities because the economic and political mechanisms for dealing with them efficiently and effectively are weak or absent. He contends that governance is a central issue in dealing with global externalities because effective management requires coordinated actions of the major countries. Among most nations, binding international agreements limiting emissions of GHG should employ combinations of regulations and taxes. This topic explores suggestions for the coordination of global policy. It describes what would make this policy work more effectively and points out the problem of economic nationalism. Finally, it laments that climate change affects the disadvantaged more severely but hopes research and development efforts respond to incentives.

An effective policy to reduce global warming entails countries harmonizing national policies. Regimes of valuing carbon prices are novel ideas. Moreover, international agreements often distinguish the responsibilities of poor and prosperous nations. Nordhaus suggests that whatever global plans policy makers settle on to slow climate change, they should confront countries' tendencies to free-ride on others' efforts.

Current auto emission rules require substantial increases in miles-per-gallon levels for new cars sold. Designing the improvement in fuel efficiency is costly to manufacturers and drivers. Nordhaus thinks regulatory approaches to reduce emissions of CO_2 are inefficient and sometimes counterproductive. Some involve institutional factors. The shortcomings of relying primarily on regulations are severe. Realistically, policy makers don't have enough information to write rules for the entire economy. So unless society implements effective policies for carbon pricing, it progresses virtually nowhere in slowing climate change.

Society can use nuclear power to generate electricity, but it is impractical for many applications, such as air travel. The most attractive options in the public's minds are renewable energy sources such as solar, wind, and geothermal power.

Nordhaus takes climate science seriously, but others are skeptical. The consensus of science is the collective judgment of the community of informed and knowledgeable scientists in a field at a given time. There are no votes on science principles, and most scientists scoff at the idea that they decide science by a vote. Of course, not every scientist or economist agrees with every finding. Still, Nordhaus feels most published and peer-reviewed literature have secure foundations.

Policies slowing climate change are economically simple, if difficult politically. One obstacle is the result of economic nationalism. The nature of the payoff in the future from the current reduction of emissions amplifies this dilemma of nationalism. Another obstacle involves unavoidable realities. For example, while roadblocks in a representative democracy are fundamental elements of open society, advocates of science or pseudo-science undermine the normal process of science.

Public opinion and substantial wings of American politics are moving in one direction, even as the views of science are moving in the other. Nordhaus ponders somber but realistic concepts of the state of debate and obstacles in implementing efficient and effective policies to slow global warming. Some barriers are structural. The consequences of climate change are costly for human societies and grave for many unmanaged earth systems. These basic themes must be qualified and constantly updated because of the uncertainties involved at all stages of the links, from economic growth through emissions and climate change to impacts and policies.

Warmer Earth

Banerjee and Duflo (2019) also think the earth will become warmer over the next 100 years. Their more important question is how much? Various scenarios project, at minimum, coral reefs will vanish. More dire predictions see rising sea levels and arable land transforming into deserts. They also suggest climate change is massively inequitable. Developed countries or the various global locations that produce what rich countries consume generate the most emissions of CO_2. But developing countries will eventually experience the most significant share of the costs.

Even with technological improvements and eliminating fossil fuel use in society, any future economic growth directly impacts climate change. This impact is because as consumption rises, the community needs the energy to produce all consumed goods. Also, circumstances position poorer countries closer to the equator, where they feel pain. On the other hand, more prosperous and technologically advanced countries can use their resources to help mitigate temperature risks. Banerjee and Duflos hope efforts of research and development respond to policy incentives.

What policy makers are seeking is a free lunch. Banerjee and Duflo doubt there are many free lunches. This notion isn't what economists want to hear. Instead, they use material consumption as a measure of well-being.

This topic explored global policy coordination and described what would make this policy work more effectively. In addition, it pointed out the problem of economic nationalism. Finally, it lamented that climate change affects the disadvantaged more severely but hopes research and development efforts respond to incentives. The section discussed the economics of climate change. It examined the basics of climate change, analyzed pragmatic mitigation proposals, and described international policy coordination. The chapter inquires into the nature of inequality, income redistribution policy, and climate change economics.

As our happy quest winds down, we can confirm economics is complicated but approachable using common sense. We looked through the microscope at human behavior in the laboratory. We examined smaller sections of the economy to see how they ticked. We saw how economies form capital and investigated the role of government. We took a deep dive into the nature of the work force and developed ideas for assembling all the pieces. We put together principles to help modernize developing economies and learned how nations interact. Finally, we discussed some of the social justice issues our global economy faces.

The contributions of Nobel laureates and others effectively narrow the unknowns of economics. Nevertheless, we also discovered that many unsolved economic issues remain. Charles Darwin and the biologists are taking a journey through a similar process when exploring the origin of our specie, except they use indecipherable terminology.

Human nature is embedded in the core engine of economics. Adam Smith (1776) captured this essence 250 years ago when he declared, "It is not from the benevolence of the butcher, the brewer, or the baker that we expect our dinner, but from their regard to their own interest."

Between Smith's wisdom and the contributions of our Nobel laureates lies the best spot to choose the perfect loaf of bread.

You can further explore the ideas discussed in this book. Please dive into the works of your favorite economists listed in the reference table.

References

Akerlof, G. and R. Kranton. 2010. *Identity Economics*. Princeton: Princeton University Press.

Allais, M. December 1997. "An Outline of My Main Contributions to Economic Science." *American Economic Review* 87, pp. 6–12.

Arrow, K. 1951. *Social Choice and Individual Values*. London: Martino.

Arrow, K. and L. Hurwicz, eds. 1977. *Studies in Resource Allocation Processes*. Cambridge: Cambridge University Press.

Aumann, R. and M. Maschler. 1995. *Repeated Games With Incomplete Information*. Cambridge: MIT Press.

Banerjee, A. and E. Duflo. 2019. *Good Economics for Hard Times*. New York, NY: Hatchett Book Group.

Becker, G. 1962. *Human Capital*. Chicago: University of Chicago Press.

Black, F. and M. Scholes. May–June 1973. "The Pricing of Options and Corporate Liabilities." *Journal of Political Economy* 81, pp. 637–654.

Buchanan, J. 1962. *The Calculus of Consent*. Indianapolis: Liberty Fund.

Coase, R. 1988. *The Firm, The Market, and the Law*. Chicago: University of Chicago Press.

Deaton, A. 2013. *The Great Escape*. Princeton: Princeton University Press.

Debreu, G. 1959. *Theory of Value*. New Haven, CT: Yale University Press.

Diamond, P. and M. Rothschild, eds. 1978. *Uncertainty in Economics*. New York, NY: Academic Press.

Engle, R., ed. 1995. *ARCH Selected Readings*. Oxford: Oxford University Press.

Evans, G., S. Honkapohja, and P. Romer. June 1998. "Growth Cycles." *American Economic Review* 88, pp. 495–515.

Fabozzi, F., F. Modigliani, and F. Jones. 2013. *Foundations of Financial Markets and Institutions*. Noida: Pearson India.

Fama, E. and M. Miller. 1972. *The Theory of Finance*. New York, NY: Holt, Rinehart, and Winston.

Fogel, R. 2000. *The Fourth Great Awakening*. Chicago: University of Chicago Press.

Friedman, M. 1962. *Capitalism and Freedom*. Chicago: University of Chicago Press.

Friedman, M. and R. Friedman. 1979. *Free to Choose*. New York, NY: Avon Books.

Friedman, M. and A. Schwartz. 1963. *Monetary History of the United States*. New York, NY: National Bureau of Economic Research.

Frisch, R. 1965. *Theory of Production*. Chicago: Rand McNally.

Granger, C. 1980. *Forecasting in Business and Economics*. San Diego: Academic Press.

Haavelmo, T. 1954. *A Study in the Theory of Economic Evolution*. Amsterdam: North-Holland.

Hansen, L., J. Heaton, and E. Luttmer. Summer 1995. "Econometric Evaluation of Asset Pricing Models." *Review of Financial Studies* 8, pp. 237–274.

Harsanyi, J. 1977. *Rational Behavior and Bargaining Equilibrium in Games and Social Situations*. Cambridge: Cambridge University Press.

Hart, O. 1995. *Firms, Contracts, and Financial Structure*. Oxford: Clarendon Press.

Hayek, F. 1944. *The Road to Serfdom*. Chicago: University of Chicago Press.

Hayek, F. 1960. *The Constitution of Liberty*. Chicago: University of Chicago Press.

Heckman, J. May 1990. "Varieties of Selection Bias." *American Economic Review* 80, pp. 313–318.

Heckman, J. May 1993. "What Has Been Learned About Labor Supply in the Past Twenty Years." *American Economic Review* 83, pp. 116–121.

Hicks, J. 1939. *Value and Capital*. Oxford: Oxford University Press.

Holmström, B. and J. Tirole. 2011. *Inside and Outside Liquidity*. Cambridge: MIT Press.

Kahneman, D. 2011. *Thinking, Fast and Slow*. London: Penguin.

Kantorovich, L. December 1989. "Mathematics in Economics." *American Economic Review* 79, pp. 18–22.

Keynes, J. 1936. *General Theory of Employment, Interest, and Money*. Hertfordshire: Wordsworth Editions.

Klein, L. 1943. *Economic Theory and Econometrics*. Oxford: Basil Blackwell.

Koopmans, T. 1957. *Three Essays on the State of Economic Science*. New York, NY: McGraw Hill.

Kremer, M. Fall 2002. "Pharmaceuticals and the Developing World." *Journal of Economic Perspectives* 16, pp. 67–90.

Kremer, M. May 2003. "Randomized Evaluations of Educational Programs in Developing Countries: Come Lessons." *American Economic Review* 93, pp. 102–106.

Krugman, P. 1995. *Development, Geography, and Economic Theory*. Cambridge: MIT Press.

Kuznets, S. 1973. *Population, Capital, and Growth*. New York, NY: W.W. Norton.

Kydland, F. December 2006. "Quantitative Aggregate Economics." *American Economic Review* 96, pp. 1373–1383.

Kydland, F. and E. Prescott. Winter 1996. "Computational Experiment: An Econometric Tool." *Journal of Economic Perspectives* 10, pp. 69–85.

Leontief, W. 1947. *Input-Output Economics*. New York, NY: Oxford University Press.

Lewis, A. 1955. *The Theory of Economic Growth*. Oxford: Routledge.

Lucas, R. 2002. *Lectures on Economic Growth*. Cambridge: Harvard University Press.

Malthus, T. 1798. *An Essay on the Principle of Population*. Oxford: Oxford University Press.

Markowitz, H. 1959. *Portfolio Selection*. New Haven: Yale University Press.

Maskin, E. and A. Sen. 2014. *The Arrow Impossibility Theorem*. New York, NY: Columbia University Press.

McFadden, D. March 2006. "Free Markets and Fettered Consumers." *American Economic Review* 96, pp. 5–29.

Meade, J. 1961. *A Neo-Classical Theory of Economic Growth*. London: Unwin University Books.

Merton, R. 1990. *Continuous-Time Finance*. Cambridge: Basil Blackwell.

Miller, M. and C. Upton. 1974. *Macroeconomics*. Chicago: University of Chicago Press.

Mirrlees, J. 2006. *Welfare, Incentives, and Taxation*. Oxford: Oxford University Press.

Mortensen, D. 2003. *Wage Dispersion*. Cambridge: MIT Press.

Mundell, R. 1964. "An Exposition of Some Subtleties in the Keynesian System." *Weltwirtschaftliches Archiv* bd93, pp. 301–312.

Mundell, R. 1971. *Monetary Theory*. Pacific Palisades: Goodyear Publishing.

Myerson, R. 1991. *Game Theory*. Cambridge: Harvard University Press.

Myrdal, G. 1944. *An American Dilemma*. New Brunswick: Transaction Publishers.

Nash, J. 1950. *Essays on Game Theory*. Cheltenham: Edward Elgar Publishing.

Nordhaus, W. 2013. *The Climate Casino*. New Haven: Yale University Press.

North, D. 1990. *Institutions, Institutional Change, and Economic Performance*. New York, NY: Cambridge University Press.

Ohlin, B. 1933. *Interregional and International Trade*. Cambridge: Harvard University Press.

Ostrom, E. 2005. *Understanding Institutional Diversity*. Princeton: Princeton University Press.

Phelps, E. 2013. *Mass Flourishing*. Princeton: Princeton University Press.

Pissarides, C. 2000. *Equilibrium Unemployment Theory*. Cambridge: MIT Press.

Prescott, E. May 2002. "Prosperity and Depression." *American Economic Review* 90, pp. 1–15.

Prescott, E. Spring 2006. "The Transformation of Macroeconomic Policy and Research." *American Economist* 50, pp. 3–20.

Romer, P. Winter 1994. "The Origins of Endogenous Growth." *Journal of Economic Perspectives* 8, pp. 3–22.

Romer, P. May 1996. "Why, Indeed in America? Theory, History, and the Origins of Modern Economic Growth." *American Economic Review* 86, pp. 202–206.

Roth, A. 2015. *Who Gets What—and Why*. Boston: First Mariner Books.

Samuelson, P. 1948. *Macroeconomics*. New York, NY: McGraw.

Sargent, T. 1986. *Rational Expectations and Inflation*. New York, NY: Harper and Row.

Schelling, T. 1960. *The Strategy of Conflict*. Cambridge: Harvard University Press.

Scholes, M. June 1998. "Derivatives in a Dynamic Environment." *American Economic Review* 86, pp. 350–371.

Scholes, M. May 2000. "Crisis and Risk Management." *American Economic Review* 90, pp. 17–21.

Schultz, T. 1949. *Production and Welfare of Agriculture*. New York, NY: Macmillan Company.

Schultz, T. 1979. *Economics of Being Poor*. Singapore: World Scientific Publishing.

Schumpeter, J. 1942. *Capitalism, Socialism, and Democracy*. New York, NY: Harper and Brothers.

Selten, R. 2015. *Impulse Balance and Its Extension by an Additional Criterion*. Koenigswinter, Germany: Books on Demand.

Sen, A. 1999. *Development as Freedom*. New York, NY: Anchor Books.

Shapley, L. 1988. *The Shapley Value*. Cambridge: Cambridge University Press.

Sharpe, W. 1970. *Portfolio Theory and Capital Markets*. New York, NY: McGraw Hill.

Shiller, R. 2000. *Irrational Exuberance*. Princeton: Princeton University Press.

Simon, H. 1945. *Administrative Behavior*. New York, NY: The Free Press.

Sims, C. June 2012. "Statistical Modeling of Monetary Policy and Its Effects." *American Economic Review* 102, pp. 1187–1205.

Smith, A. 1776. *The Wealth of Nations*. New York, NY: Modern Library.

Smith, V. 2008. *Rationality in Economics*. New York, NY: Cambridge University Press.

Solow, R. 1970. *Growth Theory*. New York, NY: Oxford University Press.

Spence, M. 2011. *The Next Convergence*. New York, NY: Picador.

Stigler, G. 1986. *The Essence of Stigler*. Stanford: Hoover Institute Press.

Stiglitz, J. 2012. *The Price of Inequality*. New York, NY: WW Norton.

Stone, R. 1961. *National Income and Expenditure*. London: Bowes and Bowes.

Thaler, R. and C. Sunstein. 2008. *Nudge*. London: Yale University Press.

Tinbergen, J. and J. Polak. 1942. *Dynamics of Business Cycles*. London: Routledge and Kegan Paul.

Tirole, J. 1988. *The Theory of Industrial Organization*. Cambridge: MIT University Press.

Tobin, J. 1997. *World Finance and Economic Stability*. Cheltenham: Edward Elgar Publishing.

Vickrey, W. 1939. *Public Economics*. Cambridge: Cambridge University Press.

von Neumann, J. and O. Morgenstern. 1944. *Theory of Games and Economic Behavior*. Princeton: Princeton University Press.

Williamson, O. 1985. *The Economic Institutions of Capitalism*. New York, NY: Free Press.

About the Author

David Simpson received a Bachelor of Arts in economics from Bethany College and a Master of Business Administration degree from Arizona State University. He is a chartered financial analyst and the founder/CEO of Simpson Capital Management, an independent registered investment adviser. He was an instructor at UCLA.

Index

www.ingramcontent.com/pod-product-compliance
Lightning Source LLC
Chambersburg PA
CBHW061144220326
41599CB00025B/4348